Borderline Justice

BORDERLINE JUSTICE

The Fight for Refugee and Migrant Rights

Frances Webber

Foreword by Gareth Peirce

PlutoPress
www.plutobooks.com

First published 2012 by Pluto Press
345 Archway Road, London N6 5AA

www.plutobooks.com

Distributed in the United States of America exclusively by
Palgrave Macmillan, a division of St. Martin's Press LLC,
175 Fifth Avenue, New York, NY 10010

British Library Cataloguing in Publication Data
A catalogue record for this book is available from the British Library

ISBN   978 0 7453 3164 5   Hardback
ISBN   978 0 7453 3163 8   Paperback
ISBN   978 1 8496 4770 0   PDF eBook
ISBN   978 1 8496 4772 4   Kindle eBook
ISBN   978 1 8496 4771 7   EPUB eBook

Library of Congress Cataloging in Publication Data applied for

This book is printed on paper suitable for recycling and made from fully managed
and sustained forest sources. Logging, pulping and manufacturing processes are
expected to conform to the environmental standards of the country of origin.

10   9   8   7   6   5   4   3   2   1

Designed and produced for Pluto Press by Chase Publishing Services Ltd
Typeset from disk by Stanford DTP Services, Northampton, England
Simultaneously printed digitally by CPI Antony Rowe, Chippenham, UK and
Edwards Bros in the United States of America

Contents

Acknowledgements

Three groups of people have been instrumental in the gestation and development of this book. First, those I represented in the immigration tribunals and the courts. It was the courage and dignity of those whose struggles for fair treatment in the UK I have referred to here, in the face of official indifference, hostility and duplicity, which made me want to write their stories. Second, the solicitors and barristers with whom I worked, and to whom I have returned for their help during the writing of the book, have been true to the collegiate traditions of the profession in their generosity with both time and knowledge. Particular thanks to Ronan Toal, who has always been ready with his help, and my 'sister in law' Stephanie Harrison, whose chaotic spelling disguises enormous legal creativity, erudition and warmth.

The Institute of Race Relations, with which I have been associated since 1969, has been a second home, a haven and a refuge from the courts (any sign of legal pomposity was met with cries of 'Take your wig off!'). If anything kept me sane and grounded during my nearly 30 years as a barrister, it was the IRR. I have been extraordinarily lucky to enjoy the friendship of all the staff there. In particular, I owe a huge debt of gratitude to A. Sivanandan for his continuing education of me over four decades. Liz Fekete has been a source of massive, unstinting support, from encouraging me to write the book in the first place to setting aside her enormous workload on demand to read chapters as they appeared and offering detailed, careful and creative suggestions. Jenny Bourne, who read an early draft of the manuscript, also provided hugely useful criticisms and suggestions which helped me to restructure the book. It is from these friends at the IRR that most of the political insights of the book emanate, and to this extent it is a collegiate work. It goes without saying that errors and deficiencies are my sole responsibility.

Thanks are also due to Teresa Hayter for her careful comments and suggestions, and the staff at Pluto Press, including Robin Virgin and my editor David Castle.

Foreword

First generation beneficiaries of international treaties enacted as the most urgent of priorities after the Second World War have within their working lifetimes been forced to confront the fragility of instruments believed to be inviolable. That each generation has to fight afresh, not just to maintain a minimum level of compliance, but to retain the treaties as meaningful instruments at all, is a realisation that has been only inadequately appreciated; the battle that has to be waged to preserve the most important of the international conventions on human rights and in particular those that relate to torture, to prisoners and to refugees, is a permanent one.

For substantial periods during the past decade we have been paralysed, in large part by our naive astonishment that fundamental protections can have been (and so easily) side stepped or ignored. Naivety in respect of this country's observance of the 1951 Refugee Convention becomes unsustainable and inexcusable now this author's richly evidenced investigations are available, put together with her own experience and her coherent overview.

It is important to recollect that only seven years ago, our government and our government's lawyers were fighting tooth and nail to establish that evidence obtained from torture was to be allowed to be used in courts in this country, arguing that all means justified the end. The cases in which these arguments were raised? Those of a handful of refugees whom we had locked up indefinitely without trial, in breach of the prohibition by another post-second world war instrument – the European Convention of Human Rights, that detention could never be imposed arbitrarily (and in those cases, furthermore, without the very essence of fair accusation – of the accused knowing the evidence against them).

As to the principle of each country using its best efforts to abolish torture – a commitment under the post-war Torture Convention – instead this country constructed new mechanisms for selected refugees in the UK to avoid those undertakings entirely, by introducing 'diplomatic assurances' by which countries (accepted as using the methodology of torture to extract information under interrogation and to terrify and punish dissidents) could be pretended to be 'men of principle' who could be trusted to behave differently.

Combine these lawless measures with the most central guarantee of the Refugee Convention (which insists that those who claim asylum in fear should be guaranteed confidentiality); realise in relation to the same people initially interned on the basis they could not be deported because they would be tortured in their country of origin, that they are now being deported on the basis of diplomatic promises that they will not be, even though the practice in those countries is still acknowledged as continuing regardless; learn that we have sent their personal and confidential asylum claims to their countries of origin and ask what guarantees in fact, any longer, are respected by the UK?

It was thus the protections of the Geneva Conventions designed to protect all captured prisoners of war disappeared when together with the US, we colluded to assist in unlawful kidnap and rendition to dark prisons, to countries that torture or to Guantanamo Bay. Claimed by the US mendaciously to have been captured 'on the battlefield', nevertheless British citizens or residents (all refugees in this country), detained and tortured in the Gambia, Zambia, Pakistan or Morocco were permitted no protections, let alone the inalienable guarantees of the Geneva Conventions, ensuring as they do that POWs need provide only name, rank and number. Instead, the US term 'unlawful enemy combatant' was accepted without protest by the UK when it claimed an entirely new category of captive in 'war' who could be interrogated at will, and by torture.

We have gone further still in our conceptual attacks; we have effectively rewritten and reinterpreted key concepts designed to protect even the most vulnerable and abused of all; the UN Charter and the UN Declaration of Human Rights redefined the fundamental right of a people to self-defence (intended as a last resort against a tyrant) and the right to self-determination. In the now expanded definition of terrorism, resistance to any government however appalling can now be and has been for some years used to justify internment, criminalisation and deportation.

At the same time there has been little in the way of on-going intelligent interpretation for the public in this country to judge the constant overall message hammering through to us – 'national security', 'war on terror', 'the means justify the end'.

In parallel with our passive astonishment, if we are aware at all of the dismantling of guarantees that were meant to hold good for all time against all comers, is a secondary level of amazement at how we seem to have little or no ability through the use of the law or through moral reaction to even the most overt of injustices, to overcome these or place them into reverse even where victories have been achieved in the courts. It is impossible to work as a lawyer, as Frances Webber has done, in the world inhabited by the recipients of what is not even borderline justice and not develop a bleak cynicism that there is no longer any certainty or relief that the most fundamental legal principles can provide.

Yet twelve years into the twenty-first century, significant numbers of refugees who until recently in this country inhabited that world without hope, have turned the wider world on its head. They, whose years of asylum here were made a hundred times worse when they were targeted by unjust legislation brought in specifically for them, have returned to the countries they fled, to complete revolutions and to make new beginnings, in Libya, Egypt and Tunisia. The personal histories that many take with them are shocking. Their treatment in a country where they had sought shelter, demonstrates only our persistence in ensuring that we are again and again on the wrong side of history.

At the time and individually, each of those refugees, many now themselves an inspirational part of the Arab Spring, could only respond through the frustratingly inadequate resources and legal strategies that Frances Webber describes here. Only once in a lifetime and accidentally will the exchanges between governments while giving paper recognition to rights of refugees, demonstrate nevertheless that they were at all times supping with the devil. Documents recently found in ransacked intelligence offices in Tripoli show how intelligence services here were initiating and orchestrating the rendition and diversion of flights of Libyans seeking asylum here to Gaddafi's Tripoli. Many of the refugees who have returned from the UK to build a new Libya, were subjected for a decade to a dizzying succession of executive experimental measures, the majority declared in turn one by one unlawful by the courts in the United Kingdom, in the European Court of Justice, and in the European Court of Human Rights. The list includes internment without trial, proscription in the UK of their dissident group as 'terrorists', the sending of detailed personal information to Gaddafi's agencies even where the refugee had been promised total confidentiality, imprisoning Libyans on secret evidence for the purpose of deportation to Libya on the basis of Gaddafi's promise, prosecuting and imprisoning in the criminal courts as terrorist activities actions taken by dissidents to help Libyan refugees across the world, placing them under house arrest (Control Orders) on secret evidence, asking the UN to impose financial sanctions on the basis of secret evidence on Libyan charities and individuals and liaising with Libyan intelligence to pressure families in Libya and individuals in the UK to become informers. After such concrete documentary proof of what our country did to individuals opposed to Gaddafi, we would do well to recognise that we have been given a rare insight into what our country actually does, and for once not as a unique instance deniable as a evidence of systemic practice but as the clearest possible policy played out in a hundred and one different ways.

What do these experiences teach us? Of what does the history contained in this book inform us? Importantly, that there must be universality in our respect for legal principles. We cannot pick and choose to whom they apply. We cannot wake up to the rights of men and the wrongs done to them only when they become the victors. Whilst it is acknowledged that the worst dictatorships often have the finest constitutions, we in large part have no experience in this country of any concept of rights at all. And so it is that at the same time that this country's criminal behaviour towards a significant number of refugees has been shockingly exposed, that a pitched battle is being fought in Parliament and the press – attacking the Court established 60 years ago in Europe to protect against governments' propensity to destroy the rights of individuals and demanding our formal withdrawal from the enabling treaty – in large part because the Court has ruled that refugees in this country are entitled to the same justice we proclaim for ourselves, neither borderline nor limited.

This book is a record, disturbing in its detail, of that pitched battle, from the perspective of those entitled, almost all voiceless, vulnerable and powerless, struggling for even the most minimal recognition that the same justice should apply to us all.

Gareth Peirce
2012

Introduction

Borderline justice is marginal justice, justice which constantly disappears and constantly has to be fought for. For the individuals and families at the border as migrants or asylum seekers, justice is regularly transformed into injustice by political or economic imperatives of exclusion. The laws and administrative practices in this field, often conceived in haste in a spirit of punitive populism, are designed to ward off the strangers or drive them out; they exclude their targets from mainstream legal entitlements, suspend normal guarantees of freedom and the rule of law, and are enacted in wilful disregard of the consequences for those targeted. It is 'borderline justice' in another sense, too; the border is no longer just the point of arrival in the country, but has been brought deep into workplaces, colleges, banks, hospitals and marriage registries, as immigration status has become determinative in many areas of daily life.

In the nearly 30 years that I have represented migrants and asylum seekers in the UK, the tensions between law and justice, between order and humanity, have been played out in battles inside and outside the courts around rights and freedoms which were believed secure. The hallmarks of a free society – universal rights not to be detained arbitrarily or without trial, access to justice, to fair and public trial with equality of arms, freedom from double punishment, freedom of movement; and those of a humane one – the principle of universal access to subsistence, shelter and health care at the point of need – have all been called into question, have had to be fought for repeatedly and are increasingly fragile and conditional when applied to migrants and asylum seekers. This book is an attempt to describe how, in my legal lifetime, the law has been deployed, developed, used and abused, stretched and strained for use against migrants and asylum seekers – but also how it has been used to resist executive abuses of power, exclusion and injustice, whether by reference to common-law precepts of fairness, the 'law of common humanity' or human rights law.

The chapters are ordered to follow the migrants' trajectory, from arrival to departure. The first section, dealing with arrival, is entitled 'Contest at the Border', and Chapter 1 examines the

1

policies of deterrence and prevention, particularly of the 'disorderly movements' of undocumented migrants and refugees. Drawing on my and my colleagues' cases, I seek to show the ways in which visa controls, carrier sanctions, biometrics and e-borders, criminalisation of unauthorised arrival and of assistance have created paper and electronic walls to accompany the military patrols, the surveillance systems and the subcontracting of controls to countries of origin and transit, making concentric fortifications around Europe – and the ways lawyers and solidarity movements have tried to resist these developments. Chapter 2 examines the distortion of officials' and judges' decision-making by the 'culture of disbelief', a colonial-style set of assumptions about applicants' dishonesty and behaviour, particularly marked in the handling of family reunion and asylum claims. I reflect on why many immigration judges find it hard to resist becoming Home Office gate-keepers, how anti-asylum attitudes infect their approach to medical and country experts, and how campaigns for fair decision-making are changing the landscape. Chapter 3 looks at other obstacles in the path of justice, including the notorious fast track system for determining 'straight-forward' asylum claims, which sets claims up for failure by the use of detention and the imposition of impossible timetables. It also discusses the visa obstacle race for non-asylum seeking migrants, the erosion of immigration appeal rights and the campaign against the abolition of legal aid. Chapter 4 deals with additional difficulties faced and battles fought by particular groups of asylum seekers, including women, children, homosexuals, conscientious objectors, those fleeing civil war and 'victims of globalisation'.

The second section, covering asylum seekers' and migrants' stay in the country, is entitled 'Battles for Fair Treatment', and starts with a look in Chapter 5 at the use of enforced destitution against asylum seekers and undocumented migrants, their exclusion from rights to work, social housing and hospital care, and the growth of coalitions of solidarity and resistance to the laws of inhumanity. Chapter 6 looks at how government attempts to make labour migration more responsive to volatile global market conditions have created insecurity for lawful economic migrants and students. Chapter 7 discusses the double standards surrounding discussion of family life, the legal battles which have raged around the rules restricting the entry of foreign partners, children and elderly parents, and the fight to protect the family life of undocumented migrants. Chapter 8 examines the growth industry of immigration detention, for asylum seekers and for others, looking at the convergence of interests between politicians seeking policies of containment, electoral imperatives and private companies seeking profits.

The final section, dealing with departure, and entitled 'Resisting Total Controls and Mass Removal', looks at the shift of emphasis to enforcement in the past decade. It starts by examining, in Chapter 9, the creation of a huge new immigration police force, with virtually none of the safeguards attending the police; the growth of a security infrastructure of information exchange and data collection and retention; and the subcontracting of immigration control functions to a wide variety of public and private sector agents who are themselves policed in an emerging totalising control. Chapter 10 describes the deportation drive in which economic and political imperatives, public and private interests converge to sweep up refused asylum seekers, irregular migrants and offenders with little regard to age, health or family ties, and the resistance to the increasingly brutal methods used in removal. Chapter 11 describes the way the legal system and the rule of law have been corrupted by secret evidence regimes which deny natural justice, deprivation of citizenship by stealth and deportation to torturing states, all justified by the demonisation of Muslims in the war on terror.

THE WAR ON MIGRATION

The genesis of the book was anger at the vilification and misrepresentation of migrants and asylum seekers by politicians and the press and the injustices they are subjected to at the hands of officials and judges. Our leaders encourage and treat as heroes those people fighting for democracy and human rights, in Burma, in Libya, in Egypt and Syria; those who fight women's oppression and religious persecution in Iran, Afghanistan, Pakistan, Nigeria. But as soon as these heroes seek sanctuary here in the 'free world', they are transformed into a hostile alien threat to our culture and our values, to be kept out by military patrols and bilateral accords and e-borders and carrier sanctions and all the paraphernalia of modern immigration controls.

Then we discover that our government – the bastion of democracy and human rights, as we thought – has been selling arms to repressive regimes including Libya, Bahrain and Saudi Arabia, Algeria, Egypt, Kuwait, Morocco, Oman, Syria and Tunisia, which have been used to suppress pro-democracy activists and minorities, and the MoD and British universities have trained soldiers from China, Sudan and Uzbekistan, Sri Lanka and Colombia. The governments of repressive regimes have in turn acted as sub-contractors in the outsourcing of torture of British and UK-based Muslims suspected of support for terrorism, and to keep asylum seekers from coming here. And we have to ask: how many other repressive regimes is our government propping up, and doing dirty deals with? How many refugees have been created by British government policies?

Many refugees don't claim asylum,[1] because of the corralling of asylum seekers in fast track detention camps and dispersal slums and the low recognition rate for certain nationalities. But among the undocumented, the 'irregulars', are also those who have migrated here over the past 30 years because increasingly there is no land, no work, no possibility of feeding, clothing and educating a family, no future at home and no legal routes to earning a livelihood anywhere else. They are the 'economic migrants', the 'bogus asylum seekers' of popular myth, hounded as 'illegals' and rounded up when they are discovered using false documents to secure sub-minimum wage work. But how valid is the distinction the law draws between economic and political desperation? Justice Collins recognised that 'the so-called economic migrants are frequently trying to escape conditions which no one in this country would regard as tolerable'.[2] What does this have to do with us? Sivanandan memorably said, 'We are here because you are there.' One way or another most of those who come to these shores without official permission are refugees from globalisation, from a poor world getting poorer as it is shaped to serve the interests, appetites and whims of the rich world, a world where our astonishing standard of living, our freedoms, the absurd array of consumer novelties, fashions and foods available to us, and thrown away by us, are bought at the cost of the health, freedoms and lives of others. This cost is felt in the terms of trade and intellectual property agreements, in the imposition on poor countries by the global economic police of policies that remove food self-sufficiency and drive small producers off the land, in the substitution by agribusiness of biofuels for food production in the vast tracts of Africa and Asia bought up by corporations for profit, in the soaring food prices in the poor world which sparked riots in Egypt and Tunisia.

The entire system of immigration controls, not just in the UK but throughout Europe, the US and Canada, Australia, Japan, South Korea, the Gulf states, is built on the most massive global injustice. At the heart of globalisation is a ruthless social Darwinism, which immigration controls reflect and reinforce. For the global elite, it has never been easier to move about the globe, as biometric technology opens gates literally at the blink of an eye, and new immigration rules smooth the path of the wealthy, even as fees have increased steeply to reflect the commercial value of UK residence. As requirements for eligibility multiply, increasingly the biblical parable is reversed, and only the rich may traverse the needle's eye to enter the kingdom. The points-based system (PBS) for immigration introduced in 2008 awards points for youth, salary, qualifications and talent. If you don't have all these attributes, you're not wanted; even if you do, your residence is increasingly contingent and precarious. If you're not computer-literate and don't speak English, in most countries you can't even apply for a visa – forms must be filled in on-line and in English. This brave new world is for the corporate class, and closed to the rest.[3]

This global mis-distribution of wealth and mobility rights is taken for granted, just as the feudal order was, and in the rich world it is the migrants, not the governments and corporations, who wear the mark of Cain, for seeking to disturb this unnatural order. The asylum seekers and migrants I have met over my career are ordinary people who decided to leave home because of intolerable living conditions, war, persecution or the fear of it – or to study at a British university, to join family members already here, to make good, to support families at home. They are as different from their tabloid caricatures as it is possible to be. But they continue to be portrayed as inherently dangerous, posing an existential threat to the body politic, to our way of life, as well as more tangible threats to our standard of living, our public services, our safety and security. For them, it is real-life militarised external border controls, to match the metaphors of invasion; a large, mobile fully-fledged and virtually unregulated internal border police force; total control and degradation for asylum seekers; segregation of foreign national prisoners, and the drive to deport the rejects and undesirables in ever greater numbers. And as society has become increasingly 'governed by immigration', in that immigration control has become prioritised as a policy aim, more and more public and private sector bodies have been recruited to perform immigration policing functions. Voluntary sector groups and charities have been co-opted, too: into the reception, processing and 'voluntary removal' of asylum seekers; into becoming accessory to the detention of children.

Immigration control has become a huge industry, employing an ever greater proportion of the workforce. And in common with many other former public services, it has become big business. Private companies are ubiquitous. Visa applicants in many countries deal not with consular staff at embassies but with Gerry's, Worldbridge and VFS, who receive the applications and increasingly perform the biometric testing required for visas. Refused asylum seekers receive Sodexo smartcards redeemable only in Tesco, Asda, Sainsbury's or Morrisons, may wear Sodexo electronic tags and may be monitored by Sodexo telephone monitoring systems. Immigration detainees are mostly held in centres run and staffed by G4S, Serco and Reliance, multinational security companies which also provide deportation 'escorts' and are now cornering the asylum hostel market. Detainees needing medical care might be seen by Primecare Forensic Medical or Nestor Healthcare Services plc staff. World-Check, Thomson Reuters and other large media groups perform terrorism financing blacklist checks. And that does not include the computer companies such as Siemens, Raytheon and IBM providing the networks, the biometrics databases and recognition systems, the international information exchanges and the software for the interfaces required by education providers; the arms and defence companies providing everything from satellite maritime surveillance systems in the Mediterranean to the handcuffs, helmets and leg restraints used in deportation ... As governments increasingly serve the interests of the corporations rather than the people, and as the revolving doors between politicians and the boards of corporations become normalised, there is more than just political capital to be made out of policies of segregation, detention, deportation, securitisation of asylum and immigration.

LAWYERS IN THE STRUGGLE

Political struggles are increasingly played out in the law courts. In parallel, more lawyers have become involved as committed partisans, forsaking the role of remote expert and consciously putting themselves on the side of historically marginalised and excluded groups, including migrants and asylum seekers. In the 1970s, the nature of the legal profession was changed by the movements sweeping through society. Law centres were set up by radical lawyers working with community activists to ensure the same access to justice as wealthy corporations had for benefits claimants, social housing tenants, compulsorily detained mental patients, parents threatened with removal of their children, sacked workers and immigrants. Young lawyers set up the Legal Action Group and the Free Representation Unit, they flocked to the Haldane Society of Socialist Lawyers and the National Council for Civil Liberties (now

Liberty). Many had worked in their local Race Relations board or Community Relations Council, as volunteers for the Joint Council for the Welfare of Immigrants (JCWI) or their local advice centre, or for women's groups such as Rights of Women. In the years that followed, groups for radical lawyers proliferated in parallel with popular and community organisations, providing an infrastructure of legal expertise for the grassroots movements fighting for civil rights, justice and equality.

Like many coming into the legal profession in the 1970s, my politics were formed by the movements of that era, primarily the anti-racist movement which embraced campaigns against the 'sus' law,[4] police brutality and racist immigration laws as well as against the fascists who swaggered through Southall and Brick Lane behind protective police cordons. Immigration law was in its infancy as a legal discipline, but was intensely politically charged, and was an area where state racism was confronted in every case. The privilege of the Bar, where formal dinners, compulsory for Bar students, always ended with port, was in stark contrast with our clients' lives, but I was lucky to get a place in a young, radical chambers. It took me a few years to begin getting immigration cases, as women were not considered clever enough for this kind of work – other than crime, the family courts were seen as the place for women barristers. However, the depth of injustice faced by our clients dwarfed the difficulties we faced as women barristers. Many radical young lawyers went into immigration law, in both branches of the profession, and the Immigration Law Practitioners' Association (ILPA) was formed in 1984 to provide a forum for immigration lawyers, discussion and training. It has grown into a powerful voice for reform, lobbying the Home Office for migrants' and asylum rights, taking test cases, conducting research and briefing MPs and peers on legislative proposals.

Immigration law in the form of statutes, rules and regulations grew exponentially in response to the arrival of large numbers of asylum seekers from the late 1980s onwards, and as demand for legal expertise in the field grew, so more and more lawyers turned to immigration, often driven by radical politics or plain dislike of the political and media witch-hunt. By the end of the millennium many lawyers from migrant backgrounds, and many more women, had come into the field to defend migrant rights. Now the number of immigration lawyers is shrinking again as legal aid cuts decimate high-street firms and specialist practices; the two major non-profit organisations, Refugee and Migrant Justice and the Immigration

Advisory Service (IAS), employing hundreds of lawyers between them and providing immigration services to tens of thousands, went under in 2010 and 2011.

Although much has changed, the institutions and language of the law, particularly the Bar, remain elitist and intimidating. The first we barristers see of a client is still a set of papers tied up in pink ribbon – a brief, containing a decision, whether a refusal of a family, work or study visa, asylum refusal or a decision to deport, supported by reasons, statements of evidence, records of interviews and correspondence. Part of our job is to articulate the sense of unfairness the decision embodies in language recognisable to a judge. Preparation for a case involves searching for the legal principles to do so, as well as (crucially) ensuring that the evidential basis is there, which means going through the facts thoroughly. If it is an asylum case, what country information has the Home Office used and is it reliable? What other country information is there? Will we need expert evidence to corroborate the client's account of events or to discuss his or her likely treatment on return? Is there medical evidence to corroborate any injuries described? If not, can we contact Freedom from Torture or the Helen Bamber Foundation or, if the client is detained, Medical Justice, for a report?

I can hear some readers asking: but are the clients telling the truth? What if they're lying? But I would respond: in what other field is lying so readily assumed? Of course, it's part of the job to test clients' accounts rigorously, questioning them in readiness for the grilling they will receive from the Home Office representative in court. But I can count on the fingers of one hand the clients I disbelieved.

Some cases involve situations that the law has simply never dealt with before, which provides the opportunity to work from first principles. If the law is unclear, the battle will be in convincing the court of the interpretation which best protects rights from unwarranted intrusion. The task then is to marshal cases, precedents and arguments in support of that interpretation. If the law (whether statute or case law) is against the client, then we must ask: is that law itself open to challenge, via the Human Rights Act or other international or common-law principles? What do the international conventions – the Refugee and Human Rights Convention, the International Covenant on Civil and Political Rights, the UN Convention on the Rights of the Child, the Convention on the Elimination of all forms of Discrimination against Women – have to say about this situation? What about UN resolutions? How have other common-law jurisdictions resolved the legal issues? If there is already a campaign against the law or provision at issue, is this a good test case, or does it have weaknesses which could result in a bad legal decision and make things worse for more people? Are other lawyers seeking to challenge the provision in other cases and if so, should we try to link up with them? Or would our case be better off standing alone? These are some of the technical and tactical questions which might arise. The legal arguments which we present to the court are informed by the politics of the movements we are involved in as well as by the obvious legal issues arising from the case. These arguments determine the shape of the case which the judges hear, and judicial creativity generally rests on the work of the barristers whose arguments frame the courts' judgments.

Legal strategies are discussed at the conferences with solicitors and clients, where, in appropriate cases, ways of 'bringing the community into the courtroom' are planned. Friends, neighbours, detention visitors, church and trade union contacts may all have a part to play in mobilising support which can be deployed in the courtroom so as to make a real difference, particularly in bail applications and deportation appeals, where community ties are important to the decision. The mere presence of people in the public gallery (friends, not hostile journalists!) improves the quality of decisions; when immigration judges know they are being watched they tend to behave with more regard for justice than when the only people in the hearing room are the appellant, the lawyers (if any), the Home Office representative and a dozing court usher. For a fighting lawyer, there is nothing more dispiriting than an empty courtroom. But the community has to be brought into the courtroom in another sense, too, by bringing the reality of clients' lives into focus as powerfully as possible to judges inevitably insulated by their position of privilege and under political, bureaucratic and time pressure to see cases as purely intellectual exercises.

Legal action necessarily proceeds through individual cases, and in this sense appears antithetical to political action, which is essentially collective. But many fighting lawyers also work with campaign groups, helping to turn cases into issues. Many battles have been fought simultaneously inside and outside the courtroom, on issues such as enforced destitution of asylum seekers, separation of families through harsh immigration rules, immigration detention and the use of secret evidence in national security deportation cases.

Most of the thousands of cases I worked on during my career raised no new points of law. If the successes had value over and above the relief they brought to individual clients and their families, it was as part of the great mass of challenges to Home Office decisions and the careless racism that informed them. Very few made legal history, and of those that did, they often didn't set out to do so. Bakhtaur Singh's case, where the House of Lords ruled that a person's value to the community should be taken into account in an appeal against deportation, is typical. A friend involved in the Asian youth movement asked me to represent Bakhtaur, a musician, priest and long-term overstayer facing deportation; he organised a 100-strong picket of the court, and many community leaders sat in the public gallery. It was this community support which provided the legal ammunition to take the case further when the adjudicator dismissed the deportation appeal saying that he couldn't take into account Bakhtaur's value to the community. The point arose organically through the legal proceedings and took Bakhtaur to the House of Lords, with veteran immigration lawyer Ian Macdonald QC now heading the legal team. Bakhtaur simultaneously stood as a parliamentary candidate on a 'no deportations' platform. Mrs Shah's case was another unplanned intervention. With its joined case of Mrs Islam, it became a leading case, establishing that women fleeing domestic violence could be refugees, but it started as a last-ditch attempt to prevent a woman being returned to a violent husband who would probably kill her. There was no public campaign around her case, but the global women's movement had led to pioneering cases in Canada and Australia changing the way women were perceived in refugee law, and this thinking was incorporated into the legal arguments which eventually persuaded the House of Lords. (It is much easier to do this now, as the jurisprudence of the Canadian, Australian, New Zealand and US courts is freely available on the internet.)

Some cases are brought more deliberately as part of campaigns against government action. When the 1996 social security regulations excluded certain asylum seekers from subsistence benefits, some of us were so alarmed that we decided to look for a way of challenging the regulations in court, and the judicial review by JCWI was the result. Organisations like JCWI could not get public funding for legal challenges, but a destitute claimant joined JCWI in the judicial review, and she was eligible for legal aid, which funded the case and enabled us to get the regulations quashed. It has now become more common for campaigning organisations such as JCWI, Liberty, Bail for Immigration Detainees (BID) and Medical Justice to get involved in test case litigation, either as claimants, or as interveners in cases brought by others, to ensure that wider policy considerations are not neglected. The work of representing such an organisation is generally unpaid or *pro bono* (short for *pro bono publico*, for the public good), but there is no shortage of lawyers willing to put as much time and effort into them as into their paid cases. Immigration lawyers are not generally interested in making big money.

MAKING EXECUTIVE POWER ACCOUNTABLE

What happened in the JCWI case on asylum and benefits illustrated the cat-and-mouse nature of the legal struggles in this field, which can lead to enormous frustration. When the courts ruled the social security regulations excluding asylum seekers illegal, the government simply re-enacted them as primary legislation, which made them immune from legal challenge because of the doctrine of parliamentary supremacy. Parliament and the media are described as the two great checks on executive power apart from the courts, but when they are supine, as parliament was in that case, or worse, support and legitimate that power, as the media, with honourable exceptions, have done in immigration and asylum, the courts' role becomes even more important.

The law is intensely dynamic and as far from the Mosaic stone tablets as it is possible to be – constantly fought over, in flux, pulled this way and that by conservatives and progressives in the courts and in the increasingly vocal struggle between the executive and judicial branches of government, and sometimes the legislature too. A growing executive contempt for the rule of law, marked by secret, unlawful detention policies, systematic failure to comply with legal safeguards for vulnerable people and attempts to muscle through measures abolishing the higher courts' scrutiny of immigration decisions, has been increasingly resisted in the past decade or so by the higher judiciary, whether because of the examples set by a few stalwart human rights defenders among them, or because some of the radical lawyers of a generation ago are now sitting on the judicial bench, or maybe the resistance is provoked by the sheer overweening arrogance of the executive. But as senior judges have shown more willingness to castigate Home Office conduct as a public disgrace, and law lords have condemned proposed legislation as an affront to the constitution, ministers complain that judges are subverting their work and making their task impossible. There is loud ministerial heckling of judges who declare legislation incompatible with human rights obligations, or overrule policy decisions which violate foreign national offenders' or asylum seekers' rights, and there are signs that more executive-friendly judges are being appointed to the highest courts as well as further attempts to insulate legislation from judicial scrutiny. The constant battle between executive and judiciary carries on a great tradition: in the words of historian E. P. Thompson, 'One way of reading our history is as an immensely protracted contest to subject the nation's rulers to the rule of law.'[5]

The cases I describe here span three incarnations of government, from the Thatcher and Major Tory administrations (1979–97) through Blair and Brown's new Labour (1997–2010) to the Cameron–Clegg Con–Dem coalition. When I started dealing with immigration cases in the early 1980s, hardly any primary (economic) immigration was permitted: it had been virtually ended by the 1971 Immigration Act. Thatcher's government imposed further restrictions, first on the entry of dependants of the Commonwealth settlers who had come in the previous decade, and later, to prevent and deter asylum seekers. As she slashed the social infrastructure, defeated organised labour and opened the country to globalised capital with her programme of privatisation, cuts and financial deregulation,[6] immigrants were the enemy without and miners the enemy within. We immigration lawyers were kept busy trying to prove that the primary purpose of marriages was not immigration, that children were related to the parents they were joining in the UK and that people arrested as illegal immigrants weren't.

From the mid-1980s, we were also seeking to show that asylum seekers were genuine refugees. Kurds, Tamils, Somalis, Iranians, Angolans and Algerians, Chinese, Rwandans and Congolese were joined by Nigerians, Croatians, Bosnians, Kosovars, Czech and Slovak Roma, and later still Zimbabweans, Ethiopians, Eritreans, Sudanese, Iraqis, Afghanis … Although governments claim that most asylum seekers are disguised economic migrants, the country-of-origin statistics for those claiming asylum tell a different story, reflecting all the zones of repression and conflict.

Initial indications of Labour progressiveness on immigration, such as the abolition of the primary purpose rule, were belied by its adoption of anti-asylum rhetoric and policies, a huge growth in immigration powers of detention, enforcement, removal and internal controls, matched by savage cuts to legal aid. Challenges to enforced destitution, deportation and detention all became common. The iniquities of 'managed migration', which recruited and discarded educated and highly skilled migrants in line with market needs, gave rise to case law too. But Labour's Human Rights Act is a powerful weapon for accountability.

The coalition government has used nationalist rhetoric to seek to slash migration of all but the wealthy. Against a background of unprecedented income inequality and attempts to dismantle the welfare state and privatise health and education, it has sought to tune immigration policy even more finely to the needs of the globalised market state. The courts hear cases of illegal capping and robotic controls, and of colleges closed down for inefficient policing of their students. The coalition came into power on a civil liberties ticket, but has forced through the almost complete destruction of civil legal aid, and proposes legislation to curtail the reach of the Human Rights Act and to wrap the veil of secrecy round more types of judicial process.

RACISM AND THE SUPPRESSION OF EMPATHY

It is often claimed that immigration law has been decoupled from racism since the bad old days of the 1960s and 1970s, when 'immigration' meant settlement of former colonial subjects from Africa, the Caribbean and the Indian sub-continent, and laws emerged from, reflected, legitimated and reproduced that colour-coded racism. But the anti-asylum laws and practices of the 1980s and 1990s were informed by a non-colour-coded but just as virulent 'xeno-racism'[7] directed against poor eastern Europeans, particularly Roma. A ferocious anti-Muslim racism underlay the national security measures of the 2000s and the debate about Britishness instituted by Labour and carried forward in Cameron's critique of multicultural-ism, which suggests that you can't be properly British and properly Muslim at the same time. A deep vein of xenophobic nationalism informs the anti-human rights campaign and the deportation drive against foreign national prisoners. Nationalism doesn't have to be racist: Scottish nationalism is evolving as a progressive cause – but in the Union Jack, nationalism and xenophobia or racism seem inextricably interwoven.

Institutional racism is alive and well in government, in the United Kingdom Border Agency (UKBA), the modern incarnation of the Home Office Immigration and Nationality Directorate, and in the immigration judiciary. It is of course important to distinguish institutional racism from personal attitudes, although the former informs the latter. Many times I marvelled at this paradox: how could presenting officers (UKBA civil servants who present their cases in the Tribunal), who were generally friendly and pleasant to me, display such contempt and lack of human understanding in their questioning of my clients? Home Office officials and immigration judges are not evil monsters, but many lose their human empathy in their dealings with migrants and asylum seekers. Sociologist Zygmunt Bauman has compellingly described the processes whereby natural human empathy is manipulated by the powerful to produce moral indifference to the fate of marginalised groups, and although he was trying to understand the Holocaust, his description of the suppression of empathy and moral responsibility resonates here.[8] He describes how physical and spiritual separation, which distance us from the effects on others of what we do (or what is done in our name), dilutes our sense of empathy, while demonisation of the targeted group puts them outside the realm of moral responsibility. We transfer our empathy and sense of responsibility to a 'mini-moral community', defined by employer, by race, class or religion. This allows decisions about the targeted group to be based on 'rational' or technical, rather than moral considerations.

This suppression of empathy underlies atrocities from Rwanda to Abu Ghraib, accounts for the widespread indifference to migrant deaths at the border and in the prisons, and allows officials to discount the humanity of those they deal with. The higher judiciary are not immune from these processes; it is not hard to find judgments from them which display a want of empathy. But these judges' prominence as defenders of common-law values of fairness and human rights against executive intrusion provides a powerful countervailing pressure. Of course, these same values enable many officials and low-level judges to resist the pressures to group loyalty over human solidarity, and to refuse to reify the people whose cases they decide. (And there are some terrible, lazy, negligent and downright crooked lawyers who see clients purely as income streams, and do untold damage to them.) But we are all up against a racist system, and in large measure, the work of lawyers in this field is part of the fight against racism. The cloak of invisibility conferred by the political and media dehumanisation of migrants and asylum seekers, which hides in plain view the struggles of people seeking safety and security, against immiseration and destitution, the psychological and physical damage wrought by detention, the known and unknown dangers of deportation, is constantly pierced by the campaigning groups who picket and blockade detention centres and airports to prevent deportations, who march against forced destitution, who lobby and harry and brief and report and protest at the treatment of people as less than human because of birth and nationality.

Although the book is about the UK, there are similar laws and policies – and struggles – across Europe, Australia, the US and Canada, South Korea, the Gulf states, Israel, South Africa – wherever, in fact, refugees and poor migrants seek sanctuary and livelihood. Migrants are, too, not the only group facing policies of marginalisation and demonisation in the global economy. The Dale Farm and Meriden evictions demonstrated how those who insist on retaining old ways, such as traveller communities, are systematically excluded and criminalised. And the poor, the sick, the disabled, the workless are today suffering similar exclusion and demonisation by politicians and the press, as those who can't work find their lives squeezed out to mere existence – just like asylum seekers. The opening of a new, state-of-the-art court building in October 2011, designed to ensure the UK's supremacy as a forum for international commercial litigation, reminds us that justice is not immune from the privatisation/marketisation process, becoming a commodity available only to those who can pay for it.

The legal struggles described in this book demonstrate how vital access to justice is – vital in restraining the executive, providing accountability and protecting and occasionally extending rights. When given the freedom to do so, the courts, particularly the higher courts, sometimes fulfil their function of doing justice. But judges' powers are limited. They cannot overrule acts of parliament; and they can only respond to the cases brought to them. The shrinking pool of immigration lawyers can't hope to help more than a fraction of those suffering injustice, a fraction which will be reduced further when immigration is taken outside the scope of legal aid. And many of the really pernicious measures against asylum seekers and migrants are contained in acts of parliament.

The myriad asylum and detainee support groups up and down the country are beginning to come together to develop new strategies, and there is room for more strategic deployment of lawyers' expertise in the new movement. But it is the tripartisan consensus on restriction of asylum and migrant rights which needs to be challenged head-on. The global injustices giving rise to migration and refugees need to form part of any public defence of migrants' and asylum rights. It is justice, not charity, which is demanded. Loud and sustained defence of the Human Rights Act and access to the European Court of Human Rights (ECtHR) is vital. The Right has been given virtually a clear run in the attack on human rights in the media; where is the voice of the anti-racist Left? The arguments for universality of basic human rights, and for the rule of law, need to be made again and again, making common cause with struggles of other excluded and marginalised groups in the process, and building solidarity against corporatist values. 2011 saw the world catch alight with resistance from the '99 per cent'; migrants' struggles for recognition and humanity form a large part of that resistance.

Part One

Arrival: Contest at the Border

1
The War on Asylum: Preventing Entry

The problem with an open Europe is how to close it – against immigrants and refugees from the Third World. (A. Sivanandan)[1]

In the late 1980s there was a furore when it was discovered that the Home Office was asking airline staff to hold on board passengers without visas, not allowing them to land, on the assumption that they might claim asylum. Luckily, perhaps with the aid of sympathetic airline staff, some Kurds held on board a small number of aircraft were able to contact perhaps the best immigration solicitor in the country, David Burgess,[2] who obtained a high court order that the men must be allowed to land and to claim asylum.[3] The same solicitor represented a Zairean stowaway on a boat which arrived at Tilbury in March 1991. Two immigration officers who saw him said they would return to register his asylum claim, but he was then locked into a cabin, and had to force the door and escape from the boat under cover of darkness to apply for asylum.[4]

Holding people on aircraft and locking them in on boats were early salvoes in the war waged against the arrival of undocumented migrants and refugees[5] for the past quarter-century. In 1948 Britain had supported the Universal Declaration on Human Rights, which proclaims the right of everyone to seek and enjoy asylum from persecution. Britain even helped to draft the 1951 United Nations Convention on Refugees and its 1967 Protocol, which bound signatory states to offer protection from persecution to refugees from racial, political, religious or social persecution. Our immigration rules stipulated that anyone arriving in the UK claiming asylum from persecution had to be allowed to stay while their claim was investigated. But since the numbers of those seeking safety and security in the UK (as elsewhere in the rich world) rose in the mid-1980s, governments have tried to get round these commitments to refugees by preventing them from getting here. In this war, the weapons have included visa controls, carrier sanctions, crimi-nalisation, advanced technology, military patrols and diplomatic

19

agreements which keep refugees away from Europe. Some of these weapons can be, and have been, fought over in court battles.

VISA CONTROLS AS A WEAPON

Looking for ways to stop refugees travelling to Britain, the government seized on the stipulation in the Refugee Convention that refugees must have left their own country to be recognised and protected. Visa requirements were imposed on citizens of countries from which many people were fleeing, preventing many from reaching safety. The catch-22 was (and still is) that until they leave their own country they are not refugees (and so are ineligible for visas) and once they have left, according to the British government, they are safe – or if not, should seek protection in the first safe country they reach.

Sri Lankan Tamils were among the first to be affected by the visa policy. From 1983, they were fleeing racial pogroms unleashed on them by the Sinhalese majority, whipped up by government ministers.[6] Amnesty International, the International Commission of Jurists and the British Parliamentary Human Rights Group were among those condemning the atrocities. But the British were training the Sri Lankan army and supplying arms to its government – and Thatcher's immigration minister David Waddington saw no persecution. *The Times* asserted that Tamils were using the 'disturbances' as a 'pretext for evasion of strict immigration controls for economic reasons'.[7] In 1985, Sri Lanka became the first Commonwealth country whose citizens – British subjects – required a visa to come to the UK, to stop what ministers described as a 'flood' (although in the previous two years only 1,000 Tamils had sought asylum in the UK, compared with 100,000 who had gone to India).[8]

The pattern was to become familiar over the next two decades: an exodus of people fleeing repression or civil war would be met by the erection of a visa requirement to stop them coming here. From 1986 to 1991 visas were imposed on citizens of Iran, Iraq, Somalia, Zaire and Turkey (as well as India, Pakistan, Nigeria and Ghana). In 1992, at the height of the ethnic wars in the former Yugoslavia, visas were imposed on all nationalities there except for Slovenians and Croatians[9] (who became subject to visa controls in 1999).[10] They were imposed on Zimbabweans in 2002, in response to the ruling party ZANU PF's murderous attacks on real or imagined opponents. But the imposition of the visa requirement didn't stop the arrival of Tamils in the mid-1980s; they simply came without visas, and asked the immigration officer for asylum on arrival. Their claims had to be investigated before they could be removed, but having arrived without visas, they could not appeal the refusal of asylum before being sent back. The only legal recourse was judicial review in the high court.

I had my baptism of fire in refugee law when, in February 1987, I was instructed to run across (literally) to the high court out of hours to obtain emergency injunctions to prevent the summary removal of 58 Sri Lankan Tamil rejected asylum seekers[11] who were even then being escorted across the tarmac at Heathrow airport. In its haste to remove them, the Home Office had ignored an informal agreement to refer the men to the UK Immigrants' Advisory Service (UKIAS) to allow representations to be made on their cases, which made the summary removal unfair and possibly unlawful. Supported by the Tamil Refugee Action movement, some of them stripped to their underpants to delay their removal for long enough to allow the legal team to get to court. The judge, whom I saw in his room, listened to my stammering explanation and willingly granted the order, but in my inexperience, I had failed to ensure that it covered all the men (I had the name of only one of them), so the Home Office took only that named man off the plane, and I had to run back breathless to the judge with a hastily compiled list of the other 57 to secure their temporary reprieve.[12]

The high court intervention which stopped the Tamils' removal outraged the tabloids for days. Home secretary Douglas Hurd told parliament that the Tamils' claims were 'manifestly bogus',[13] despite the London representative of the United Nations High Commissioner for Refugees (UNHCR) and the director of UKIAS concluding that a significant number bore the scars of torture and qualified for refugee status. The government used the Tamils' case to push through legislation to introduce the next weapon in the war against refugees: carrier sanctions.

CREATING ILLEGALITY THROUGH CARRIER SANCTIONS

Just a month later, in March 1987, the Immigration (Carriers' Liability) Act was rushed through parliament, imposing fines of £1,000 on airlines and shipping companies for each passenger they brought in who did not possess valid passports and visas for travel to the UK. (In 1993 the fine was doubled to £2,000 per passenger.) In parliament, Hurd described as a 'loophole' the ability to arrive visa-less on UK soil and claim asylum and claimed that the introduction of carrier sanctions would not affect genuine refugees, 90 per cent of whom claimed after arrival in the UK as visitors or students.[14] But as Michael Meadowcroft MP pointed out, 'If all countries took the same line as ourselves, there would be no means of travelling in an emergency in the way people are forced to do when fleeing from terror.'[15] The government was oblivious, rebuffing attempts to exempt carriers from penalties for passengers subsequently recognised as refugees (although providing a discretionary waiver of the penalty in very restricted circumstances). Involving carriers in immigration control was not new; since the 1905 Aliens Act they had been liable for the costs of detaining and returning inadmissible passengers. But the new carriers' liability went further, by forcibly recruiting airline and ships' captains as immigration officers – but immigration officers who were obliged to ignore passengers' protection needs, focusing only on checking their documentation. Airlines complained but complied.[16]

As airlines turned them away, undocumented travellers were forced to travel overland, by train or hiding in lorries, to get to the country they believed would offer sanctuary and respect for their rights. A typical journey, described by an Afghan teenager, had taken a year, through the mountains to Iran, then from Turkey to Greece and Italy, on trains across France to Calais where he had tried five times in the past week to cross the Channel by clinging to the underside of a lorry. 'Forty of us left Afghanistan,' he said, 'only three of us are here now. Some of our group died crossing the mountains, we had to abandon the weaker ones. We couldn't stop to bury the corpses, we had to leave them in the snow.'[17] In 1998, carrier sanctions were extended to Eurostar, and the following year, despite the protests of the Road Haulage Association, to road hauliers who inadvertently carried stowaways.[18] Thousands of people, including many children, congregated in Calais, destitute and homeless, waiting for a chance to creep into a freight train at Coquelles, cling to the underside of a lorry, walk under or paddle across the Channel. The Red Cross opened a centre for them at Sangatte, which became a centre for solidarity action for asylum activists across Europe. Eurotunnel became subject to fines in 2001, and in response, erected at the French end of the tunnel two 12-metre watchtowers and an electric fence capable of delivering an 8,500-volt shock. After huge pressure from the British government and a battle in the French courts, the Red Cross centre at Sangatte was closed in 2002. The would-be asylum seekers, once more destitute and homeless, constructed makeshift camps in the woods outside Calais, which became known as 'the jungle', or lived rough along the Nord-Pas-de-Calais coast. The jungle was bulldozed in 2009.[19]

Despite carriers' liability laws, asylum seekers arrived in ever larger numbers throughout the 1990s.[20] Over four-fifths were granted refugee status or exceptional leave to remain, demonstrating that the increase reflected conflicts and repression abroad – although ministers including prime minister John Major still spoke of 'bogus asylum seekers'.[21] In 1991, senior ministers proposed withdrawal from the Refugee Convention. But the combination of visa controls and carrier sanctions created a market for two new growth industries: document forgery and human smuggling. Desperate people paid huge sums, generally thousands of pounds, for false documents – British or EU passports, sometimes stolen and with the passenger's photograph substituted, or the home country's passport with a forged visa, to get on to a plane, ship or train. In parallel with this, human smugglers, initially small-scale and often working with political opposition parties in countries of persecution, provided an 'alternative travel service' using small boats and container lorries.

CRIMINALISING HUMANITARIAN SMUGGLERS AND SHEPHERDS

The government now declared war on the human smugglers. It increased prosecutions and pushed up the maximum sentence for facilitating illegal entry (i.e., involvement in people smuggling) from seven to ten years in 1996, and to fourteen years in 2002 – the same maximum sentence as was set for human trafficking. Acting with European governments, it pushed for the UN anti-smuggling and anti-trafficking Conventions in 2000.[22] It is now an international offence to assist any person in an illegal border crossing, regardless of whether he or she is a refugee in need of protection. In all this, there is no acknowledgement of the fact that recourse to smugglers is the only option for the vast majority of asylum seekers trying to reach safety. And treating smugglers the same as traffickers, who always use force or deception and exploitation, endangers the long and vital tradition of 'underground railway' humanitarian smuggling, which has historically been the expression of human solidarity in response to persecution of others, whether to spirit away escaped slaves in the US in the nineteenth century, or Jews in occupied Europe in the twentieth. That is not to deny the role now played by criminal gangs in smuggling, and the extreme callousness with which some smugglers treat their charges. But humanitarian smuggling does not deserve a prison sentence.[23]

The courts, more concerned with deterrence than rescue, have consistently held that smugglers should go to prison, and motive is relevant only to the length of the sentence. In 1995, when convictions at Maidstone Crown Court for people-smuggling were running at two or three a week, the average sentence was two to three years for commercial smuggling, and twelve months for humanitarian smuggling. The tariff has gone up steadily since; commercial operators sometimes get seven years, while non-profit smugglers get up to two and a half years – including a man who smuggled in his own brother.[24] Juries would sometimes acquit those who claimed not to know that their car contained unauthorised passengers. I enjoyed representing the Frenchwoman who exclaimed, 'Mon Dieu! Je ne savais rien!'[25] when the boot of her hired Citroen was unlocked at Dover immigration control to reveal two Tamils crouching inside. She was acquitted after a vehicle examiner we called as an expert witness showed how they could have got there via a one-inch opening in the car window.[26] But the courts' increasingly severe treatment of non-commercial smuggling was reflected in my caseload. In 1995 Jim P, a British man working in Germany, was given a three-month suspended sentence for bringing in a Croatian teenager who had run away to Germany to get away from the war and had made friends with Jim's family. But a decade later, a Sudanese refugee from Darfur was sentenced to two years' imprisonment, and was threatened with deportation, after he bought a false passport to bring in his young wife. She was at risk from marauding rebel gangs on the Sudan–Chad border and had no means of obtaining a (genuine) passport for travel to the UK.[27]

In the early 1990s, meanwhile, the net was widened to criminalise people who simply helped would-be asylum seekers to get round carriers' pre-boarding checks, typically by lending a falsified passport to enable them to board an aircraft, taking it back before the plane touched down in the UK, where their charges claimed asylum. There was no deception of the immigration officer, and the passengers did not enter clandestinely – the two recognised modes of illegal entry.[28] So what offence had been committed? A legal battle ensued.

Mr Kanesarajah, a Sri Lankan, was prosecuted for responding to the desperation of a family friend by putting her photo in his wife's passport, to get her out of Sri Lanka. He took the passport back after she boarded the plane with her young children, and she claimed asylum without documents on arrival at Heathrow. But the Crown Prosecution Service (CPS) said her arrival without travel documents made her an illegal entrant, and Mr Kanesarajah's help made him guilty of assisting her illegal entry. The Court of Appeal allowed his appeal. The CPS appealed to the House of Lords.[29] The law lords mocked the prosecutor's argument: 'You mean that if I fall off a boat in the Channel and arrive at Dover dripping wet and without my passport, I'm an illegal immigrant?' Their judgment was definitive and binding: persons simply arriving and claiming asylum at the port of entry, rather than entering clandestinely or presenting false documents, could not be treated as illegal entrants, and those bringing them to the UK for this purpose committed no offence.[30]

Refugee and migrants' rights groups were delighted. But three years later, with anti-asylum feeling whipped up to fever pitch and racial violence against migrant and refugee families soaring,[31] the government legislated to criminalise the 'shepherds' who brought asylum claimants to the UK.[32] There was outrage: how could it be criminal to help someone exercise a fundamental right? In parliament, home secretary Michael Howard insisted that the offence was aimed at profiteers, exempting from its scope assistance 'otherwise than for gain, or in the course of ... employment by a *bona fide* organisation whose purpose it is to assist refugees'. Nevertheless, many people motivated by friendship or common humanity found themselves in the dock, having to prove their innocence of a commercial motive.[33] One such was D, a refugee from Gaddafi's Libya who spent five months in prison awaiting trial for helping fellow citizens get to the UK. The prosecutor at his trial said he had to prove he had gained nothing from organising their travel – but how do you prove a negative? After a fierce legal argument, the judge accepted that, in accordance with the presumption of innocence, the prosecution had to prove that he had acted for gain, and D was acquitted.[34]

Successful cases and campaigning meant fewer prosecutions of 'shepherds', although hundreds of humanitarian smugglers continued to be prosecuted each year. The criminalisation strategy spread across Europe: in 2002 the EU adopted a directive requiring all member states to provide 'effective, proportionate and dissuasive penalties' for those assisting unauthorised entry, although in a hard-fought concession to humanity, smugglers bringing in family members, and those acting for humanitarian motives, could be exempted from penalty.[35] The Home Office told parliamentary committee members who were concerned about penalising humanitarian smugglers that British law did not criminalise persons or organisations bringing asylum seekers here 'otherwise than for gain' – but failed to point out that humanitarian smuggling remained a criminal offence.[36] A colleague in chambers used the defence of necessity to secure the acquittal of a Kurdish refugee who smuggled his nephew into Britain, showing the jury the reality of Turkish state repression of Kurds to persuade them that he really had no choice but to help the young man get out, but jury cases set no precedent, and the acquittal was a one-off. Even rescuing refugees at sea and bringing them here was seen as a hostile act, if not a crime (since international maritime law requires rescue); the captain of the container ship *Clementine Maersk* was severely criticised when in 2005 the ship picked up 27 mostly Somali refugees from a stricken boat which had drifted for eight days in the Mediterranean without help. The captain brought the refugees to Felixstowe, its next scheduled stop, into a storm of tabloid criticism and a massive Home Office security operation.[37]

THE CRIMINALISATION OF REFUGEES

Meanwhile, the government had extended its criminalisation strategy to asylum seekers themselves: those caught presenting false documents to immigration officers at the port found themselves prosecuted and imprisoned. From 1994 to 1995 the number of arrests at Heathrow quadrupled to 450 (the figures were similar for Gatwick and Dover).[38] By 1998, it was estimated that over half of all criminal cases heard at Uxbridge magistrates' court, one of the closest to Heathrow, were of asylum seekers trying to enter on false documents.[39] Many refugees'[40] introduction to the country was a prison cell and a sentence of three to twelve months. This alarming trend put Britain in breach of the Refugee Convention stipulation, in Article 31, that refugees should not be penalised for illegal entry because, as the UN Secretary-General said in 1950, 'A refugee whose departure from his country of origin is usually a flight, is rarely in a position to comply with the requirements for legal entry (possession of national passport and visa) into the country of refuge'. Refugee and rights groups began fighting on this new front, and Chouku Adimi's case became a major test case. Adimi was a young Algerian who fled the country in 1997 in fear of an armed group, travelling to the UK via Italy and France, where he obtained false travel documents which he proffered on arrival at Heathrow. The immigration officer was not fooled, and Adimi admitted his identity and claimed asylum. He was arrested and charged with an offence of possessing a false instrument (the passport) with intent, which carries a ten-year maximum sentence (the charge was later changed to simple possession, carrying a two-year maximum). In January 1998 he appeared at Uxbridge magistrates' court. He was represented by a young, feisty pupil barrister, Sarah Vine, who realised that the prosecution contravened the Refugee Convention and argued that it should be postponed until his asylum claim was determined, and if his claim to be a refugee was upheld, should be dropped. Mr Adimi met the criteria for the protection of Article 31, she argued (that the refugee has come directly from the country of persecution and presented himself promptly following the illegal entry); he would not have been granted protection in Italy or France (because neither country at that time accepted as refugees people who feared non-state-sponsored persecution), and he had claimed asylum immediately the false documents were detected. The case-hardened magistrates gave this novel argument short shrift. She launched a legal challenge to the prosecution and the magistrates' rejection of the argument, asking me to take over the case, and the prosecution was halted to await the outcome. Meanwhile, Mr Adimi was granted refugee status, but the prosecutor still refused to drop the charge.

The challenge was heard in July 1999 in the Divisional Court, along with two others, involving Mr Sorani, an Iraqi Kurd and Mr and Mrs Kaziu, an Albanian couple, who had travelled through the UK on false documents to seek refuge in Canada, where they had family, when they were stopped at Heathrow. They too argued that Article 31 should have been applied to protect them from prosecution. The cases were an important test of the UK's compliance with its legal obligations towards refugees. It emerged during the hearing that no one in the Home Office or the criminal justice system had given the least thought to Article 31. The judges were shocked.[41] 'One cannot help wondering', observed Lord Justice Simon Brown, 'whether perhaps the increasing incidence of such prosecutions is yet another weapon in the battle to deter refugees from ever seeking asylum in this country.'[42] As he noted in his judgment, the need for Article 31 had not diminished: 'The combined effect of visa requirements and carrier's liability has made it well-nigh impossible for refugees to travel to countries of refuge without false documents.'[43] The judges rejected the government's argument that Article 31 applied only to refugees who sought asylum in the first safe country they reached,[44] accepting that they had an element of choice as to the country of asylum, reflecting ties of family, language or culture, and that refugees who stopped over in a transit country for a short while should not forfeit protection. They accepted that 'where the illegal entry or use of false documents or delay can be attributed to a *bona fide* desire to seek asylum whether here or elsewhere, that conduct should be covered by Article 31', and should not be prosecuted.[45]

The ruling was a vitally important and unqualified victory for refugee protection. But the government hated it for undermining the useful 'first safe country' doctrine, which enabled it to return asylum seekers to transit countries. So although it created a new statutory 'asylum defence' to charges of presenting false documents,[46] it restricted the defence to those who could not have obtained asylum in any transit country, denying the element of choice of asylum country which the judges had found in the Convention. But at least Mr and Mrs Kaziu were awarded £80,000 for wrongful imprisonment, paving the way for many other wrongly convicted refugees to obtain compensation.[47]

Prosecutors got round the ban on prosecuting falsely documented refugees by using different charges, as happened to Ms Asfaw. A student who had been imprisoned and tortured for her activism in Ethiopia, she was arrested at Heathrow in transit to the US, where she intended to claim asylum. The asylum defence applied to the charge of using false documents, but not, the judge ruled, to the additional charge of attempting to obtain air services by deception, which was not listed in the 1999 legislation, and she was sentenced to nine months' imprisonment on the latter charge. The House of Lords ruled in 2008 that, as someone fleeing persecution, she should not have been convicted of any offence.[48] Following the ruling, refugee support organisations such as Asylum Aid asked the attorney-general to review all similar convictions so they can be quashed, since they affect employment and citizenship prospects as well as travel to the US and Canada.[49] But a decade after *Adimi*, widespread ignorance of the asylum defence was still causing many refugees to be wrongly convicted. In October 2010, the Court of Appeal ruled that three refugees – two Iranians and a Somali woman – had suffered miscarriages of justice by being detained on arrival, charged, prosecuted, convicted and sentenced to between eight and fifteen months' imprisonment for using false identity documents. No one – immigration officers, police, CPS, duty solicitors or judges in the magistrates' or crown court – had realised that they should benefit from the asylum defence.[50] In *Adimi* the government had been forced to concede that asylum rights took priority over controlling entry. But in 2004, the government unveiled a new initiative against asylum seekers. Return of the passport provided by 'shepherds' left asylum seekers with no document to present to the immigration officer. A new law made it a crime punishable by two years' imprisonment to fail to produce a valid travel document to the immigration officer on arrival or at an asylum interview, unless the traveller never had a travel document, or had a 'reasonable excuse' for getting rid of one. But obedience to the instructions of an agent would generally not count as a reasonable excuse under the section.[51] The government's rationale was that asylum seekers were destroying travel documents in order to make false claims and to prevent their removal. The Home Affairs Committee expressed concern that 'genuine refugees may be convicted', JUSTICE and the Law Society argued that the new offence breached Article 31,[52] and Lord Avebury pointed out, '[P]utting [someone] in prison ... seems to be a curious way of helping someone to resettle when he has escaped from a foreign dictatorship.'[53] But a strong campaign did not prevent the clause's enactment.

Despite Baroness Scotland's promise that the new offence 'is not there to catch the innocent or the unwary',[54] 18 months later over 200 asylum seekers, including children, elderly people and victims of torture had gone to prison under the section.[55] One of these was Ms E, an Eritrean Pentecostalist who fled religious persecution in her own country and forced marriage in Sudan, where she sought refuge. When she arrived at Heathrow, she could produce no travel documents, having returned to the agent, on demand, the false passport he gave her to board the plane at Khartoum. She was convicted of not having a valid passport at her asylum interview, and went to prison for three months, despite being accepted as a *bona fide* refugee. She appealed the conviction, arguing that the refugee defence ought to apply. Her case was heard with that of a 19-year-old Afghan asylum seeker who, like her, had returned the passport to the agent 'because he said if I disobeyed him I would not get to my destination'. It was rudely dismissed by criminal appeal judges who knew little and cared less about refugee protection and seemed affronted by my and my colleague's arguments. For them, parliament was perfectly free to legislate in breach of the Refugee Convention if it wanted to. The new law was clear and left no room for a refugee defence.[56] The House of Lords refused permission to appeal – the same law lords who, twelve years earlier, had mocked the idea that arrival without a passport could be a criminal offence. In just twelve years, the absurd had been given the force of law.

The campaign to stop refugees being penalised by the new law met with more success the following year, when the Lord Chief Justice ruled that disposal of a false passport, used to leave the country of persecution, was not a criminal offence under the statute if the asylum seeker had never had a genuine, valid passport. The judgment virtually put an end to prosecutions under this section.[57] But the courts continued their refusal to give protection to humanitarian smugglers of refugees, rejecting the argument of Rudolph Alps, who used his British nephew's passport to help his Kurdish nephew escape persecution in Turkey, that Article 31 should give immunity from prosecution to the smuggler as well as to the smuggled.[58]

EXTENDING THE BORDERS

Resistance from refugee and rights organisations and success in the higher courts largely defeated the deterrent strategy of criminalising asylum seekers. But the government, working with other EU states, has had far more success using technology, diplomacy and military might, against which legal strategies have so far failed. Technology to detect both false documents and stowaways hiding in vehicles was introduced not just at UK ports but also at ports and railway stations in France and Belgium, through juxtaposed controls, introduced in 1993 and extended in 2003, to stop asylum seekers embarking for the UK.[59] In 2003, immigration minister Beverley Hughes claimed that the controls had reduced numbers of undocumented passengers by 90 per cent.[60] Home Office airline liaison officers (ALOs) trained and advised airline staff at airports abroad on checking for forged documents – but not on Refugee Convention obligations. According to the 2002 White Paper *Secure borders, safe haven*, the ALOs were responsible for preventing over 22,500 inadequately documented passengers from boarding in twelve months. There is no way of knowing how many of these were fleeing persecution. So successful were the ALOs in preventing undocumented travel that by 2009, now known as immigration liaison managers (ILMs), they were deployed in 49 airports in four continents.[61]

In 2001, to stem the arrival of Czech Roma fleeing skinhead violence, the Home Office went further, sending immigration officers to Prague airport to examine passengers before they boarded the aircraft.[62] Looking not for false documents but for likely asylum claimants, they targeted Roma passengers, whom they questioned closely about their intentions in coming to the UK. Ninety per cent of the Roma passengers were refused boarding, as against 0.2 per cent of the non-Roma. Six refused Roma passengers took the Home Office to court, supported by the European Roma Rights

Centre.[63] They argued that the Refugee Convention imposed at least an implicit obligation to allow refugees to reach a country of asylum, and preventing boarding frustrated the Convention's central protective purpose and violated their right to claim asylum. They also argued that subjecting only Roma passengers to intensive questioning was racially discriminatory. In its judgment of December 2004, the House of Lords agreed that the immigration officers' conduct unlawfully discriminated against Roma passengers on racial grounds. But on the main issue, they were against the claimants, maintaining that sovereign states were perfectly entitled to take measures to prevent the arrival of refugees and that the Refugee Convention had no application outside the borders of host states.[64]

The judgment dealt a severe blow to refugee protection, definitively legalising all the prevention strategies of successive governments. It cleared the way for e-Borders, a fully integrated system of pre-screening of all incoming passengers by UK-based immigration officers before they travel, using detailed passenger information demanded from carriers. Passenger and crew lists have been required from carriers since 1905, but with their increased information-gathering powers, UKBA officials can now demand such details as when and where the ticket was issued, who booked it, how it was paid for, the passenger's visa expiry date and travel itinerary and the names of all other passengers on the reservation.[65] Carriers must supply the information requested, if they have it, on pain of penalties.[66] Officials will then authorise or deny the passenger's travel, using information from the European Information System and other databases. This is the 'authority-to-carry' scheme. Marry this with biometrics in visas – fingerprints have been required from all visa applicants since 2006 – together with the digitised information in the machine-readable zone of passports, require carriers to build computer interfaces to transmit all this data to UKBA in real time,[67] and you have e-Borders. When it is fully implemented,[68] anyone whose biometric data does not match that in the travel document, or whose data shows an adverse immigration history or other 'undesirability', can be refused boarding, wherever in the world that person is and whatever perils he or she faces, at the click of a mouse of an immigration officer sitting at a computer terminal in the UK.

As more and more resources have gone into the technology of detection and prevention – heartbeat scanners, carbon dioxide detectors, fibre-optic cameras, thermal imaging, millimetric wave imaging; as these technologies have been exported to 'vulnerable' borders;[69] and as carrier penalties have spread to cover anyone with any means of transport which migrants can use, so refugees' journeys have become longer, more hazardous, with more unknown casualties. Thousands have died trying to reach Spain, Malta, Lampedusa or the Canary Islands in small boats from Africa,[70] or as stowaways thrown overboard on discovery by ships' captains unwilling to pay the fines they would incur if they allowed them to land.[71] Others have been killed by landmines as they tried to enter Greece, shot by border guards at the Spanish Moroccan enclave of Ceuta,[72] frozen to death in the wheel arches of planes, electrocuted trying to get into the Channel Tunnel, fallen from or crushed by trains.[73] Survivors and relatives of the dead are, however, rarely treated with compassion. Twenty-two-year-old Pardeep Saini, who survived ten hours at temperatures of minus 60° in an aircraft wheel bay in which his 19-year-old brother died, was interviewed within hours of his arrival in November 1996 and detained at Harmondsworth for return to India despite his severe hypothermia, shock and grief. Immigration minister Mike O'Brien responded to campaigners by expressing 'reluctance to reward someone for using extreme methods to evade immigration control'.[74] And in June 2000, the UK-based families of 58 Chinese migrants who suffocated in a lorry arriving at Dover were prevented from identifying relatives' bodies unless they gave information about their own immigration status and the travel route of the victims.[75] The government has occasionally recognised that refugees have no legal and safe way of getting here, but the 'solutions' are based on keeping them out, save in minuscule numbers.[76]

OUTSOURCING BORDER CONTROLS

As migration is increasingly managed globally, controls are outsourced to countries of origin and transit. The EU first recruited eastern European countries seeking accession as 'buffer states' to stop refugees travelling to western Europe through their territories, and supplied them with the latest military and technological paraphernalia.[77] Then, Mediterranean states such as Morocco and Libya were given EU funding to improve their border controls and detention facilities.[78] Most recently new 'buffer states' – Western Sahara, Mali, Niger, Chad, Sudan, Georgia, Armenia, Iran, Turkmenistan, Kazakhstan, Mongolia, Senegal and Mauritania, under pressure to adopt EU 'standards' on control of migration through 'migration management' clauses in trade and cooperation agreements, are funded to police migrants' movements by land and sea, with the International Organization for Migration (IOM) running 'technical assistance' programmes in transit countries. These measures are having a serious knock-on effect on migrant and refugee movements in Africa. According to Fortress Europe, detention centres in Libya and Mauritania held 60,000 migrants in 2008, in appalling conditions; there are mass expulsions to the desert, and forced repatriations increased tenfold between 2003 and 2006.[79] It used to be possible to travel without documents right through the countries of the Sahel (Senegal, Mauritania, Mali, Burkina Faso, Algeria, Niger, Nigeria, Chad, Sudan, Somalia, Ethiopia and Eritrea), but not anymore.[80] Many of the military and technological barriers against undocumented migrants familiar in Europe have been exported to African countries which never had immigration controls, locking populations in to their own countries and jeopardising their ability to find safety even in their own continent.

The UK has also joined EU programmes intercepting and turning back the boats bringing refugees from Africa. From joint military operations such as Operation Ulysses, which included British aircraft and warships, the EU has developed a fully-fledged militarised border force, Frontex,[81] which watches migrants' movements in the Sahara and on the Mediterranean and Atlantic coasts of Africa using satellite surveillance and deploys land and sea patrols to stop them.[82] But all the surveillance does not prevent refugee deaths from drowning, hunger and thirst.[83] The 'push-back' operations involving the interception and return of refugees to Libya and Tunisia from Italian waters were declared unlawful by the ECtHR in February 2012, since the crew of the military vessels made no attempt to identify those fleeing persecution, who should not have been returned to a country with no refugee law.[84] The impact of the court's judgment remains to be seen. But until the recent exodus of refugees from north Africa,[85] the patrols dramatically reduced the numbers arriving in Europe, and during the 'Arab spring', when the Italian and Greek governments sought help in receiving the sudden influx from Libya and Tunisia, Britain refused to take a single refugee.[86] The number of asylum seekers reaching the UK has steadily declined to around a quarter of the 100,000 recorded at their peak in 2002. The world is not a less dangerous place, but the government has rendered most refugees invisible by keeping them at a distance. The refugee 'problem' has been offloaded onto the countries of southern Europe, to countries such as Turkey, Libya and

Syria, which are not full signatories of the Refugee Convention,[87] and to the Caucasus, the Middle East and sub-Saharan Africa.

RESISTANCE

An ever-growing network of resistance exposes and challenges the hypocrisy, immorality and injustice of the anti-refugee policies. Since the 1990s, European refugee and migrant organisations and solidarity groups have run border camps on the EU's eastern borders to document and protest human rights abuses there. UNITED for Intercultural Action, based in the Netherlands, has monitored migrant deaths at sea since 1993. People's tribunals such as the Basso Tribunal (the Permanent People's Tribunal), sitting at Berlin in 1994 with a distinguished jury, have condemned European anti-asylum policies. In the 2000s, solidarity groups formed around Calais, supplying food, clothing and medical care, refugee groups from across Europe have held conferences and joint actions, and Civil Rights Caravans have toured Germany and the UK in support of refugee rights. Groups such as European Roma Rights have become involved in test case litigation, and many civil society groups, including the Institute of Race Relations in the UK, Migreurop, UNITED and PICUM in Europe, document developments and exchange information with migrant rights groups in the US, Asia and Latin America. The movement for refugees and migrants has gone global, and has forged links with anti-arms trade, environmental and anti-globalisation campaigns to fight all these interconnected forms of global injustice. But the legal, military, technological and diplomatic barriers to refugee movements are formidable. We need to up our game, finding creative ways to highlight and challenge the systematic closing off of routes to safety.

2
Struggles for Fair Decision-making

In February 2010 whistle-blower Louise Perrett, an asylum caseworker, disclosed the pervasive anti-asylum seeker culture in her Cardiff office, epitomised by the 'grant monkey' put on the desk of any official who granted refugee status. Asylum seekers were 'mistreated, tricked and humiliated' by UKBA officials, who conducted interviews without lawyers, independent witnesses or tape recorders, she claimed, and caseworkers were advised to refuse 'difficult' cases and 'let a tribunal sort it out'.[1] Although an internal investigation rejected her accusations, her portrayal was instantly recognisable to the asylum seekers of many nationalities who have been subjected to contempt and rejection in the asylum system, not just from officials but from immigration judges too. The bread-and-butter work of immigration lawyers involves tackling the myths, assumptions and attitudes collectively referred to as the 'culture of disbelief' which distorts official and judicial decisions.

Asylum seekers are just the latest group to be so treated. In 1979, immigration officers were found to be virginity-testing brides from the Indian sub-continent as they arrived at Heathrow. A Home Office medical inspector explained, 'The abuse of immigration laws is ... common and the assumption of false identity an ever-present problem ... an inspection of the introitus or a vaginal examination may be indicated to clarify matters.'[2] A vigorous community campaign by groups including the Indian Workers' Association, AWAZ and Southall Black Sisters forced home secretary Merlyn Rees to put a stop to the practice,[3] and the Commission for Racial Equality (CRE) launched a formal investigation into race discrimination in the immigration service. Its report, issued in 1985, confirmed what was already well known in migrant communities: visitors from the black Commonwealth were overwhelmingly more likely to be refused entry than those from the white Commonwealth or the US; entry clearance officers in the Indian sub-continent started from the premise that applicants seeking entry as dependants were probably lying; nationals of poor countries were subject to more intensive scrutiny that those of rich countries. The CRE concluded that the administration of immigration control 'concentrated to an excessive degree' on the prevention and detection of evasion, which obscured and overrode rights.[4] Its report changed nothing; in 1989, Jamaican visitors were still a hundred times more likely to be refused leave to enter at the port than Australians. In 1993, I represented one of an entire charter flight of Jamaican passengers who were all refused entry for a Christmas visit. Solicitor Louise Christian phoned a judge on Christmas Day to prevent the passenger's removal, and we eventually won damages for his three-day detention, which the judge held 'so unreasonable as to be unlawful'.[5] A Jamaican interviewed in 2010 revealed the same exclusionary culture at work when he said, 'I don't like that you are actually on your knees begging these people to get into their country and they just refuse you.'[6] South Asians and West Africans, particularly Nigerians, the *bêtes noires* of the immigration service, were treated just as badly.[7]

Political leaders consistently set the tone, from Enoch Powell and his 'rivers of blood' in 1968 and Margaret Thatcher's 'swamped by a different culture' speech in 1978, to ministerial references since the 1980s to 'bogus asylum seekers' and in the 2000s, 'bogus students'. Electoral politics and media coverage are shamelessly based on anti-immigration 'common sense' reflecting and amplifying popular racism. In this relentlessly hostile climate, it is not surprising that Home Office officials take the tone of their political masters, or that indifference and contempt are manifested in massive delays, mountains of lost files, hostile questioning, bullying and decisions based on ignorant and unwarranted assumptions. Asylum seekers are repeatedly told they are lying. Sometimes immigration officers just won't let go of apparent contradictions: one Libyan asylum claimant was interviewed 15 times, over a period of a hundred hours.[8] Children interviewed in 2011 by the Children's Commissioner said they were frightened by lengthy asylum screening interviews, sometimes conducted without an independent adult,[9] and a torture survivor was told at screening that she was lying through her teeth.[10] But as often, there is just a lack of interest – answers are not fully or properly recorded, apparent non-sequiturs or contradictions not pursued at all, so no opportunity is given to explain; and the tone of the questions actively discourages disclosure of painful and humiliating events, non-disclosure of which can be fatal to an application.

THE BATTLE FOR DUE PROCESS

The refusal letter to an Afghan asylum seeker which read 'the Secretary of State considers your claim to be a pile of pants' became notorious,[11] but refugee groups have condemned the abysmal quality of asylum decisions for decades. The first battle, in the 1980s, was for reasons to be given for refusal of asylum, which was rare despite well-known principles of fairness requiring reasons for important administrative decisions. Worse, those refused asylum at the port, or after entering the country illegally, had no right of appeal, and adverse decisions could only be challenged by judicial review in the high court, on narrow grounds of illegality, irrationality or procedural irregularity. Such a challenge was impossible without knowing the reasons for refusal.

As refugees from Cyprus, Sri Lanka, Turkey and all corners of Africa began to organise themselves in the 1980s, umbrella groups such as the Migrants Rights Action Network and Refugee Forum made demands for due process rights such as reasons and appeal rights – demands taken up by the support groups springing up to defend migrants and refugees, and later by mainstream human rights groups such as Amnesty International and the National Council for Civil Liberties (now Liberty), and adopted by lawyers working with these groups. The high court accepted in 1986 that reasons for refusal of asylum would be 'highly desirable',[12] and the following year, the House of Lords emphasised the need for 'anxious scrutiny' of decisions affecting rights to life and liberty.[13] Sierra Leonean asylum seeker and Hackney council worker Marion Gaima made legal history when, supported by her union, NALGO, she challenged the refusal of asylum without the opportunity to answer objections to her story. Her barrister Ian Macdonald successfully argued that officials must give applicants a chance to deal with objections before refusing claims.[14] The Home Office was forced to issue provisional refusals, termed 'minded to refuse' letters, setting out the objections which, unless successfully addressed by the asylum seeker, would defeat the claim. Finally, in 1993, an appeal on the merits of asylum claims before removal was provided, when the European Court of Human Rights looked about to demand one.[15] While the appeal right was vital, it had unintended consequences: the 'minded to refuse' procedure fell into disuse, and unfair and absurd points were relied on to refuse claims, on the basis that they could be corrected on appeal. But the independent authorities to whom immigrants and asylum seekers appealed[16] were immersed in the same culture and many shared the same attitudes.

The 'old guard' of adjudicators were appointed by the Home Office and were frequently ex-colonial judges or civil servants, with attitudes to match. In the 1980s, when I began representing migrants, one old, titled adjudicator was famous for asking appellants' representatives what right they had to be in the country. Adjudicators became independent of the Home Office in 1987, but nothing really changed. They could display extraordinary coldness and inhumanity; when a witness broke down while giving evidence, the adjudicator brusquely told me to control my witness, and on another occasion, Tribunal members coolly stepped over an appellant who had collapsed sobbing on the floor. Some displayed overt racism, remarking that West Africans should not be accountancy students, for example. These attitudes were not confined to low-level judges either: I have witnessed a senior judge in a packed high court repeatedly bellowing 'Can you read?' at a black barrister whose written pleading did not comply with new guidance. Although such openly racist attitudes have become culturally and legally unacceptable, there are still immigration judges who (privately) boast that they have never allowed an appeal; many have cosy relationships with Home Office presenting officers whom they see daily, many relish their power and brook no challenge to it; and many become quickly and permanently case-hardened.

As entry to the judiciary has broadened in race, class and gender terms, a decent number of immigration judges now bring a refreshing open-mindedness and humanity to the job. Their decisions are the ones that are routinely appealed by the Home Office. It used to be rare for the Home Office to appeal a positive decision by an immigration judge, but it has become routine, although a further appeal should only be brought if the immigration judge has made a legal error.

Entry to the UK depends on satisfying officials (or on appeal, an immigration judge) of a particular state of affairs – if you are a visitor, that you have funds to support yourself and will leave at the end of your visit; if seeking family reunion, that you are related to the British sponsor, who will support you, and if seeking asylum, that you have a well-founded fear of racial, religious, social or political persecution (that is, there is a real risk you will be persecuted) if forced to return.[17] Establishing the facts is central. But too often immigration judges, like Home Office officials, say simply, 'I don't believe you'. This widespread disbelief has put into question the basis of judicial decision-making. In this field, 'instinct' or 'intuition' is often a tangled ball of unexamined, preconceived ideas of how people behave, informed by prejudice and whether they look you in the eye. So despite warnings of the dangers of reading too much into demeanour,[18] immigration judges still describe as 'evasive' and 'unworthy of belief' witnesses who hesitate, ramble, have difficulty remembering, or who for cultural reasons avoid eye contact. And the higher courts will not interfere with immigration judges' evaluation unless it is obvious that it is badly defective because, for example, no reasons are given or important evidence has been left out of account altogether.[19] This leaves a lot of room for subtle, unstated, often unconscious prejudices and assumptions.

DISCREPANCIES USED TO JUSTIFY REJECTION

The 'discrepancy-counting' approach to decision-making assumes that discrepancies in accounts between different tellings or different witnesses point to fabrication rather than normal variations in recall. In the 1970s and 1980s it was the main weapon used to refuse visas to children in the Indian sub-continent seeking to join fathers in Britain. In a grotesque parody of a TV game show, family members were questioned in turn about the family home – how many rooms, who occupied them, what livestock were kept – and visas refused when answers didn't tally, for failure to satisfy the entry clearance officer that the family were 'related as claimed'.[20] As community groups fought the anti-immigration rhetoric and vicious racial attacks in the east London Bangladeshi community, Tower Hamlets Law Centre coordinated the legal resistance to the refusals.

The approach should have been fatally discredited when the arrival of DNA testing in the late 1980s proved that most of the claimed relationships were genuine. But instead, discrepancy-counting was transplanted to areas not susceptible to scientific falsification – the primary purpose of marriage or a couple's intention to live together ('disproved' by differing recollections of first meeting or of who said what to whom and when) – and then to asylum claims. Since in this field, eye-witnesses are rare, it is more often applied to differences between claimants' first and subsequent accounts. On matters such as dates of significant events, the duration of a claimed detention, the precise methods of torture used on each occasion, discrepancies damage credibility. On appeal, Home Office presenting officers often resort to the advocate's trick of forcing the witness to choose between the different versions: 'Well, were you released in June or July? Which was it?' And then, signs of confusion, hesitation or self-contradiction in trying to answer are seized on to confirm the conclusion that the witness is fabricating. The problem is exacerbated by delays in the process. A Turkish Kurd who claimed asylum in 1991 had been active in left-wing politics since the late 1970s, and had as a result been arrested and tortured on numberless occasions. Meeting him, it was obvious he lived and breathed politics, which would have marked him out for persecution. But his inability to recall the exact dates and durations of every single period of detention, and the exact manner of his torture on each occasion – whether electric shock, or *falaka* or Palestinian hanging – exacerbated by the length of time he had to wait for interviews, and the intervals between, meant that his claim was disbelieved. He was expected to have total recall in 1997, when his appeal was heard, six years after his application and over 20 years since his first arrest.

Discrepancy-counting as an approach to asylum decision-making has been very difficult to challenge. But academic researchers and psychiatrists have produced a hugely valuable body of work demonstrating the vagaries and unreliability of memory,[21] among trauma sufferers in particular,[22] and describing the difficulties victims of violations sometimes have in telling their story. The failure of a claimant to mention something significant at the first opportunity, such as torture or rape, seems fatal to credibility: how could anyone forget something so traumatic? But in 1997, medical evidence obtained by Women Against Rape in support of a rape victim demonstrated that survivors frequently find it impossible to talk about their ordeal until they have been through a sometimes lengthy healing process. Ms E's asylum claim was refused and her appeal dismissed before she could reveal her rape and sexual enslavement as a young girl by Ugandan soldiers. She made a fresh claim. The rules said that evidence in support of a fresh asylum claim had to be 'previously unavailable' or it would be disregarded. The psychiatric report convinced the high court judge that the shame she felt had prevented her from revealing her ordeal until then. He ruled that the Home Office was wrong to discount the evidence.[23] The Centre for the Study of Emotion and Law, set up in 2007, trains lawyers to understand why memories are frozen by horrendous events, but there is a long way to go in persuading judges that late claims of rape or torture are not necessarily fabricated.

In recognition of children's vulnerability, it was the practice not to interview unaccompanied children on their asylum claim, but to rely instead on objective evidence, in line with UNHCR guidance. But even here, the discrepancy-counting approach appeared, causing injustice. DS had no idea why his family had sent him away from Angola, just that his mother had died. Once here, he learned some of his family's history from Angolan exiles. When after five years he was asked to complete an asylum questionnaire, he set out what he had heard. Without interviewing him, the Home Office refused his claim – and without questioning him, the adjudicator dismissed the appeal because of the 'discrepancies' between his screening interview, held on arrival, and the asylum questionnaire completed five years later.[24]

ASSUMPTIONS UNDERLYING REFUSALS

Many asylum refusals are based on unstated, so-called 'common-sense' assumptions shared by Home Office caseworkers and immigration judges about the way people 'should' behave – assumptions born sometimes of ignorance, laziness or arrogance, and applied within a framework which denies asylum seekers full human agency. Here is a sample of the most common assumptions encountered in my own practice:

- *Political activists must be fervent.* So a Nubian activist, journalist, poet and songwriter whose phrases became anti-regime graffiti on Khartoum walls was disbelieved because he had 'none of the fervour of the revolutionary or frustrated nationalist in exile'.[25]
- *If a political party is not banned, its members are not persecuted.* So members of opposition parties in Kenya or Democratic Republic of Congo (DRC) who describe an escalating pattern of intimidation, detention and ill-treatment, are routinely disbelieved on the basis that 'your party is legal', 'multi-party elections have been held'. (Ironically, 'good governance' clauses in trade or aid agreements often insist on multi-party democracy, so repressive governments allow opposition parties to register, but harry, intimidate and sometimes kill their members.)
- *Men involved in banned opposition parties in traditional societies tell their wives what they are doing.* So if a Kurdish or Algerian wife does not give evidence in support of her husband's claim, or says she knew nothing of her husband's activities, his claim is dismissed as fabricated.
- *'Uncle' always refers to a biological relationship.* So a Tamil who says he has no relatives in Colombo, but that his 'uncle' helped him, must be lying. (In fact the term is used in many cultures to denote older family friends.)

- *No one acts out of anything other than rational self-interest.* So claims that a stranger or neighbour sheltered someone wanted by police, or that a prison guard allowed a prisoner to escape through pity, or political or tribal solidarity, are frequently disbelieved as fabricated and incredible.
- *Police from repressive regimes always behave efficiently* ('it is incredible that the police would fail to secure the block of flats').[26] This argument is also used to counter claims of escape.
- *A political party a Home Office caseworker has not heard of does not exist.* So YS, who said he had been condemned to death in his absence after his opposition group had been discovered, had his claim rejected because 'there is no reference in our sources to the political group you claim to belong to'. The appeal succeeded following expert evidence about the party.[27] A year later, another activist from the same party was turned down on exactly the same basis: 'we are unaware of the existence of this party'.[28]
- *Someone wrongly suspected of gun-running for armed militant groups in Algeria could 'go to the police and sort it out'.* This is a classic example of 'home counties' thinking afflicting immigration judges.[29]
- *Someone fleeing persecution would go to a neighbouring country, and no one who crosses continents to claim asylum in the UK is genuinely fleeing persecution.* These related assumptions ignore the fact that neighbouring countries are often not safe; the Turkish authorities, for example, regularly return 'illegal entrants' across the border to Iran, and the persecuting country's own security forces don't always stay their side of the border. Genuine refugees frequently come to Britain for reasons of family, language or culture, or a belief in British justice, or just to get as far away as possible.
- *A genuine refugee knows how to claim and will claim asylum on arrival at the port.* So 'no one deciding to seek asylum before he left his own country could be telling the truth if he says he did not make a claim through ignorance of the correct procedure'.[30] But the procedure is not that obvious, and fear of officials frequently prevents immediate claims.

Some assumptions are double-sided:

- *Someone involved in political opposition has an encyclopaedic knowledge of the party, its history and its policies* (and a convert to Christianity similarly knows the Bible). So failing the 'knowledge' test means refusal of asylum. But knowing the party history or the Bible doesn't guarantee acceptance: the claimant might have obtained the information from others or from the internet.

- *Someone facing persecution would leave their country as soon as possible.* So staying on because of family, friendships or political commitment, or risking a last meeting with family, undermines the claim. A Turkish political activist, who remained to continue the struggle for 15 years until he was compelled to leave in fear for his and his parents' life, was refused on this basis.[31] But those who left when they saw the writing on the wall, like veteran communist MY, who left Sudan after warnings from three different sources, are told 'you have not been persecuted'; 'the risk is speculative'.[32]
- *Someone fleeing persecution would not bring children on such a dangerous journey.* Or the reverse: they would not leave their children behind to face such danger alone.
- *The use of a false passport to enter the UK* generally leads to an adverse finding on credibility,[33] and since 2004 to a statutory presumption of adverse credibility.[34] But the use of one's own passport is equally likely to lead to refusal – 'if they were genuinely interested in you, the authorities would not have given you a passport or allowed you to leave'.[35]
- *The fact that claimants are still alive* has been held to undermine their claim: 'Your enemies have had ample opportunity to kill you, but they have not done so'; 'The threats against you were not carried out'.[36] Yet I was rebuked in court for describing the Home Office attitude as 'the only good refugee is a dead one'.

Yet oddly, a government attempt to create a legal presumption of adverse credibility fell flat. A Labour statute required decision-makers and judges to 'take into account as damaging asylum seekers' credibility' behaviour 'designed or likely' to mislead, obstruct or delay the handling of a claim (including failure to produce a valid passport or destruction of travel documents, failure to seek asylum in a 'safe' country or at the right time).[37] Immigration judges felt the presumption trespassed directly on their role of weighing up all the evidence in assessing credibility. The section was quickly marginalised, and the higher courts ruled that, provided the listed behaviours were considered, their weight in credibility assessment was a matter for the judge.[38]

Campaigns by refugee groups and organisations such as Asylum Aid and the Medical Foundation have exposed the assumptions underlying decisions in a series of reports,[39] and lawyers have challenged them in court, so that the higher courts at least have begun to accept that decisions based on the perceived implausibility of asylum seekers' accounts are very dangerous when taken in ignorance of conditions in very different societies.[40]

THE BIAS OF COUNTRY INFORMATION

Another campaign has focused on the misleading and dangerous information issued by the Home Office on refugee-producing countries[41] and used by caseworkers deciding asylum claims, immigration judges and sometimes hard-pressed appellants' representatives. The country reports are crucial to the decision-making and appeal process, and their accuracy and reliability are essential. Life can depend on it, as the case of AA demonstrated. An Iranian political activist arrested in anti-regime demonstrations in 1992 and tortured in the notorious Evin prison, AA was released on bail, got his passport renewed through bribery and left Iran overland. The reasons for refusing asylum included the fact that he had been released ('you would not have been released if you were suspected of opposition'); that he had then been summonsed rather than arrested ('if the Revolutionary Guards wanted you they would not have written to you'), and that he could not have renewed his passport by bribery – the Home Office country report on Iran said this was impossible. We won his case with the help of a distinguished scholar and Iran expert who confirmed that people suspected of serious crimes against the regime were frequently granted bail, frequently summonsed rather than arrested, and were able to extend passports through bribery and corruption, which were endemic. But four years later, the Home Office relied on the same unreliable information in another Iranian case in which the appellant claimed to have left the country through bribery. Officials had not bothered to change the country report to reflect the true position.[42]

Home Office country assessments have long been condemned as partial, inaccurate and unreliable. The Refugee Council reported in 1995 that they were 'fundamentally flawed' – the assessment of Nigeria was 'an acutely distorted picture of the political and human rights conditions',[43] and in 2003 the IAS found Home Office assessments of 21 countries including Afghanistan, Algeria, Ethiopia, Iran, Rwanda, Sri Lanka, Zimbabwe and DRC flawed by basic inaccuracies.[44] In the climate of hostile disbelief of asylum seekers, reliable country information against which to judge their accounts was not seen as important. They weren't worth it.

Faced with official incredulity and misleading Home Office country reports, refugee support organisations and lawyers realised the need for authoritative country evidence. Informal networks developed to collate and exchange reports from human rights groups and UN bodies, and renowned academic experts were commissioned to prepare reports for individual cases. For the first time, the appellate authorities were given real insight into the situation for political opponents, religious or racial minorities and had thorough, objective information against which to assess appellants' accounts. Expert country reports really came into their own when the Tribunal (the second-tier appellate body, now the Upper Tribunal) bowed to the higher courts' complaints of inconsistent and chaotic decision-making, and began designating particular cases as 'country guidance', authoritative assessments of the human rights situation for specific minorities in particular countries against which to judge individual cases.[45]

But Tribunals fed on anodyne Home Office assessments, and anxious to preserve their own authority, lashed out at appellants' experts, calling them 'too critical', 'too gloomy' about the human rights situation in the countries they reported on. Reports by world-renowned academics were dismissed as 'partial', 'speculative', 'unsourced'. The Court of Appeal delivered a stinging rebuke to the Tribunal in a 2000 test case where four expert witnesses gave evidence on the risks facing Tamils on return to Sri Lanka: '[I]t was completely wrong for the tribunal ... to dismiss considerations put forward by experts of the quality who wrote opinions on this case as "pure speculation."'[46] One of the first country guidance cases, involving ethnic Serbs in Croatia, had to be sent back to the Tribunal because of its failure to address significant expert evidence,[47] and wilful disregard or unwarranted dismissal of experts' evidence continues.[48]

Evidence from the Foreign and Commonwealth Office (FCO) or the British Embassy usually receives a far less critical reception. In 1996, the Tribunal relied on an upbeat FCO assessment, contradicted by all the other reports, to dismiss a Sudanese Christian's appeal. His fear of arrest on return was also rejected, despite a Sudanese security service document indicating that returnees were routinely detained – the Sudanese government and the security service head had assured the British Embassy that the document was forged. The

Court of Appeal observed that in asylum cases, information from government sources was hardly reliable, and chided the Tribunal for being 'over-impressed' by FCO and Embassy material.[49] The battle against double standards still raged over a decade later. The Tribunal asserted in 2007 that diplomats' opinions, unlike experts' reports, could be accepted without knowing their sources of information, and neither the potential conflict of interest in a diplomat, professionally friendly to the host state, giving evidence about its human rights abuses, nor the partiality of government sources, caused it concern.[50] In 2011, the Court of Appeal had to remind the Tribunal that FCO evidence is not to be given any special status or taken at face value.[51]

Campaigning by refugee support groups and judicial criticism have not yet achieved the demand of an independent resource providing unbiased and comprehensive country information to all parties, on the Canadian model. But in 2002 the Advisory Panel on Country Information (APCI) was set up to monitor Home Office reports for accuracy and reliability using independent academics. In 2009 it became the Independent Advisory Group on Country Information, part of the new inspectorate of the UK Border Agency. It, and groups such as *Still Human Still Here*, have forced UKBA to improve its own country information by publishing their own critical reports.

THE QUEST FOR SUPPORTING EVIDENCE

Failure to produce supporting evidence is a common but wrongful reason for refusal of an asylum claim. As senior judges have observed, jailers do not write to confirm asylum seekers' accounts of torture and incommunicado detention, while the risk of jeopardising the safety of others often precludes obtaining supporting evidence from hospitals, relatives or comrades at home. But even when there is supporting evidence, getting it before a court is not always straight-forward. AM's case is an extreme example of the difficulties asylum seekers encounter trying to produce evidence in the teeth of judicial pig-headedness. It is also an object lesson in tenacity.

A Cameroonian woman, AM claimed that she was arrested, beaten and imprisoned when she refused to disclose her activist husband's whereabouts. The Home Office rejected her claim as incredible. There were two witnesses in Cameroon, a human rights activist and her lawyer, who could verify her account. There was no funding to bring them to the appeal, the postal service from Cameroon was very unreliable, and little weight is given to statements from witnesses who cannot be questioned, so her representative applied to the immigration judge for their evidence to be taken by live telephone link. Told there were no facilities for such a link, and receiving no response to his request that the Tribunal use the county court's telephone link (on the same floor of the same building), he sought and obtained Legal Services Commission (LSC) funding to install a link in the courtroom. But the judge repeatedly refused the application, accusing him of going behind his back in getting the link installed – a refusal backed by a senior immigration judge. No reasons were given.

On the day scheduled for the hearing, the immigration judge refused to adjourn it for written statements from the Cameroon witnesses. Despite medical evidence showing that the appellant could die if her blood pressure rose sharply (making her ability to give oral evidence doubtful), the judge, banging his fist on the table, said there had been plenty of time to obtain the statements (for which funding had been received two days earlier) and insisted the case went ahead that day whatever happened. AM 'became at this stage very afraid of the judge ... I felt my body suddenly became weak and heavy. I was getting dizzy and my vision was blurry. I was becoming confused.' She was taken from the hearing room in a semi-collapsed state and, losing consciousness, was admitted to hospital with dangerously high blood pressure. Only then did the judge agree to adjourn the case – but only for a week, scheduling it for a day no representative could attend and insisting on hearing it himself. On the appointed day, an application to adjourn again, supported by evidence that AM had chest pains and uncontrolled blood pressure which needed urgent investigation, was rejected. Faced with this situation, the firm's ad-hoc representative, who did not know the case and had attended purely to get the case adjourned, in the absence of AM's own representative, withdrew from the hearing – which proceeded without the appellant and without any evidence from the Cameroon witnesses, whose statements had not yet been signed and returned. Although the solicitors sent the judge the signed statements from the Cameroon witnesses confirming AM's account immediately they received them (the following day), he refused to take account of them and dismissed the appeal. The Tribunal refused to consider reopening the case, claiming the application was made late. The Court of Appeal quashed the decision as a denial of justice.[52]

I believe all immigration lawyers are familiar with the attitudes displayed in this case, although few confront them with the tenacity shown by AM's representatives. What possesses judges to conduct themselves in this way? Clearly, the judge felt his authority challenged, but it is hard to escape the conclusion that colonial and racist attitudes which deem Africans 'lesser breeds' and asylum seekers opportunistic liars also played a part.

When supporting evidence is produced, it is frequently treated with the deepest suspicion and scepticism. Statements from family members are rejected as not independent, or self-serving, and arrest warrants, party membership cards and even local press cuttings are routinely rejected by disbelieving immigration judges unless authenticated by experts. But for the Home Office, unsubstantiated allegations can be enough to deny refugee status, as S's case showed. S's asylum claim, refused by the Home Office, was allowed on appeal, and the Home Office did not appeal the immigration judge's decision. But when allegations that S's claim was false appeared on a TV programme, the Home Office issued a deportation notice, with no inquiry into the cogency of the broadcast material.[53]

MEDICAL EVIDENCE MARGINALISED

The scepticism of Home Office officials and adjudicators created a need for expert documentation of injuries, physical and psychological, and the Medical Foundation for the Care of Victims of Torture (now renamed Freedom from Torture) was founded in 1985 by members of Amnesty International's medical group. Under Helen Bamber's leadership, Medical Foundation documented torture, treated survivors, trained medical professionals and campaigned against human rights violations, growing over 25 years to 170 staff and 190 volunteers in five cities. Twenty years later, the Helen Bamber Foundation was founded to perform a similar role for the survivors Medical Foundation couldn't help; and a third organisation, Medical Justice, does the same for detained asylum seekers.[54] These organisations and their physicians are acknowledged as experts in documenting and treating torture injuries. But the fight against the routine rejection or marginalisation of their evidence is constant. A 1995 report showed that many Zairean asylum seekers' injuries, including scars from electrodes, handcuffs and whips, were deemed 'accidental' by Home Office officials.[55] On appeal, the intellectual contortions that some immigration judges engage in to reject plain, clear evidence supporting claims of torture suggest fundamental problems with accepting that Africans can be genuine refugees. An immigration judge who did not believe a Zairean asylum seeker's oral testimony ruled the man's stab wounds and burns 'self-inflicted'.[56] A medical report on another DRC citizen found a 'mass of scars', consistent with beatings from a belt, being kicked with booted feet, leech bites (he recounted a punishment of being thrown into a barrel of leeches), and having electrodes attached to his genitals. The immigration judge decided that the appellant's account of his ordeal was 'wholly not credible' and concluded that the medical evidence 'does not assist the appellant ... [W]hilst noting ... numerous scars ... [the report] does not consider ... whether the scars could be the result of ... childhood illness or skin disease'.[57]

Another way of discrediting expert evidence is to doubt the expertise of its author. Helen Bamber, who started her career working with concentration camp survivors in 1945 and has worked with traumatised people ever since, regularly comes to court to testify about the extreme psychological distress of those she sees. But Home Office presenting officers sometimes start their cross-examination with, 'You don't have any psychiatric qualifications, do you?' GPs documenting torture injuries for Freedom from Torture or Medical Justice often have their expertise queried.[58] Even when medical evidence is accepted at face value, it is often marginalised. A decision letter refusing asylum to a Ugandan woman read: 'there is reference [in the report] to perineal scarring consistent with very violent sexual abuse of an unprepared young woman. The Secretary of State is prepared to accept your client may have suffered some degree of sexual abuse but he does not accept this occurred in the manner put forward or that this gives rise to a well-founded fear of persecution under the Convention.' This reasoning is frequently deployed: the person has been horribly injured but has not proved 'persecution'. Psychiatric evidence is easily rejected on the basis that the psychiatrist is merely repeating what the appellant has told them.[59]

The work of refugee support groups in exposing the perversity of these decisions and supporting litigation in the higher courts, has forced the Home Office and the Tribunal to take the issue seriously. Caseworkers and immigration judges have been warned not to judge claimants' credibility before looking at the medical evidence – 'putting the cart before the horse',[60] and not to make their own alternative diagnoses unsupported by medical evidence.[61] But many people considered by medical charities to be victims of torture still lose their appeals against refusal of asylum, even with supporting medical evidence – over half, in a 2011 study.[62] That study persuaded UKBA to conduct a pilot project under which receipt of a positive report from Freedom from Torture or the Helen Bamber Foundation bound UKBA to accepting the fact of torture or serious harm in the absence of significant reasons for rejecting it.[63]

UNSPOKEN RACIAL HIERARCHIES

Although I am not aware of any academic studies on this, practitioners know that certain nationalities are much less likely to be believed by Home Office caseworkers and immigration judges than others. I spoke of colonial attitudes in the context of AM's case. The fact is that a fairly primitive racist culture persists in the immigration courts. White witnesses are more likely to be believed than black ones; every advocate knows that an asylum, deportation or human rights appeal has a much greater prospect of success if white (preferably British) witnesses to fact or character are there to lend their aura of unruffled honesty and reliability. But there are hierarchies of credibility within non-white populations, with Africans and, within Africans, Nigerians at the bottom of the credibility table. In 1995, two years after General Abacha seized power and brutally suppressed dissent, only two out of 1,495 applications for asylum from Nigeria were granted, and three months before Ken Saro-Wiwa's execution by the military dictatorship the Home Office was still saying Ogonis in the Movement for the Survival of the Ogoni People (MOSOP) did not face persecution.[64] In a typical Nigerian case heard that year, OB, who claimed he was wanted for pro-democracy articles he had written for the Campaign for Democracy, was deemed 'not credible' by the adjudicator: 'the account is littered with discrepancies, or it is just plain implausible. It's rehearsed, and he has made things up'.[65] Asylum seekers from the Democratic Republic of Congo (formerly Zaire) also have a hard time being believed.

Roma (regardless of nationality) were, unsurprisingly, at the bottom of the European league.[66] From top to bottom, the judiciary – even the liberals – turned its collective back on the Roma fleeing vicious skinhead violence which flared in Poland, the Czech Republic, Slovakia and Romania in the mid- to late 1990s following the disintegration of the Soviet bloc. It was not true, as home secretary Jack Straw claimed at the height of the political and tabloid hysteria of that time, that not a single Roma had had a claim recognised as genuine – but certainly very few were granted status. This was not because their claims were not genuine, but because of 'creative interpretation' of the Refugee

Convention for the purpose of rejecting their claims. Immigration judges hearing evidence of beatings and taunts such as 'Gypsies and Jews to the gas chambers' were forced to accept that there was 'popular feeling against gypsies' but said the police would provide protection. Faced with overwhelming evidence of police hostility or even complicity[67] and *de facto* impunity for skinheads, the House of Lords developed a new doctrine – that when the state was not the persecutor, available 'machinery of protection' (a functioning criminal justice system which did not formally exclude Roma) was enough to deny victims of persecution refugee status.[68] The ruling provoked a national demonstration by Roma groups.[69]

In one case, involving a 50-year-old Czech Roma, his 'white' wife and 10-year-old 'mixed-race' son who had suffered years of threats and assaults escalating in seriousness and had given up on police assistance, the Court of Appeal recognised the historical context – of 'pervasive, lifelong discrimination and increasing intimidation during the last few years', and the significance of the police failure to apprehend a readily identifiable perpetrator of serious crime, instead blaming the victim.[70] For once the court acknowledged the reality of Roma lives. But for the most part, even the higher courts, whose judges are generally more concerned with the law and not as susceptible to popular racism, found it inexpedient to recognise that Roma were persecuted in these countries. Recognition that racist persecution existed in Europe forced uncomfortable questions about skinhead violence and racist policing closer to home. If what Roma were experiencing was persecution, what about the black (African, Caribbean and Asian) experience in Britain not so long ago, and the enduring reality for gypsies and travellers in Britain and Ireland?[71] The Roma cases demonstrated that judges' construction of the Refugee Convention depended on their sincerely held belief, belied by daily evidence, that Britain leads the world in upholding the rights of vulnerable minorities.

Yet cutting across the racial hierarchy, I also observed a strange inverse relationship between the known dangerousness of any particular country and the credence given to asylum claimants from there. A large number of similar claims by many people from the same ethnic, political, religious or social group ought to suggest serious human rights abuses directed at that group. But for the Home Office and the immigration judiciary, it suggests instead an epidemic of false claims. Claims from Iran, Afghanistan, Eritrea, Sri Lanka, Zimbabwe and Sudan all suffered from a lower threshold of disbelief as the situation in those countries worsened (and as numbers claiming rose), and those fleeing appalling events found themselves accused of bandwagon-jumping. Only 13 Tamils were granted refugee status between 1986 and 1988.[72] In 1996, 94 per cent of Iraqi Kurds' claims were accepted – but by 2001, despite Saddam's bombing attacks, all Iraqi Kurds' claims were rejected, provoking tent protests and hunger strikes outside parliament and pickets of the Home Office.[73] When numbers of Zimbabwean asylum seekers surged in 2002 in response to Mugabe's murderous violence against real or imagined opponents, at first almost a third were recognised as refugees; but within two years the proportion had fallen to a tenth, despite the continuing violence.[74] Since no one could safely be returned, many Zimbabweans denied any form of status became utterly destitute, and some resorted to crime to live (see Chapter 5 below).

In 2001, public officials were brought within the scope of anti-discrimination legislation for the first time, in belated recognition of the reality of institutional racism.[75] The satisfaction of campaigners who had fought for decades was tempered by the exemptions allowing immigration officials to discriminate on grounds of nationality or ethnicity under ministerial authorisation. Immediately after the Act was passed, the Home Office authorised discrimination allowing more intensive questioning and more rigorous checks on Tamils, Kurds, Somalis, Afghans, Albanians, ethnic Chinese and Roma (all nationalities high in the asylum league tables) than on other passengers. Ten years later, we are not even allowed to know which national or ethnic groups are singled out under the latest authorisation.[76]

SCIENCE MISAPPLIED

In parallel with this legalised discrimination has come the development of quasi-scientific methods of finding out where people are from, such as language, isotope and mitochondrial analysis, to detect 'nationality swapping' (Kenyans claiming to be Somalis, or South Africans claiming Zimbabwean nationality). Unlike DNA testing for relationship, which was welcomed by applicants as a more reliable method of proving relationship than 'discrepancy-counting', these new 'scientific' tools are strongly criticised. Language analysis for the determination of origin (LADO) has been used since 2003, but despite the Tribunal's approval,[77] linguists have condemned it as brief, careless, lacking in supporting evidence, unreliable and unconvincing.[78] It rests on shaky assumptions – that everyone from a particular country or territory speaks the same standard (non-dialect) language. Some appeals dismissed by the Tribunal are now being reopened in the light of the experts' criticisms.[79]

Isotope analysis has been used in archaeology to determine characteristics of the area someone grew up in from teeth and bone samples. After the Met police used the technique to determine the provenance of a murdered child whose body was too badly mutilated to identify, the Home Office seized on it to establish 'nationality swapping' by claimants.[80] The announcement of a 'human provenance' pilot project, testing volunteers' hair and nail samples and taking mouth swabs for mitochondrial and Y-chromosome DNA testing (for ancestry), led to howls of outrage, both on scientific and legal grounds.[81] Apart from the unreliability of samples other than bone for assessing provenance, it is obvious that knowing where someone has been is not the same as knowing their nationality (a legal category) – the proposed purpose of the tests. The outcry forced the Home Office to renounce use of the pilot in decision-making on claims.

NEW MODELS FOR DECISION-MAKING

The combination of dogged campaigning by refugee and migrant groups and the mass of legal challenges has made a public issue of bad Home Office decision-making, and has led to some improvements. Procedures have been standardised and made more transparent. Detailed instructions for caseworkers on the conduct of interviews and the assessment of claims have been published on the internet since about 2000.[82] Asylum seekers are entitled to have a lawyer at their interview to ensure that nothing is omitted or misconstrued (although few can afford it; legal aid for most asylum interviews was withdrawn in 2004), and unrepresented asylum seekers may request tape-recording of the interview (although they aren't told of this right, so few ask).[83] Claimants get a copy of the interview (although since 2000 it is no longer read over at the end to ensure prompt correction of mistakes – which can be many). From 2004, asylum decisions have been monitored for quality by UNHCR's UK representative, whose recommendations include better training, rigorous testing and accreditation of Home Office caseworkers. But most refused asylum seekers interviewed for a 2006 report said they had not been able to tell their story fully, either to the Home Office or on appeal, because of poor legal advice, poor interpretation and the disbelief they faced.[84]

Under the New Asylum Model (NAM), introduced in 2007, specialist case managers ('case owners') deal with a case from application to conclusion. The immigration rules require caseworkers to know the law and to have access to 'reliable and up to date' country information. But their training is absurdly short; 25 days to learn relevant legislation and case law, interviewing, assessment of evidence and reasoning decisions (reduced from 55 days), with no input from refugees.[85] And under the target-driven approach adopted to tackle the huge backlogs of the late 1990s and early 2000s, the number of claims determined in a week is paramount,[86] an approach inconsistent with fair or careful decisions. UNHCR has expressed concern. The NAM has not done away with the 'culture of disbelief' which the Independent Asylum Commission (IAC) found to be alive and well and leading to 'perverse and unjust decisions' in 2008.[87]

In 2006 a pilot scheme in Solihull tried a completely different approach to deciding asylum claims, in response to a decade of campaigning around early access to legal advice.[88] This approach ensures that all asylum seekers have legal representation, and brings together the caseworker and the claimant's legal representative before, during and after the asylum interview to define the issues, to work together on obtaining evidence and to conduct the interview jointly, so as to ensure that caseworkers have all the relevant evidence, including the claimant's written statement, before taking a decision. Although the priorities used for evaluation of the project were meeting time- and cost-saving targets, and only secondarily achieving high-quality, sustainable decisions, the pilot apparently achieved all these objectives – greater involvement by the asylum claimants, a much higher rate of positive decisions by caseworkers and a clearer understanding by claimants of negative decisions, as well as faster decisions and cost savings.[89] Following the evaluation, the new approach was adopted over the Midlands and east of England UKBA region in October 2010, covering around a sixth of new asylum seekers, with a promise to extend it over the whole country.[90] This cooperative approach to asylum decision-making is the best hope yet for real change in the attitudes and assumptions underlying refusal of claims – but its effects will remain limited without a real change in the political discourse.

The most dangerous development in refugee determination is the spread of fast track procedures, which contain a fraction of the normal safeguards and where more and more asylum seekers find themselves. To this, among other obstacles to justice for both migrants and asylum seekers, I now turn.

3
More Obstacles to Justice

In July 2006, a group of Pakistani women held in Yarl's Wood Immigration Removal Centre wrote to detention support group BID: 'We ... have been put on fast track, which is not understandable and entirely confused system for us which is not enabling us to get any support and approach to solicitors. We are feeling like our hands are cut off, and we are terribly in the desperate situation and we can't do anything helpful, supportive in regard to our cases because we have not provided any solicitors and without solicitors we are unable to deal with our cases. We are very helpless here.'[1]

The desperation that letter expresses is heard daily from asylum seekers held in the 'detained fast track' (DFT), a factory system processing asylum claims at breakneck speed where a large and increasing proportion of asylum claims are dealt with. The fast track is one of a multitude of measures designed to reduce delays and address demands to slash asylum numbers, which have created massive obstacles to justice. Non-asylum seeking migrants face obstacles too, in visa procedures, and both groups have suffered erosion of appeal rights and legal aid.

'YOUR APPLICATION IS BEING HELD IN A QUEUE ...'

The first enemy of justice was delay. Applicants for family reunion were early victims of deliberate delays used as part of a policy of deterrence. Family members applying to join relatives in the UK in the 1970s had to wait 30 months just for an interview.[2] In 1976, Mrs Phansopkar, an Indian national, made legal history when, fed up with a 14-month wait for a certificate of patriality to prove her right to join her British husband, she flew to the UK (this was before the days of carriers' liability) and claimed the right to enter. She was told to go back and join the queue in Bombay. She declined, and sought judicial review. Vindicating Mrs Phansopkar's right to enter without inordinate delay, Lord Denning quoted Magna Carta, 'To no one will we sell, to no one deny or delay right or justice'.[3] Denning's stirring rhetoric was, alas, limited to those with a right to enter (patrials).[4] For those with no such right, the years-long queues were better fought politically than through the courts.

In 1994, the Home Office was accused of 'shameful laxity' when it was revealed that 80 or so asylum seekers had been waiting for over five years for their claim to be determined.[5] By 2000, there was a backlog of over 100,000 claims. The huge rise in asylum applications in the 1990s coincided with a mishandled computerisation programme, lay-offs of experienced staff and a move of headquarters.[6] Thousands of claimants waited for over five years, in limbo and separated from families who could not join claimants until refugee status was granted, while files were rumoured to lie rotting in flooded and rat-infested basements at the Immigration and Nationality Directorate's Croydon office. Some Turkish Kurds got their applications decided by going on hunger strike in protest at the delays and the enforced separation from families, and we lawyers launched hundreds of judicial review challenges, which forced decisions on those cases. But individual challenges were costly and ineffective, just pushing the applications of others further back. Labour tried to clear the backlog by the first of three 'one-off' regularisation programmes, for which it was slated by the tabloids. It introduced a two-month target for asylum decisions – but 'old' claims were just pushed to the back of the queue, which as the Court of Appeal held in 2007, left those affected in a 'cruel limbo'.[7] This was an important judicial recognition of the cruelty of delay. Politicians and the media see asylum seekers as beneficiaries of an undeserved reprieve from removal. But between application and decision, life cannot be lived fully. Everything is on hold. The uncertainty of the future makes decisions impossible: how to study, furnish a room, buy clothes, make friends, plan a future, when everything is provisional and insecure? For survivors of persecution, this limbo is another torture: the constant, daily uncertainty embraces the possibility of forced return.

For those seeking a visa, delay can be fatal. A two-month delay between the approval of an application and the issue of a visa for vital medical treatment killed nine-year-old Nigerian Chijoke Ekenguru in December 2001.[8] Some of the worst cases in my practice were those of Somali children and elderly parents of refugees in the UK, festering in refugee camps in Ethiopia and Kenya for years and years while applications for family reunion visas sat on entry clearance officers' desks in Addis Ababa or Nairobi or wound excruciatingly slowly through the appeal system. Children died of preventable disease waiting for visas. A Somali orphan of 15 who applied to join his sister in the UK was waiting three years later for his appeal against refusal of the visa. In that time his house had been destroyed, he had been shot twice while scavenging for food in Mogadishu, and he had seen his infant nephews and nieces die of starvation. Children don't understand the bureaucratic obstacles and feel rejected by their families. Yet politicians who allow these delays to build as a means of control of numbers, an unofficial quota, condemn those children as criminals when, carrying their experiences with them to the UK, they reject their families and join gangs. Delays like these were not exceptional but routine.

Delay in deciding asylum claims profoundly damages children who have suffered traumatic events, been uprooted from home, sometimes from parents, and desperately need security and settled status. The immigration rules recognise this, and require children's asylum applications to be prioritised.[9] But these considerations are frequently ignored – as in the case of SS, a profoundly traumatised 15-year-old Iranian girl who claimed asylum in November 2005 but whose solicitors' repeated reminders went unheard, as did her own self-harming. After six months an asylum interview was scheduled, but no staff were available to conduct it; they had been moved to processing of deportation cases, a more urgent political priority. Four months later, more solicitors' letters, complaints and an MP's intervention elicited the response that the file had been mislaid. Gritting his teeth, the solicitor sent a copy, but another five months passed with no action, which only came after a judicial review was lodged.[10] Similar delays still occur despite the new statutory commitment to children's welfare: in 2011, the Children's Commissioner found children waiting 20 months for a decision, in limbo without papers.[11]

The appeal process, too, is drawn out by the pathological inefficiency of the Home Office – not (as the tabloids would have it) abuse by bogus claimants. In my practice, it was routine for Home Office presenting officers to seek adjournments because files were lost, or appellants' documents hand-delivered to their offices had not arrived on their desks. Algerian Ahmed Benkaddouri attended court seven times over three years for his appeal hearing; each time it was adjourned because the Home Office had not complied with the judge's directions.[12] I have seen immigration judges reduced to impotent fury over Home Office failures over months to respond to their requests for basic information. And even after an application has been approved or an appeal won, there are further delays in obtaining papers. In 1999, a test case was brought by Turkish Kurd

Deniz Mersin, who waited five years for an initial decision, a further two years for an appeal, which he won, and another seven months for refugee papers. A doctor's report that the stress of waiting could precipitate collapse of his compromised health drew the tart response that his illness was not life-threatening. The judge ruled that the delay following the successful appeal had been unlawful: the appellant was entitled to refugee status, and 'it would wholly undermine the rule of law' if the Home Office could 'simply ignore the ruling of the adjudicator without appealing it'.[13] But since then delays have got worse, not better. The parliamentary ombudsman's 2010 report cited the case of a Somali who waited eight years for his refugee documents – vital for everything from work and benefits to health care and travel – after being told he qualified for refugee status and indefinite leave to remain.[14]

Delay, as Magna Carta recognised, can cause serious injustice. Kosovan Arben Shala arrived and claimed asylum in 1997, at the height of the ethnic cleansing there. He should have received refugee status immediately, but his application was sat on until 2001, by which time Kosovo was safe and his claim refused. By this time, he had been living with a Czech refugee and her two young children for three years and was about to marry. He was told to go home to apply for a visa to join them. The Court of Appeal said no; the four-year delay in deciding his claim had unfairly deprived Mr Shala of residence rights, and he should not be penalised.[15] Later, the House of Lords went further, ruling that where delay is 'shown to be the result of a dysfunctional system which yields unpredictable, inconsistent and unfair outcomes', it could be used to resist removal.[16]

THE ILLUSION OF 'SAFE' COUNTRIES

If judges sought to remedy injustices caused by delay, the government's responses magnified them. An early response was to offload as many asylum seekers as possible to other countries. I described in Chapter 1 how governments have made use of the 'first safe country' concept to reduce the numbers of asylum seekers coming to the UK by sending those who had travelled through other European countries back there without looking at their claims.[17] This was done in disregard of asylum seekers' preferences, language and family ties[18] and frequently their health. In 1993 I represented a Somali who had spent two hours in a transit lounge at Rome *en route* to Britain, and who collapsed on landing in the UK. He was found to have shrapnel lodged in his head and neck. He was given painkillers and detained for ten days while we tried unsuccessfully to persuade the Home Office to allow him to claim asylum in the UK, where he could receive hospital treatment – unavailable to asylum seekers in Italy. The day before his scheduled return, he collapsed again. But on judicial review, the judge said the Home Office was not acting unreasonably in putting a severely injured refugee back on the plane to Rome without allowing him to claim asylum.[19] He was one of tens of thousands summarily returned to a transit country.

From 1993 there was an appeal against such returns, where asylum seekers could argue that the asylum procedures in that country were deficient and they would end up back in the country they had fled from. The high rate of successful appeals showed up serious flaws in refugee reception and assessment in many EU member states – but the appeal right was abolished three years later, and in 1999 Labour enacted a legal presumption that all EU countries were safe and would deal with asylum claims properly.[20] It was a dangerous presumption, masking huge disparities in the way asylum claims were dealt with.[21] With mounting evidence of appalling conditions for asylum seekers in Greece, and unsafe procedures which resulted in refugees being sent back to persecuting states, lawyers repeatedly challenged returns there through judicial reviews, but failed to persuade the higher courts, whose classically trained judges perhaps still revered Greece as the cradle of democracy – until the ECtHR and the European Court of Justice (ECJ) forced their hand, calling a halt to returns to Greece in 2011.[22]

Back in 1996, the Tory government had also created a 'white list' of 'safe' countries of origin, whose asylum seeking citizens were given fewer appeal rights in a speeded-up procedure.[23] It followed a recommendation from accountants KPMG Peat Marwick, called in to suggest ways of dealing with the mounting asylum backlog.[24] The proposal, in the Asylum and Immigration Bill 1996, caused a furore. As the Bill went through parliament, an independent inquiry set up by groups including the Asylum Rights Campaign, Asylum Aid, Justice and ILPA and chaired by former appeal court judge Sir Iain Glidewell, took evidence from over 90 organisations and concluded that the 'white list' would damage race relations and would put lives and freedom in jeopardy.[25] Baroness Williams, leading opposition in the Lords, inserted a clause exempting those with a credible claim to have been tortured, or coming from countries with a recent record of torture, from the accelerated appeal procedure. In a telling riposte which confirmed suspicions that the Bill was an anti-asylum rather than an anti-abuse measure, the government complained that the amendment 'defeated the object' of the Bill, and vowed to overturn it. But the amendment survived, in modified form: full appeal rights would apply where the evidence established a reasonable likelihood that the appellant had been tortured.

The first 'white list' countries were Bulgaria, Cyprus, Ghana, India, Pakistan, Poland and Romania.[26] Given the documented persecution of Sikh and Kashmiri militants in India, of Ahmadis, Christians and others in Pakistan, and of Roma in Poland and Romania, the 'white list' remained a focus of campaigning and litigation. Three Pakistani asylum seekers – an Ahmadi and two men who had suffered political violence – challenged the inclusion of Pakistan as irrational and unlawful, and the high court agreed.[27] In 2001, the Court of Appeal dismissed the Secretary of State's appeal, and Pakistan came off the 'white list'. This was an important check: ministers could not deprive asylum seekers of appeal rights by simply deeming the countries they came from safe, even with parliamentary approval, if they patently weren't. But the 'white list' itself survived.

When Labour came to power in 1997, it faced a barrage of demands by migrant and refugee groups for fairer procedures, restoration of full appeal rights for all and abolition of the 'white list', as well as the massive backlogs and a right-wing press and front-bench Tories continuing their anti-asylum diatribes. Labour promised a thorough review of asylum procedures. The passage of the Human Rights Act, which brought the guarantees of the European Convention on Human Rights to the domestic courts, and the introduction of a human rights appeal against immigration decisions,[28] which provided broader protection than the Refugee Convention, made some feel that a new era of universal human rights was dawning. But new immigration and asylum measures quickly disillusioned them.

FAST TRACK LEADS TO FAILURE

In March 2000, Labour opened Oakington Barracks near Cambridge as a new 'fast-track facility' where over 13,000 asylum seekers annually were to have their 'straightforward' claims processed speedily.[29] Following interview, applicants were given up to five days to submit evidence in support of the claim, refused (in over 99 per cent of cases) on the seventh day, then released pending appeal. The fast track built on a Tory pilot of 1995 in which all but three out of 5,700 claims had been rejected in a year.[30] Following the courts' rejection of a challenge to the use of detention for speedy processing of claims,[31] the scheme was extended in 2003 to men at Harmondsworth detention centre, and made even faster, with only 24 hours between interview and decision. Under the new model, detention was 'end to end', from the making of the claim through refusal and appeal to removal – a process designed to take no more than five weeks in total. The Refugee Legal Centre challenged the system as too fast to be fair, but the Court of Appeal ruled that the procedure could be fair provided it was applied flexibly.[32] Encouraged, the government extended the system to women at Yarl's Wood detention centre in Bedfordshire. Fifty-five nationalities were listed as suitable for the process, but nationals of any country could be fast tracked if their claim could be decided quickly.[33] 'It is a mystery of the fast track process,' said ILPA, 'how the straightforwardness of claims can be accurately assessed when the screening interview elicits no or virtually no information about ... the claim.'[34] Human Rights Watch found women with complex gender-based claims in the fast track, including trafficking victims, women fearing forced marriage or female genital mutilation and a trans-gender person threatened and attacked in Pakistan.[35]

Fast track is an inspired self-fulfilling prophecy. Set up to deal quickly with 'unfounded' claims, its combination of detention and the breakneck speed of the process gives claimants needing to recover from the odyssey of illegal travel no time to compose themselves, to prepare a claim or to find and present evidence in support, and little or no access to legal help. Appeals are subject to the same impossible timetables.[36] The resulting dismal success rate (around 1 per cent of claims accepted by the Home Office, and a further 3 to 6 per cent on appeal) is used to justify the assumption that the claims are unfounded.[37] At Yarl's Wood, applications for removal from fast track by women who had suffered rape or torture or were suicidal were routinely refused.[38] Once I had to go in armed with a ready-drafted high court judicial review application to wave at an immigration judge who was refusing to release a suicidal West African lesbian woman. Fortunately, the judge released the client, so I didn't need to use it. A colleague was less lucky; she arrived for the appeal hearing to find a client with severe mental health problems and unable to communicate, and an immigration judge who refused to take the case out of the fast track or to adjourn for medical evidence. The appeal was dismissed for 'inconsistencies'.[39]

The fast track is a travesty of due process, yet even with asylum claims running at a quarter of their 2002 volume, it survives.

In 2002, Labour crossed the fast track with the 'white list' to create the 'non-suspensive appeal' for asylum seekers from a new list of 'safe' countries of origin who could not convince the Secretary of State that their claim was not clearly unfounded.[40] They could only appeal after they had left. Labour's first 'white list' contained the ten countries accepted for membership of the EU in 2004,[41] and within days of the Act's passage and before it was even published, the first Czech and Slovak Roma were being bundled out of the country. I was involved in the first legal challenge to the new procedure, for Mrs L, the matriarch of a Czech Roma family who had suffered repeated abuse and injury from skinheads, and who had been raped by police when she tried to report a crime to them. She and her adult son claimed asylum in November 2002 and were sent to Oakington, where within three days their claims were certified unfounded, and they were told they could appeal only after removal. With the support of the European Roma Rights Centre, we challenged the procedure as a denial of justice with potentially fatal results. Both the high court and the Court of Appeal rejected the challenge,[42] and soon asylum seekers from India, Gambia,[43] Jamaica, Nigeria[44] and a score of other African, Asian, South American and European states were denied appeal rights before removal.[45] In January 2010, the government announced its intention to opt out of an EU directive on minimum procedural standards for dealing with asylum claims, because signing the directive would mean abandoning the fast track and non-suspensive appeals regime.[46]

BUREAUCRATIC HURDLES

Asylum seekers who were not detained were also subjected to increasing bureaucratic pressure in the new millennium. Just as they were being dispersed *en masse* out of London and the south-east, to places where virtually no legal or linguistic help was at hand, they were given a new, 20-page 'Statement of Evidence' (SEF) form to complete in English and return within 14 days, on pain of refusal for 'failure to provide prompt disclosure of material facts'. So desperate was the situation in Newcastle that a law centre worker who agreed to attend an asylum hostel one afternoon found 200 asylum seekers waiting for his help. And a Farsi interpreter described being mobbed by dozens of Iranian asylum seekers when she went to help one man in a holiday camp turned asylum hostel.[47] Even a couple of days' delay in returning the form meant rejection of the claim. A claimant who was in hospital having a baby when the form was due was refused, and only the launch of a judicial review persuaded the immigration officer to retract the notice.[48] Failure to attend the scheduled asylum interview also meant refusal – but it was impossible to reach caseworkers by phone to reschedule the interview.[49] By March 2001, a third of all asylum claims were refused for 'non-compliance', many wrongfully. AS's failure to attend an asylum interview, in 'blatant disregard of asylum practice', led to the caseworker rejecting his claim for 'non-compliance' – and maintaining the refusal even when it was pointed out that the interview notice had been sent to the wrong address.[50]

Appeal procedures, too, often seemed calculated to tie appellants in knots and make them miss their hearings.[51] Many appellants, told not to worry if they heard nothing for over a year,[52] learned that their appeal had been dismissed in their absence only when it was too late to do anything about it, sometimes when they were detained for removal. The Court of Appeal said one rule was a denial of the fundamental right of access to the legal process,[53] but another example of egregious unfairness soon emerged. This was the Home Office practice of refusing asylum claims – and cutting off asylum support – without telling claimants. Lithuanian asylum seeker Nadezda Anufrijeva had her support withdrawn with no explanation until five months later, when she received a refusal notice. The practice, condemned by Lord Steyn in the House of Lords as a denial of the right of access to justice ('a fundamental and constitutional principle of our legal system'), was 'consistently and deliberately adopted ... It provides a peep into contemporary standards of public administration. It is not an encouraging picture.'[54]

In a system devised for speedy disposal of claims, for each injustice fought and remedied another emerges. The government has now made claiming asylum itself more difficult, for those who do not claim at the port. A claim could previously be made by letter, but since 2009, claimants must go to the Asylum Screening Unit in Croydon, with all their dependants, at their own expense, no matter where in the country they are and however destitute they may be. Staff have been accused of obstructive tactics to prevent claims being made. An elderly Zimbabwean woman who caught a bus at 3 a.m. to arrive at Croydon for 7 a.m. was told she was too late to be seen that day. Booking an appointment is impossible too; the phones are constantly engaged. In September 2011 the Law Society, which represents solicitors, complained of 'degrading treatment' of asylum seekers at Croydon, and said that lawyers have to threaten judicial review for their clients to be allowed to register their claim.[55] New rules also stipulate that failure to attend an asylum interview is taken to imply withdrawal of the claim (with no appeal) unless circumstances beyond the asylum seeker's control can be proved.[56] Despite all the campaigning by refugee support, human rights and practitioners' groups, these procedural obstacles to asylum claims, with their manifest and rampant injustice, remain like cancer cells in the legal system.

OBSTACLES TO GETTING VISAS

It is not only in the asylum field that applicants have found obstacles erected against them. Many internationally acclaimed performers are now boycotting Britain in protest at their treatment when they apply for visas. Pianist Grigory Sokolov objected to the fingerprinting and eye scans he had to give whenever he sought a visa. Iranian film director Abbas Kiarostami said he would not return after being fingerprinted twice. Artists coming to the UK as visitors must now give assurances that they will not do anything creative during their stay, on pain of removal and a ten-year ban.[57] Apart from the delays discussed earlier, the main obstacles to getting a visa – particularly for people from Africa, Asia and the Caribbean – used to be difficulties in travelling to the British consular post, hostile treatment from entry clearance officers and racist assumptions leading to unjustified refusals. Now, the main obstacles to obtaining visas are the extremely high fees, requirements to fill application forms in English[58] and (in many countries) on-line, over-rigorous biometric and documentary demands, and racist assumptions leading to unjustified refusals. Fees have gone through the roof in the last five years or so, with the replacement of the public service model by a frankly commercial one in which the fee charged is designed to reflect 'the value of the product'.[59] A student bringing a partner and two children pays over £1,000 for their visas; business persons and skilled workers can pay from £800 to £6,000 (the 'super premium' fee), while it costs over £800 to bring a spouse or child, and £1,800 to bring an elderly parent, for settlement.

While fees have rocketed, the number of British consular posts deciding visa applications has been slashed under the 'hub and spoke' system, whereby applications made in, say, Pakistan are couriered to the consular post in Abu Dhabi, which also decides applications from the Gulf states and Iran, while the post in Amman (Jordan) decides applications from Syria, Iraq, Israel and Palestine. Few applicants are interviewed, although all must attend a visa application centre in their own country (often run by commercial companies such as Gerry's in Pakistan and VFS Global in Indonesia), to submit a printed copy of their application, pay the fee (and a further handling fee to the commercial agent) and be fingerprinted. Delays in getting appointments and in processing applications are now in the order of weeks or months rather than years (although they are still significant enough to miss start dates of courses, conferences and family events such as weddings). But 'risk profiling' and simple prejudice mean additional evidential requirements for so-called high risk applicants and nationalities, such as Pakistanis – requirements they are not told about in advance, and are not in the immigration rules, such as identifying the source of the funds in their bank account.[60] The new, expensive, online visa application system offers improved access for the globalised middle classes and reflects a change in policy from generalised exclusion to 'a more selective approach ... which brings in more of the brightest and the best who will make a real difference to our economy',[61] but deters and prevents the rest.

APPEAL RIGHTS ERODED

When in 1991 the Tories proposed to remove appeal rights for visitors and short-term students, Tony Blair protested, in words which would be quoted back at him a decade later, 'It is a novel, bizarre and misguided principle of the legal system that if the exercise of legal rights is causing administrative inconvenience, the solution is to remove the right'.[62] Lord Donaldson, the lead Court of Appeal judge, said the 'draconian' and 'vicious' proposals had 'a certain brilliance ... for ten years I was ... striving in every way to make the Court of Appeal civil division more efficient. It never occurred to me that one of the simplest and best ways would be to abolish certain categories of appeal or, if possible, all categories of appeal.' He added, 'There is either a naivety or an arrogance in the attitude of the Home Office that its immigration officers must inevitably be right. Yet if they are not right, what is to happen?'[63] In power, Labour repeatedly sought to cut down migrants' access to the higher courts. In 2002, it pared down judicial review rights, making successful challenge to poor decision-making in the Tribunal more difficult, and a legal challenge to the changes was rejected.[64]

But it overreached itself with its attempt in 2003 to restrict migrants' appeal rights to just one appeal, with an 'ouster clause' to prevent any further appeal or review to any court – a restriction imposed nowhere else in the legal system. A huge public campaign embraced not only migrants' and rights groups[65] but also senior lawyers and judges, roused by the attempt to oust the jurisdiction of the higher courts – including the House of Lords, whose rulings on important issues of principle had world-wide significance – to the defence of the constitution itself. The Constitutional Affairs Committee observed: 'As a matter of constitutional principle some form of higher judicial oversight of lower Tribunals and executive decisions should be retained. This is particularly true when life and liberty may be at stake.' Law lords mobilised peers; Lord Steyn said the Bill 'attempts to immunise manifest illegality'.[66] The weight of opposition forced the government to back down.

But attempts to deny access to the higher courts, and to exclude judicial review, continue. In an important test case following the 2010 integration of immigration appeals into a new statutory framework, the supreme court upheld the continuing right of claimants to seek judicial review to resolve important points of principle.[67] But the idea that migrants have too many appeal rights has continued to inform government policy, and since the introduction of the PBS in 2008, appeal rights for those refused visas as students and skilled workers have been abolished.[68] Only family visitors and family members refused settlement visas can now appeal – and family visitors' appeal rights are next in line.

THE LOSS OF LEGAL REPRESENTATION

The huge importance of legal representation was demonstrated by a study in which over half of represented appellants succeeded on appeal, compared with a general average of 23 per cent.[69] Yet competent advice and representation have never been more difficult to obtain. The two largest not-for-profit providers of immigration and asylum advice and representation, Refugee and Migrant Justice (RMJ, formerly the Refugee Legal Centre) and the IAS, between them representing something like 20,000 clients, closed down within a year of each other in 2010 and 2011 with huge cash flow problems, and scores of legal aid firms either closed their doors or stopped providing publicly funded services. When fast track asylum processing was introduced, the government pledged that on-site legal advice and representation would be available. But in 2010, no information about legal rights and no up-to-date legal materials were available in Harmondsworth. A legal surgery open for just ten hours a week could deal with only 20 clients, and was booked up a fortnight in advance – so by the time legal help was available, detainees' asylum claims had been refused and appeals dismissed.[70] Legal aid, an important part of the welfare state, is being destroyed. So what has gone wrong?

Before 1998, when legal aid became available for representation in immigration and asylum appeals, free immigration and asylum advice was provided either by IAS, formerly UKIAS, then Home Office funded, or by the ranks of dedicated and underpaid solicitors whose payment came from the 'green form', legal aid which funded advice but not representation on appeal. In these 'bad old days', migrants were frequently gulled into paying thousands of pounds to unqualified high street advisers, who became notorious for exploiting and cheating migrants. One man I knew (and refused to work for) also colluded behind the scenes with the Home Office to ensure clients were deported. The advent of public funding for representation, together with a new regulatory scheme which criminalised unauthorised immigration advice,[71] cleaned up the field and ensured a good supply of qualified and competent legal advice and help for asylum seekers and others seeking to stay in the UK, to bring in family members or to fight deportation. But this 'golden age' of legal aid lasted a very short time indeed.[72]

The dispersal of asylum seekers from 1999 (described in Chapter 5) led to chaos, as claimants found their former solicitors could no longer represent them,[73] and many dispersal areas were advice and interpretation deserts. Many firms in these areas took on asylum and immigration work for the first time, and public money went into training lawyers in this new field. But in 2004, as costs rose with the numbers assisted, tight cost limits were imposed which meant that asylum seekers needing a new representative after a move were no longer eligible. At the same time, payments for lawyers to attend asylum interviews were stopped unless the client was a child or otherwise particularly vulnerable. The government insisted that asylum seekers didn't need lawyers to tell their story, a common-sense view at odds with reality. It now accepts that early legal advice and representation at interview is vital to good quality decisions,[74] but the changes did enormous harm to the asylum process and led to 'injustice, destitution, illegal working, frustration, loss of faith in the justice system, desperation and exploitation'.[75] Many law firms pulled out of asylum and immigration work.

Things were to get much worse. In 2005, appellants' representatives were made to bear the cost of challenging immigration judges' decisions, on a contingency basis; and further changes the following year discouraged innovative, 'borderline' or risky cases (often those which establish important new legal principles), and left thousands unrepresented. Asylum seekers in fast track saw their chances of winning an appeal reduce to vanishing point as solicitors refused representation, unable to risk losing appeals – and their legal aid contracts.[76]

Then, in 2007, fixed fees replaced hourly rates, rewarding 'factory' firms with a speedy through-put of cases, and discouraging conscientious preparation, complex cases or those involving vulnerable clients who cannot be hurried. The Constitutional Affairs Committee warned that specialist providers could not afford to carry on and 'will be lost to the legal aid system'.[77] The blow which caused the demise of the RMJ in 2010 was the move to retrospective payment for cases, which jeopardised the financial viability of immigration firms. With 13 regional offices, 270 staff and 10,000 clients (including 900 children), RMJ went into administration because it could not pay its staff, although it was owed nearly £2 million by the LSC for work done in ongoing cases.[78] In the same year, over a third of the 410 firms seeking renewal of their legal aid contracts were turned down or had contracts cut, including many of the best of the surviving firms and not-for-profit organisations. Some areas, including Kent, were left with no legal aid immigration and asylum solicitors at all,[79] while elsewhere, a tiny number of appropriately qualified and accredited lawyers tried to deal with the vast ocean of unmet legal need. The LSC and the ministry of justice were unconcerned: people could, they said, go to Citizens' Advice Bureaux (who can't provide representation, and were themselves to face the hit the following year).

Voluntary organisations responded by providing what help they could – BID, for example, set up in 1998, has a pool of young lawyers who provide free representation on bail applications, but such is the volume of demand that it encourages detainees to make their own bail applications, with a self-help guide. In similar vein, Crossroads Women's Centre has produced a guide for asylum seekers to help them present their own asylum appeals, while the National Coalition of Anti-Deportation Campaigns (NCADC) provides practical advice and guidance for those facing deportation. But the legal restrictions imposed to counter the sharks make it difficult for voluntary organisations to provide advice and help. With resources stretched, they are less and less able to afford the costs of regulation and training of advisers in such a complex area, and so migrants and asylum seekers are again vulnerable to exploitation by profit-driven firms and back-street charlatans.

In June 2011, following a consultation in which 90 per cent of the 5,000 respondents objected, the government introduced a bill to remove all publicly funded advice and representation in civil cases including immigration (other than asylum, detention and national security). The proposals are a frontal attack on the principles of social solidarity. Even cases raising significant public interest concerns (such as an unlawful policy affecting many applicants) are excluded from legal aid. Abusive practices are to go unchallenged, and all but the wealthy excluded from legal redress for bad decision-making. Although the government insists that asylum seekers and detained migrants are not affected, their access to legal help will be further eroded since the remaining specialist firms cannot survive the removal of all their other immigration work, and are likely to fold or get out of publicly funded work. As the government bids to make London the world centre for international high-value legal disputes with a brand-new, £300-million, all-electronic law court,[80] justice is rapidly becoming, in the well-worn quotation of nineteenth-century judge Mathews, 'open to everyone in the same way as the Ritz Hotel'.

4
You're Not a Refugee!

Another obstacle for asylum seekers is the narrow legal definition of who is a refugee. This was not too much of an issue in the post-second world war years when there was just a trickle of deposed monarchs, ex-dictators and their secret police making their way to Britain. But with the growth of mass travel, mass migration and mass movement of refugees, the refugee definition has become highly contentious. The Home Office and refugees' lawyers are engaged in constant struggle in the courts over the breadth of the definition, the people and the situations it covers.

Although 80 per cent of the world's refugees (using the word in its ordinary, not legal sense) are women and children fleeing war or violence, most of them are not eligible for refugee status. This is because under the Refugee Convention, not everyone who is fleeing danger or violence qualifies as a refugee. In Chapter 1 I discussed the requirement that refugee claimants be outside their own country. They must also demonstrate that they are unable or unwilling to return home 'owing to a well-founded fear of being persecuted' – so that fear of the indiscriminate violence of civil war,[1] or of starvation through famine, does not qualify someone as a refugee. The roots of civil war and famine might lie in the west's proxy wars and attempts to overthrow leaders seen as undesirable, in the arbitrary frontiers and ethnic rivalries which are part of the legacy of colonialism, in the arms trade which has pumped billions of dollars of arms into unstable countries, in resource wars or in expropriation, displacement or the planting of biofuels for globalised markets, but the responsibility of the rich world is not reflected in the refugee definition, which is firmly rooted in the twin concepts of nation-state responsibility and 'persecution'. There must be persecution (or a real risk of it) for refugee protection: the risk of serious, targeted harm, serious human rights violations against which no protection is forthcoming from the refugee's own state.[2] But even this is not enough; the persecution must be 'for reasons of race, religion, nationality, membership of a particular social group or political opinion'. These are the 'Convention grounds' which since 1951 have delimited those owed international protection as refugees.

REFUGEES FROM CIVIL WAR

The civil war in Somalia, which has pitted clans against each other following the fall of dictator Siad Barre in 1991, has produced hundreds of thousands of refugees and provoked legal battles in the UK. Most Somalis were not granted refugee status but exceptional leave to remain, a status which did not allow family reunion for many years. They argued they were entitled to be recognised as refugees: since any clan membership carried the risk of killing by members of an opposing clan, then all were at risk of persecution for reasons of membership of a 'particular social group' (a clan). No, argued the Home Office; the Convention is not designed to protect whole populations. No, agreed the House of Lords, in 1998, reversing the Court of Appeal: 'the language of the Convention did not apply to those caught up in a civil war where law and order had broken down and every group was fighting some other group or groups ... the individual has to show a well-founded fear of persecution over and above the risk to life and liberty inherent in a civil war'.[3] The judgment applied not just to wars fought between clans, but those fought along religious, political or ethnic lines. From then on, only 'underdogs' – in Somalia, members of minority clans without the firepower to defend themselves, and generally, those at the mercy of groups controlling territory – could be considered refugees in a civil war. Serious risks to life through the indiscriminate violence of civil war entitled claimants only to humanitarian protection (which replaced exceptional leave from 2003 onwards), temporary (but renewable) residence inferior to refugee status, which carried rights to permanent residence and immediate family reunion. (Refugee status itself became temporary in 2005, when both refugees and those given humanitarian protection received a five-year renewable permit and immediate family reunion rights.) Now, under the European Qualification Directive (which harmonises refugee and other protections among member states), humanitarian protection is granted to those facing real risk of indiscriminate, life-threatening violence from armed conflict. In test cases, the Tribunal has ruled that ordinary civilians can be returned to Iraq and Afghanistan, as in neither country is the armed conflict so intense that everyone in the country is at risk of death or serious injury.[4]

WOMEN AND 'GENDER PERSECUTION'

Women seeking asylum face particular difficulties over and above all the 'normal' obstacles for asylum seekers. The omission of sex or gender from the Convention grounds reflects the widespread historical view of the public sphere as 'male' and the private sphere as 'female' – with persecution seen as something necessarily conducted in the public sphere. The Convention was until relatively recently interpreted to fit a quintessentially male model of a politically active refugee – persecution meant the knock on the door at night, the brutal treatment by state thugs (although of course many women are committed political activists who have faced 'political persecution' in this orthodox sense). But in the 1990s, women began arriving in increasing numbers, fleeing different forms of violence – rape in war, unremitting private (domestic) violence from husbands, forced marriage, honour killing or sex trafficking. Women in these situations did not fit the template, and what they suffered was not seen as 'persecution' within the Refugee Convention. Although they had suffered terribly, were often deeply traumatised and were terrified of return, they could not get the right to stay as refugees.

Women involved with refugee issues began to ask: why are these different ways in which women are harmed not recognised as persecution by those interpreting the Convention? Why should the idea of 'persecution', with its suggestion of serious, targeted harm, not cover customary practices of traditional societies which inflicted grave harm on women, such as female genital mutilation (FGM), bride burning, forced marriage and honour killing? Or the newer practices reflecting the globalised market which treats people as commodities, such as international trafficking of women for forced prostitution? Are serious domestic violence or rape, against which no protection is available, not instances of persecution?

The idea that these kinds of harm could qualify a woman as a refugee was initially met with disbelief and derision from Britain's (overwhelmingly male) decision-makers and judges. After all, they were essentially private matters, far removed from the world of politics and state power. The overwhelming majority of women I represented in asylum claims had been raped, frequently repeatedly; they had been brutalised, battered and beaten – sometimes abducted as children by rebel soldiers in Uganda or Congo and treated as sex slaves, or raped by regular soldiers looking for rebels and their supporters, or sometimes by husbands twice or four times their age after being sold into marriage in Afghanistan or Tanzania, or by traffickers after being sold or abducted for prostitution in Albania or Kenya. The almost invariable response of (mostly) male judges to these claims was 'this is dreadful lust', 'a one-off', 'an isolated criminal act', 'a private matter'. Allegations of sexual impropriety in women from traditional societies may give rise to violence from outraged relatives, but claims based on fears of such violence were generally dismissed in the 1980s and 1990s. A Sikh girl who was left with her grandparents in the UK at 13 years old told officials, after her arrest as an overstayer five years later, that her grandmother had thrown her out and told her parents she had had sex and had Muslim friends. As a result her parents would not have her back in India and she feared honour killing if she tried to go back. Her appeal was rejected.[5]

Women facing life-threatening domestic violence fared no better. A 44-year-old Colombian woman arrested as an illegal entrant in 1994 described a culture of violence towards women in Colombia of which she, her mother and her sister had been victims. She had suffered extreme violence from her husband for over 20 years, including beatings during pregnancy, imprisonment in the house and, after she escaped, threats to kill her and her children and attacks on the house where she had taken refuge. Police simply refused to help – it was a 'matrimonial matter'. She fled to the UK, living without papers. Her husband followed her. He grabbed her on the street in Shepherd's Bush, but fearful of being deported, she did not report him. When he vandalised her house, her daughter called the police and he was arrested and deported. He said he would kill her when she returned – but despite the evidence of his violence and tenacity, and the complete lack of protection, she was refused permission to stay. Her appeal was dismissed and representations to the minister were rejected.[6]

Women such as these did not claim asylum until they were forced to, in desperation, by the threat of imminent deportation – there seemed no point, as their claims were doomed to failure. Desperate to remedy this grim situation for women, refugee groups and women's groups such as Southall Black Sisters and Crossroads Women's Centre joined forces with lawyers at Asylum Aid, the Refugee Legal Centre and ILPA to form the Refugee Women's Legal Group (RWLG). In 1997 RWLG published a legal handbook, *Women as asylum seekers*.[7] Drawing on Canadian, US and Australian guidelines for women's refugee claims published earlier in the decade, and on ground-breaking claims by women in these countries and in New Zealand, the *Handbook* introduced the legal community to a way of looking at the Refugee Convention which did not marginalise or discount women's experiences. They argued that there were *forms* of serious harm amounting to persecution which were specific to women – FGM, bride burning, sexual and domestic violence, forced marriage and forced abortion. (Of these, some are literally specific to women, such as FGM and forced abortion, while women are the overwhelming majority in others such as sexual and domestic violence.) In addition, women's sex or gender[8] is the *reason* (or one of the reasons) for many gender-specific forms of persecution, which frequently occur in the context of institutionalised, deep-seated discrimination against women in the societies concerned. They argued that gender-specific forms and reasons for persecution should be recognised for the purpose of refugee status.

The appearance of the *Handbook* reflected the increasing numbers of women asylum seekers, and of women concerned with the advocacy and promotion of women's rights in the legal profession and even the judiciary. The arguments began to fall on sympathetic ears. The *Handbook* was followed in 1998 by the RWLG's *Gender guidelines for the determination of asylum claims in the UK*, with input from more groups including JCWI, Amnesty International and UNHCR. In 2000, the Immigration Appellate Authority (IAA) published its own *Asylum gender guidelines*, co-authored by adjudicator (now senior immigration judge) Catriona Jarvis.[9] The gender guidelines put gender-specific and gender-based persecution on the map.

Yet how could gender-based persecution fit within the refugee definition? It is relatively easy to understand and recognise racial, nationality-based, political and religious persecution, but for many decades the Home Office and the courts were confused about the other ground qualifying a victim of persecution as a refugee, 'membership of a particular social group'. They argued that people had to be associated in a club or association to qualify under this head. In 1999, it was established that the words just meant a group defined by a recognisable characteristic, similar to race or religion – which meant that a group defined by gender could be a 'particular social group', and someone persecuted for such a reason could qualify as a refugee.

The breakthrough case for women's asylum claims revolved around two women who had suffered male violence in Pakistan. Mrs Shah had been subjected to constant, severe domestic violence and then thrown out of her village home after bearing her husband six children. Realising when she arrived in the UK that she was pregnant again, she was sure that if she went home, her husband would suspect her of adultery and kill her, or hand her over to the authorities or to mob justice, possibly to be stoned to death. Her lawyer argued at her appeal that she faced persecution as a 'battered wife' and could not be returned to Pakistan. The adjudicator accepted that she had been persecuted (subjected to serious harm) by her husband and would face more of the same, or worse, on return, and that she could not get protection from the authorities, who might even put her to death for adultery, but said she was not a refugee. She did not fear persecution for a reason within the Convention. 'Battered wives' were not a 'particular social group' under the Refugee Convention; a group could not be defined by the persecution they feared.[10] The Tribunal refused permission to appeal, and in 1996 I was asked to challenge the refusal in the high court.

There, a new argument found favour with Mr Justice Sedley,[11] probably the most progressive judge sitting at that time – that Mrs Shah faced persecution as a woman suspected of adultery. She belonged to a 'particular social group' defined by gender and transgression (real or perceived) of social mores. Sedley agreed that this could be so, observing that, 'Unless it is seen as a living thing, adopted by civilised countries for a humanitarian end which is constant in motive but mutable in form, the Convention will eventually become an anachronism.'[12] The Home Office appealed, and Mrs Shah's case was joined in the Court of Appeal by that of Mrs Islam, who also faced violence and an accusation of adultery, although the two women were very different – Mrs Islam was a teacher, urban and educated. Her claim had been dismissed by the Tribunal. Senior barrister Nick Blake QC (now a high court judge and president of the Tribunal) led me and my colleague Stephanie Harrison in the Court of Appeal, and later in the House of Lords. The appeal court – three conservative male judges – showed little interest in the arguments, and rejected the cases. Women who did not know each other and merely shared a common experience could not, they ruled, be refugees.[13]

We appealed to the appellate committee of the House of Lords, showing the judges Canadian and Australian cases where women's experiences of male violence in societies which failed to protect them had qualified them as refugees. (Because the Refugee Convention is an international Convention adhered to by the majority of the world's states, the decisions of courts from many countries are used to help the UK courts in interpreting it, and *vice versa*.) This all-male court, of five judges led by Lord Steyn and including the maverick Lord Hoffmann, responded positively. They accepted that members of a 'particular social group' did not have to know each other. Lord Hoffmann introduced the then heretical notion that women in a given society could constitute a 'particular social group' defined by their gender and by institutionalised discrimination against them. It was unnecessary for *all* the women in that society to be persecuted, he explained, for some women to face persecution for being women. The Home Office barristers argued that it was their husbands, not the state, whom the women feared – it was a private matter. Lord Hoffmann spelled out why this argument was wrong, pointing out that, while women may be subjected to male violence for any number of (private) reasons, the state's failure to protect them because of their gender brought the violence into the public domain:

> What is the reason for the persecution which the appellants fear? Here it is important to notice that it is made up of two elements. First, there is the threat of violence to Mrs Islam by her husband and his political friends and to Mrs Shah by her husband. This is a personal affair, directed against them as individuals. Secondly, there is the inability or unwillingness of the State to do anything to protect them. There is nothing personal about this. The evidence was that the State would not assist them because they were women. It denied them a protection against violence which it would have given to men ... the legal and social conditions which according to the evidence existed in Pakistan and which left [Mrs Islam] unprotected against violence by men were discriminatory against women. For the purposes of the Convention, this discrimination was the critical element in the persecution. In my opinion, this means that she feared persecution because she was a woman.

The judges agreed that the Refugee Convention protected groups defined by sex, gender or sexuality, and by a four to one majority allowed the appeal.[14] This was a huge victory for women and for the recognition of the particular forms of violence they face as giving rise to refugee status. Since this ground-breaking decision, women fleeing 'private' violence have been recognised as refugees on the basis of the entrenched discrimination and lack of state protection in their countries of origin, in Europe, Asia, Africa and Latin America.

A different kind of violence, that of female genital mutilation, was tackled a few years later in the case of *Fornah*. The appellant, a 15-year-old girl, came from Sierra Leone, where girls are routinely cut to initiate them into womanhood. The procedure is performed by older women, without anaesthetic or sterile knives, is excruciatingly painful and often leads to long-standing gynaecological problems. Many United Nations resolutions condemn it and it is a criminal offence in a number of countries (including the UK). Women in many traditional societies have fought for abolition of the practice, but there are powerful interests seeking to perpetuate such customs. Ms Fornah had run away from home at the age of ten when she heard her parents discussing her initiation. The country was in the throes of civil war and she was captured by rebels and repeatedly raped by a rebel leader, by whom she became pregnant. She was helped to escape to the UK, and feared that if she was returned to Sierra Leone her family would subject her to FGM. She was granted limited leave to stay, but not as a refugee, and the Court of Appeal upheld the refusal of refugee status. For that court, the fact that the procedure was a one-off and that it was performed by women proved fatal to the appellant's claim. My colleague Kathryn Cronin and I represented her in the House of Lords in July 2006. The first woman to be appointed to the judicial committee, Baroness Hale, was one of the five law lords who heard the case, and she brought expertise and interest in discrimination and family law. With two women representing Ms Fornah and a woman on the bench, the atmosphere of the hearing was far less forbidding than in Mrs Shah's case seven years earlier. The Lords unanimously allowed Ms Fornah's appeal, with Baroness Hale expressing astonishment that the case had needed to come to them for a correct decision – particularly since other courts in the UK, the US and Canada had already recognised FGM in different societies as gender persecution giving rise to refugee status. The law lords agreed that FGM 'powerfully reinforces and expresses the inferior status of women as compared with men' in Sierra Leonean society, under whose customary law, women were obliged to obey their husbands, could refuse sex only in limited circumstances, and could lawfully be beaten by them.[15] This victory was particularly satisfying because of the fillip it gave to women's groups fighting FGM and institutionalised discrimination in their own societies.

In another ground-breaking decision in 2008, the House of Lords accepted that a mother and her 12-year-old child should not be forced to return to Lebanon, where the courts would hand the child over to a violent father whom he did not know under custody laws which discriminated against women. The pair's removal, they ruled, would result in the destruction of the family life they enjoyed together since the boy's birth.[16] But despite these pioneering decisions of the higher courts, for many more women seeking protection in the UK, little has in reality changed. Home Office decision-making on women's claims continues to be abysmal. In a 2011 study, 87 per cent of women in a sample examined by the Refugee Women's Resource Project had their claims rejected, most on credibility grounds.[17] In most of the refused cases, the caseworker also got the law wrong, saying that even if the claim was true the woman would not qualify, ignoring the developments in the interpretation of the Convention described above, and some displayed alarming ignorance about issues such as forced marriage and FGM.[18] Considering that refusal decisions are supposed to be vetted by senior immigration officers, these findings are extremely worrying. As the higher courts have shown themselves more open to innovative and women-friendly interpretations of the Refugee Convention, so the Home Office – and immigration judges too – have responded by trying to pull the doors shut again. They have made particular and undue use of the concepts of 'sufficiency of protection' and 'internal relocation' to deny status to women.

The 'sufficiency of protection' concept was invented in the 1990s to deny refugee status to east European Roma on the basis that there was a criminal justice system in their home country which could and occasionally did prosecute their attackers.[19] It uses the theoretical availability of protection in the refugee's home country as a figleaf to cloak the reality that there is no effective protection for certain groups. So women faced with violence are told to seek the protection of their own authorities, although country reports show that that protection is more apparent than real. In a few cases, the Court of Appeal has said as much, overturning adverse Tribunal decisions on cases including those of Kenyan women fearing domestic violence (where only public pressure had forced police action against murderous husbands),[20] and young Ethiopian girls brutalised in forced marriage.[21]

The internal relocation doctrine is much older and, used sensibly, is uncontentious: if persecution is localised, and the targeted person can easily avoid it by moving to another part of his or her own country, refugee status – protection from the international community – is not needed. The test as to whether internal relocation is reasonably possible has been expressed as: 'Can the claimant, in the context of the country concerned, lead a relatively normal life without facing undue hardship?'[22] But it has not been used sensibly in relation to women's claims.[23] In most traditional societies where FGM, forced marriage or honour killings take place, a person's survival depends on family networks around the country. Extended family members will provide shelter and support even if they have never met you. But where the family is not protector but persecutor, those networks, with their speedy word-of-mouth communications systems, spell danger for a lone woman returned from the UK. And in traditional societies, women simply don't live on their own – or if they do, they are assumed to be immoral and ripe for sexual exploitation. Life without family support, away from the family home, is not an option in many countries. Experts amply attest to these facts – but the Home Office and the Tribunal have repeatedly and wilfully ignored gender issues and evidence in applying 'internal relocation' to women, relying instead on assumption and conjecture. Where evidence is provided by the Home Office it is often misleading. In one case involving FGM in Kenya, the Home Office produced a list of 30 organisations which they said could protect the appellant on her return. My solicitor went through the list, checking websites, phoning contact numbers – and found that of the 30 bodies, only three in the whole country provided practical help, to a minuscule number of women.[24]

Perhaps the most grotesque use of the internal relocation doctrine related to a young woman from the north of Uganda, whose parents were killed by the Lord's Resistance Army. It was accepted that her life would be at risk if she returned to northern Uganda, where civil war still raged, so the issue was whether she could live in the capital. The evidence showed that with little education, no training and no job experience, she would probably be reduced to homelessness, destitution and enforced prostitution. But for the immigration judge, formerly known for her feminism, this was not an obstacle to the appellant's return, but a 'relatively normal life' for young women and therefore not 'unduly harsh'. The decision outraged women's and refugee groups, and the Court of Appeal overruled it, saying that enforced prostitution did not 'come within the category of normal country conditions that a refugee should be expected to put up with'.[25]

The huge gulf between how the higher courts say women's asylum claims should be treated and the way UKBA officials and immigration judges continue to treat them appears almost unbridgeable. It is as if, when a positive decision comes from the higher courts, the UKBA and the Tribunal embark on a damage limitation exercise to reduce its impact, perhaps, like rank and file police distrustful of the 'higher-ups', believing the senior judges to be idealistic and out of touch with the reality of 'bogus refugees'. This is seen very clearly in the treatment of rape. In a 2005 House of Lords case relating to an ethnic Albanian couple, Baroness Hale acknowledged the use of rape as a weapon of war, and extended the notion of persecution to the stigma within one's own community of having been raped in the context of ethnic cleansing:

> All four members of the B family suffered persecution at the hands of the Serb police ... But the persecution of Mrs B was expressed in a different way from the persecution of her husband and sons. She was raped in front of her husband, her sons and twenty to thirty of their neighbours ...
>
> Women are particularly vulnerable to persecution by sexual violence as a weapon of war ... It is important to recognise that sexual violence and rape may be an actual weapon or a strategy of war itself, rather than just an expression or consequence. In the context of armed conflict or civil war, the rape of women is also about gaining control over other men and the group (national, ethnic, political) of which they are a part ... To suffer the insult and indignity of being regarded by one's own community (in Mrs B's words) as 'dirty like contaminated' because one has suffered the gross ill-treatment of a particularly brutal and dehumanising rape directed against that very community, is the sort of cumulative denial of human dignity which to my mind is quite capable of amounting to persecution.[26]

This was a sensitive and thoughtful reflection on the reality of rape in wartime, its impact and effects. But to the Home Office and too many immigration judges, women alleging rape are, first of all, not to be believed unless there is strong supporting evidence (and not always then), and even if they are believed, rape is still too often treated as individual misbehaviour by indisciplined soldiers or police, or as a criminal matter, as something unlikely to be repeated and with no consequences. A good judge who understands the issues can make a huge difference, as where the Tribunal rejected as not evidence-based an adjudicator's finding that the sole reason for the rape of a young Afghani woman from a Communist-sympathising family, all of whose members had been targeted in various ways, was that her assailant found her attractive.[27] But often, decisions such as this are upheld.

Baroness Hale's references to the stigma and shame felt by rape victims was an important, if oblique acknowledgement of some of the procedural difficulties faced by women asylum claimants, around which organisations such as Black Women's Rape Action Group, Southall Black Sisters, RWLG, the Refugee Women's Resource Project, Women for Refugee Women and WAST (Women Asylum Seekers Together), as well as ILPA and other lawyers' groups, have campaigned for (in some cases) decades. This shame prevents prompt disclosure, it prevents disclosure to men, disclosure in front of family members – often, rape victims (male and female) can only reveal what happened to them to a counsellor or therapist after a long period of building trust. I referred in Chapter 2 to the case of Ms E, who could not disclose her rape for years. In an asylum case of mine in 1993, a Romanian woman alleged minor harassment on the part of government officials, but showed extreme, disproportionate distress. Gentle questioning achieved nothing, but the night before the hearing, in the pub, she revealed that the officials had subjected her to sexual humiliation and degradation. She had never been able to tell her husband, and was now utterly distraught. But the following day, although the Home Office representative was sympathetic, the adjudicator was not, and an application for the case to be adjourned for medical evidence was refused. The adjudicator reduced the appellant to tears with his hostile, intimidatory, sarcastic and rude manner, and dismissed the appeal, making it clear he did not believe the allegations – because the woman had never told her husband, and could produce no supporting medical evidence. Eventually, following further legal hearings, she was granted refugee status – but by then she and her husband had given up on the UK and had gone to Canada.[28]

Some of the issues have been addressed as a result of women's campaigns – a new UKBA interviewing protocol is supposed to make caseworkers aware of and able to deal with sensitive issues around women's claims; women pursuing asylum appeals based on gender violence are now able to request a female immigration judge and a female Home Office presenting officer, to enable them to give their accounts freely, without having to recount matters about which they would be unable to speak to males.[29] But there is still a huge gulf between women asylum seekers' needs and a decision-making process driven by the imperatives of speed and efficient throughput. Time and trust are in short supply in the asylum process – particularly if, as in so many cases, women are shunted into the detained fast track, where they must within 48 hours reveal matters causing intense shame and anguish to a harried, indifferent or suspicious official, on pain of refusal. While the fast track survives, it makes a dreadful mockery of women's asylum claims.[30]

GAY CLAIMS AND 'DISCRETION'

Meanwhile, if *Shah and Islam* had opened up refugee claims for women with the recognition that a 'particular social group' could be based on gender, by the same reasoning it opened up claims based on sexuality. Homosexuals from countries where gay sex was severely punished, formally or informally, could now be recognised as refugees, fearing persecution as members of the particular social group of homosexuals. But legal recognition of the possibility of refugee status was just the beginning of a long struggle for many gay men and women. In several cases of homosexuals from Iran, where the penalty for homosexuality was death, the Home Office representative at court made areas of Tehran sound as gay-friendly as California. Apart from this sort of blatant misrepresentation, the Home Office used the idea of 'discretion' to refuse claims. People who had been flogged, whipped or chased out of town were told to go home, move to an area where they were not known and avoid trouble by living 'discreetly'. If they kept their sexuality to themselves, they would not be persecuted for it, even in a rabidly homophobic country. This was rejected by refugee and gay rights groups as self-induced oppression, accepting the denial of the fundamental rights to private life, equality and non-discrimination in order to avoid persecution. The courts had accepted that hiding one's beliefs to avoid religious or political persecution could not be demanded of refugee claimants,[31] so why should they be told to hide their sexual orientation? The argument was finally accepted by the Court of Appeal in 2006 and by the supreme court four years later.[32]

PUSHING THE BOUNDARIES

Some feminists were angry about the terms of the victory in *Shah and Islam*. They argued that the persecution in that case was political, not social, motivated by the women's resistance (real or perceived) to the structures of male oppression, and that our pigeon-holing of the women as a social group perpetuated that oppression. The argument was inappropriate to the facts of Mrs Shah's case, but it did raise questions about the definition of the political for other situations and cases, and led to a string of cases where the Tribunal and the courts accepted a much broader definition of what was political, taking in any action or opinion that challenged existing power structures.[33]

The struggle by other groups for recognition as refugees has been less successful. Law-abiding citizens who publicly oppose crime in countries where corruption and violence create dangers for the honest, have failed in their bid to be considered persecuted members of a 'particular social group'.[34] In a 2003 test case, the House of Lords rejected the claim to refugee status of conscientious objectors facing punishment for principled refusal to fight for their country. The law lords ruled that sovereign states are still entitled to demand their citizens to risk life and limb in their service, even against their conscience. It would only be if military service was likely to involve 'internationally condemned actions contrary to the basic laws of human conduct,' such as the commission of war crimes, that punishment for refusal to join up, or for desertion, would constitute persecution.[35] This proviso helped a courageous Iranian soldier who had deserted rather than obey an order to lay landmines in an area where civilians, including children, were likely to be killed or injured by them. He had been captured, served a sentence for desertion and then sent back to the same area and given the same order. This time, he left the country. Following a lengthy saga lasting over five years and involving three trips to the Court of Appeal, the judges finally recognised that laying anti-personnel landmines in this situation was a grave violation of human rights, and punishment for refusing to participate would be persecution, making the deserter a refugee.[36]

Frankly political considerations sometimes inform decisions, particularly where an embarrassing precedent could be created by a successful appeal in the Upper Tribunal or the higher courts. To avoid this danger, the Home Office sometimes concedes a case. VF was an Israeli who did not want to join the Israeli army (the IDF), as a Christian, as a pacifist, and because he did not want to kill innocent Palestinians in the Occupied Territories. His claim was refused and his appeal dismissed; there was 'no evidence' of war crimes or gross human rights violations in Palestine. With the help of conscientious objector groups in Israel, we submitted a huge bundle of UN resolutions, official reports from the UN and other international organisations, reports from human rights groups and monitors of international humanitarian law, demonstrating massive and long-standing international condemnation of Israel's military actions in Palestine, many of which amounted to war crimes or crimes against humanity outlawed by the 1949 Geneva Conventions.

At the Tribunal hearing, the judges inexplicably declined to hear the case, which had been listed for months, on the ground that it was 'too complex', and needed a 'legal panel' (one where all members, not just the chair, are senior lawyers). Months went by without re-listing – then VF got a letter saying (without explanation) that he had been granted refugee status, which avoided the possibility of a public legal ruling that Israeli soldiers are engaged in gross violations of the laws of war.[37]

The struggles over the people and situations covered by the Refugee Convention are changing the legal landscape, particularly for women. The advent of other forms of international protection for those affected by armed conflict, although drawn too narrowly at present, provides another vital legal recourse.[38] But the law still excludes most of the world's refugees from international protection.

Part Two

Stay: Battles for Fair Treatment

5
The Erosion of the Law of Humanity

The phrase 'the law of humanity' comes from a 200-year-old case, R v. *Inhabitants of Eastbourne* (1803), in which the then Lord Chief Justice said,

> As to there being no obligation for maintaining poor foreigners ... the law of humanity, which is anterior to all positive laws, obliges us to afford them relief, to save them from starving.

The quotation was used by Lord Justice Simon Brown in the Court of Appeal in 1996, in a case challenging social security regulations which denied basic welfare benefits to most asylum seekers (those whose claims were not made within three days of their arrival, and those refused asylum and awaiting appeal). It was the first time (at least in recent times) that the government sought deliberately to deprive a group of people of the means of life, by preventing them from earning a living and denying them access to welfare benefits – but not the last. It was a defining moment, when judges were asked 'Whose side is the law on?'

There was a time, as Lord Hoffmann observed in 2002, 'when the welfare state did not look at your passport or ask why you were here. The state paid contributory benefits on the basis of contribution and means-tested benefits on the basis of need ... immigration status was a matter between you and the Home Office, not the concern of the social security system.'[1] Migrants and asylum seekers were eligible for income support at the 'urgent cases' level, which was 90 per cent of the basic rate, to other benefits such as housing benefit and free prescriptions, and to public housing including emergency accommodation if they were homeless.[2] But by the late 1980s, ministers' rhetoric about immigrants and 'bogus refugees' attracted by the honeypot of Britain's generous welfare benefits,[3] played to the drumbeat of media stories like 'Fury as luxury block let to refugees'[4] and 'It cost £400 millions to keep 30,000 immigrants on social security',[5] created a popular racist myth of British generosity abused by hordes of undeserving, grasping foreigners.

Free NHS hospital treatment had been linked to immigration status since 1982, by regulations[6] charging patients in the UK temporarily (for a year or less) for non-emergency hospital treatment. Although the regulations only applied to hospital care, and did not apply to asylum seekers (who by law are assumed to be refugees until final refusal of a claim), by 1989 Kurdish asylum seekers reported being denied medical treatment by doctors in Hackney, who were refusing to register them.[7] In August 1993, the father of an Iranian refugee died following refusal of treatment at Hammersmith hospital after a row over payment,[8] and in 1995, Carlos Padilla, a Chilean refugee, was found dead in a hospital plant room a month after he had gone missing from the ward, apparently after hearing staff discuss fees for treatment for a ruptured appendix.[9] There were reports that HIV/AIDS sufferers were being denied life-saving triple combination therapy because of their uncertain immigration status.[10]

Social housing was the next casualty. In the charged political climate of the 1980s and 1990s, local authorities adopted policies designed to exclude migrants from public housing. Some would not allow migrants to put their families on the housing list until they were in the country, or refused emergency accommodation to homeless migrant families on the grounds that leaving their home countries made them 'intentionally homeless'. These rules created nightmares for people such as the Kurdish refugee from Turkey who lived in a six by nine foot room equipped with just a bed and a sink for two years after being granted refugee status. When his wife and two young children came to join him in 1992, his landlord and the environmental health officer said they couldn't stay there. But Hackney Council refused to rehouse the family.[11]

Following a legal battle over councils' restrictive housing policies, in April 1993, the Court of Appeal ruled that councils had no duty to house undocumented homeless migrants, no matter how desperate their need.[12] The Asylum and Immigration Appeals Bill meanwhile proposed reducing local authorities' housing duties towards asylum seekers and their dependants. Despite sustained campaigning, including marches by thousands in January, March and November 1992, the measure became law in July 1993.[13] No housing duty arose if asylum seekers had access to any accommodation, however temporary. Bed and breakfast 'hotels' from Hoxton to Hastings filled up with asylum seekers, who could never expect a place of their own where they could cook their own food and have some privacy.

DESTITUTION AS A WEAPON

Then social security was targeted. One of the worst aspects of the asylum system in the UK has been the ban on working. The policy, created to stop 'bogus refugees' coming over to 'take our jobs', saps confidence and self-esteem among often well-qualified refugees already disoriented and depressed at having to flee their own country. It creates an artificial dependency as well as fuelling the hysteria which sees asylum seekers as 'scroungers'. In 1995, the ban was only lifted if a claim had been awaiting a Home Office decision for six months. This was the context in which social security minister Peter Lilley introduced proposals to withdraw basic welfare benefits from in-country[14] and refused asylum seekers at the Conservative party conference in October 1995, to acclaim from the party faithful. He said refused asylum seekers 'can appeal, but not at taxpayers' expense'.[15] The *Sun* applauded the 'tough warning to the world's scroungers',[16] although its stablemate *The Times* said 'Mr Lilley's soundbite is populist and xenophobic nonsense ... The 1993 Act already imposes conditions on asylum seekers so stringent that they give the UN Human Rights Committee cause for concern'. The tacit hope behind the proposals, it said, was that 'genuine refugees will make some other country their destination'.[17]

The proposals horrified refugees and migrant support groups. Downing Street was picketed and asylum seekers embarked on a hunger strike, saying their choice would be to 'beg or starve'.[18] UNHCR warned that the UK risked breaching its international obligations to refugees. Two hundred and fifty organisations gave evidence to the government's Social Security Advisory Committee, arguing that the proposed regulations were inhuman, irrational and monstrous, and the committee warned that they were 'racially divisive' and should be scrapped.[19] Even on the government's own argument, the blunt instrument of denial of basic benefits would hit genuine refugees; figures showed that the same proportion of in-country claimants proved their claim as those claiming at the port. The government insisted that genuine refugees would not be deterred by lack of means of subsistence, but never explained how they would stay alive. The question was brushed aside as an irrelevant distraction from the all-important aims of cutting numbers and demonstrating the Tories' toughness on immigration.

It was the refugee communities themselves who, with the churches, temples and mosques and the voluntary sector, picked up the tab, opening soup kitchens and emergency housing when

Lilley's regulation came into force and benefits were withdrawn in February 1996. Ms B, a Zairean asylum seeker denied benefits because she claimed asylum at the Home Office in Croydon on the day she arrived, rather than at immigration control at Waterloo, launched a legal challenge, joined by JCWI. I was junior counsel, with Nick Blake QC leading me, for solicitor Louise Christian. The effect of the regulations on asylum seekers caught by them was described by Lord Justice Simon Brown, summarising the evidence garnered by refugee organisations:

> (1) They have no access whatever either to funds or to benefits in kind. (2) They have no accommodation and, being ineligible for housing benefit, no prospect of securing any. (3) [T]hey are invariably forbidden from seeking employment for six months and, even assuming that thereafter they ... obtain permission to work, their prospects of obtaining it are likely to be poor, particularly if they speak no English. (4) They are likely to be without family, friends or contacts and thus in a position of peculiar isolation with no network of community support. (5) Their claims take on average some 18 months to determine, on occasions as long as four years. An individual has no control over this and no means of hastening a final decision ... (6) Quite apart from the need to keep body and soul together pending the final determination of a claim, expense is likely to be incurred in pursuing it. Applicants must attend for interviews with the Home Office and with any advisers they may have. They must have an address where they can be contacted with notices of appointments or decisions. To miss an appointment or the time for appeal is to forgo their claim.

We argued that the regulations effectively deprived refugees of their rights to claim asylum and to pursue appeals, rights protected under the Refugee Convention and given effect by domestic law, and this was a use of the minister's power to make regulations that was not intended by parliament when it passed the 'parent' social security legislation. The argument failed in the high court, but in June 1996 our appeal to the Court of Appeal succeeded. By a 2:1 majority, the Court declared the regulations *ultra vires*:

> A significant number of genuine asylum seekers now find themselves faced with a bleak choice: whether to remain here destitute and homeless until their claims are finally determined or

whether instead to abandon their claims and return to face the very persecution they have fled ... Parliament cannot have intended a significant number of genuine asylum seekers to be impaled on the horns of so intolerable a dilemma: the need either to abandon their claims to refugee status or alternatively to maintain them as best they can but in a state of utter destitution. Primary legislation alone could ... achieve that sorry state of affairs.[20]

For good measure, the same court held unanimously the following day that destitute asylum seekers were 'vulnerable' and so eligible for homeless persons' housing.[21] But our celebrations were premature, as Lilley was determined to beat the judges.[22] Another Asylum and Immigration Bill going through parliament was already finally removing migrants' and asylum seekers' entitlement to any public housing or homelessness provision, and a clause was added to the Bill to achieve the same effect as the impugned regulations.[23] As primary legislation, it was protected from judicial interference under the doctrine of parliamentary sovereignty (which does not apply to ministerial regulations, even those needing parliamentary approval). By the end of July 1996, asylum seekers were back on the streets. The Refugee Council reopened its Holborn night shelter (residents could stay for a fortnight but were then on the streets again for five weeks).[24] The Medical Foundation said two destitute patients had attempted suicide and others were forced into prostitution. A Kenyan woman was reportedly found attempting suicide in a public lavatory; she had been given a bed in exchange for sex but was thrown out when she became pregnant.[25] The Red Cross announced distribution of food parcels to asylum seekers – the first time in 50 years it had distributed food in the UK.[26] The battle continued.

Campaigners and lawyers next found an overlooked but still subsisting section of an old law, the 1948 National Assistance Act, which obliged councils to care for certain mentally or physically ill residents and other vulnerable people.[27] They argued that the duty extended to asylum seekers, who were vulnerable because they were destitute and without relatives or other sources of assistance. In October, the challenge succeeded. The high court ruled that local authorities had to provide housing and basic support to asylum seekers with nowhere else to turn.[28] The judgment was good news for asylum seekers, but not for local authorities, unfairly saddled with housing and caring for an estimated 10,000 asylum seekers with little central government help.[29] As the incoming Labour government promised an urgent review, councils began looking round for the cheapest ways of fulfilling their duty. As Camden put Ghanaian and Romanian asylum seekers in old people's homes and Hammersmith considered a tent city, Westminster moved over a hundred asylum seekers to Liverpool, and other hard-pressed London authorities followed suit. It was cheaper to rent accommodation in northern towns and faded seaside resorts and to send asylum seekers there than it was to house them in their own boroughs.[30] The policy of dispersal was born.

NASS: DETERRENCE, DISPERSAL AND RACISM

Whereas the Tories had simply closed off parts of the welfare state to migrants and asylum seekers, Labour came up with a system of institutionalised inhumanity. It accepted responsibility for providing support, but its anxiety to appease the right-wing press and to create opportunities for the private sector created a monstrous system which had a lot in common with the workhouse: bare subsistence and a deterrent system of coercion, control and stigmatisation.

The 1999 Immigration and Asylum Act removed migrants and asylum seekers from all mainstream welfare benefits, and even from support under the National Assistance Act if their vulnerability was caused solely by destitution or its physical effects.[31] A new Home Office agency, NASS (National Asylum Support Service), was set up to provide support to destitute asylum seekers at the rate of 70 per cent of the 'safety net' of income support.[32] It was avowedly deterrent, to 'minimise the attraction of the UK to economic migrants'.[33] Support was to be in kind rather than cash; supermarkets were encouraged to sign up to a voucher scheme by being allowed to keep the change from the vouchers. The policy of dispersal was universalised: asylum seekers were sent away from London and the south-east to the north, the south-west and Scotland, where there was surplus housing. They had no choice about where they lived – the law specified that their preferences were not to be heeded[34] – and seven days' absence from allotted accommodation meant loss of support. Charities were invited to form consortia to provide emergency support and assistance in 'one-stop shops', which some, including the Refugee Council and Refugee Action, did.[35] Private landlords were given incentives to contract with NASS or with local authorities to provide asylum accommodation, support and services.[36] There was a lot of money in asylum support, although asylum seekers saw none of it. One of the most profitable, the Angel Group, which faced allegations of squalid and unsafe conditions, generated £700,000 profit in two years housing asylum seekers, and by the end of 2003 was a multi-million pound business.[37]

In Liverpool, high-rise blocks sold off semi-derelict by the council in the 1980s for 10p per flat were bought up for asylum accommodation by another private company, Landmark. They had no heating, lifts in 18-storey blocks didn't work, stairs were littered with rubbish and water did not reach the top floors. There were infestations of fleas and mosquitoes. Managers barged in to private rooms. Conditions like these, on top of compulsory dispersal away from friends and family in London, led to mental breakdown, self-harm and suicide. Iranian refugee Ramin Khaleghi killed himself in his room at the International Hotel in Leicester, which housed 400 asylum seekers in decrepit, unhygienic conditions.[38] He was in despair after being refused asylum and without family support after being forced out of London. Protests by Iraqi asylum seekers at conditions at Angel Heights in Newcastle led to the arrest of seven men on charges of violent disorder.[39] Those whose asylum claims were refused were summarily evicted. With no duty towards destitute refused asylum seekers, councils began evicting vulnerable people like E, an Eritrean refused asylum seeker who had applied to remain because of his fear of torture. Despite his hepatitis, he was thrown out of the hostel Lambeth had put him in and spent three months homeless and utterly destitute before the council was ordered to take him back.[40]

The voucher system capped the degradation. Asylum seekers not fed in hostels received vouchers worth up to £36.54 a week to spend on 'essential living needs', with no change given. They had to shop at specified supermarkets, sometimes an hour's walk away. Without cash they could not shop at cheaper street markets. Presenting vouchers at the check-out was humiliating, and assistants sometimes vetoed the purchase of meat, fruit, cigarettes, yoghurt or shampoo as queuing customers tutted impatiently. A Tanzanian refugee observed, 'There is no cash because you are deemed untrustworthy ... What about halal food for Muslims? And what if we need a bus fare to get to a hospital or to see a legal representative? And what about shoes, socks or underwear? Surely those who designed this policy do not regard us as humans.'[41] Mothers of babies could not afford nappies; warm winter clothing was unaffordable.[42] An Audit Commission report of June 2000 warned that the lack of effective support for asylum seekers in dispersal areas could lead to a 'cycle of social exclusion and dependency'.[43]

Labour might have believed that dispersal would appease the right-wing press, which had been stirring up popular racism to fever pitch in the late 1990s. Headlines like 'Good life on asylum alley', 'Brutal crimes of "asylum seekers"', 'Kosovo-on-Sea'[44] and descriptions of Roma as 'scum of the earth' and 'human sewage'[45] had led to vicious racist attacks – including being pushed under cars and hit with iron bars – in towns like Dover.[46] But the dispersal policy, far from appeasing the Right, merely spread xeno-racism[47] throughout the country – not surprisingly, as Labour had adopted the view of asylum seekers as an unwanted burden to be shared.[48] With Tory 'liberal' Michael Heseltine accusing 'bogus asylum seekers' of stealing British people's housing and home secretary David Blunkett pledging to 'blitz society of asylum cheats',[49] and the tabloids spreading myths that asylum 'scroungers' were given cash, computers, free sports facilities and TVs, the clear political message was that the nation was 'on its knees', exploited by a conspiracy of soft-hearted liberal officials, other western European countries (who had dumped their asylum problem on us) and 'money-grabbing gypsies'.[50] The *Oxford Mail* ran an anti-asylum campaign as the leader of the Tory group on the city council proposed isolating asylum seekers out at the Upper Heyford RAF base;[51] residents' associations across the country, fearful of rampaging criminals, opposed asylum hostel plans; and the far Right cashed in. Racist attacks soared in dispersal areas. In the Sighthill area of Glasgow, where asylum seekers were housed on a run-down and until then mainly white council estate, anti-racist activists monitored 70 racist attacks in the 14 months before the fatal stabbing of Kurdish asylum seeker Firsat Dag in August 2001.[52] Many asylum seekers fled their NASS accommodation and went back to London where, refused further NASS support, they relied on family or community support, and by the end of 2000, fewer than 10,000 of the 65,000 asylum seekers targeted for dispersal were outside London.[53]

G, a Turkish Kurd suffering from depression as a result of torture and abuse, was sent with his family in September 2001 from London to the Toryglen estate in Glasgow, a white area known for racial violence. The family were shouted at in the street, spat at, threatened with dogs and the twelve-year-old son was bullied at school. G became so distraught that he tried to throw himself out of the window. In October three men attacked their home and tried to stab the youngest boy. The family fled back to London, but NASS told them to return to the Glasgow flat or they would lose support. They refused to return, and received nothing at all from NASS for two months. Only after receiving a Medical Foundation report detailing the impact of the racism on G's mental health did NASS withdraw the instruction. But the high court refused to intervene, saying NASS could not be criticised for sending the family there; racism on Toryglen was no worse than anywhere else.[54]

Dispersal and the impossibly low level of support was leading to deterioration in asylum seekers' health and putting pregnant women and unborn children's health at risk.[55] T, a pregnant HIV-positive Ethiopian asylum seeker dispersed to Wolverhampton, had her baby delivered by caesarian to avoid the risk of transmission of the disease, and was told not to breast-feed, but NASS refused to pay for formula milk,[56] leaving T unable to afford this basic precaution against transmission of HIV to her child, until the high court overruled its refusal.[57] The All-Party Parliamentary Group on AIDS and its sister group on refugees complained in July 2003 that poverty and dispersal were exacerbating asylum seekers' poor health and that NASS 'consistently disregarded the opinions, expertise and professional medical reports of ... doctors, psychiatrists and psychologists'. Doctors were not notified of patients' dispersal, and the sudden dispersal of an HIV-positive pregnant woman resulted in her giving birth to an infected child.[58]

The common experience of dispersal created solidarity among asylum seekers across differences of nationality, race and religion and, as protests grew, solidarity from residents, as anti-racist and migrant support groups sprang up across the country to oppose inhuman policies and tabloid racism. The Civil Rights Caravan of 40 refugees, migrants and their supporters, organised by the Campaign Against Racism and Fascism and the National Civil Rights Movement, toured many of the dispersal areas in the autumn of 2000, taking testimonies from asylum seekers and building resistance.[59] In Norwich, a refugee support group stopped a slum landlord obtaining a contract to house 1,000 asylum seekers.[60] In Glasgow, trade unions and community organisations formed the Glasgow Campaign to Welcome Refugees.[61] In Liverpool, protests and hunger strikes by asylum seekers, supported by Merseyside Refugee Action, churches, the local MP and eventually even the *Sunday Express*,[62] forced Liverpool council to declare Landmark Towers and the Inn on the Park unfit for human habitation; dispersal to the blocks was suspended and Landmark ordered to rehouse the occupants.[63] Meanwhile, the campaign against vouchers was a resounding success. It started with angry asylum seekers and their supporters picketing Tesco and Quiksave in places like Gateshead and Benwell. It was taken up by unions – in the north-east the regional Trades Union Congress (TUC) supported demonstrations and the shop workers' union USDAW was brought in to emphasise that the campaign was not an attack on their members. A national campaign was launched by the Refugee Council, Oxfam and the TGWU (later Unite), supported by children's and housing charities, faith groups and trade unions. Supporters bought asylum seekers' vouchers to give them much-needed cash. In October 2001, David Blunkett announced the scrapping of the voucher system.[64] But the cash payments were pitifully small, leaving many hungry, unable to get warm in winter or to clothe themselves or their children adequately.[65]

Legal challenges were mounted to dispersal of individuals needing to be in London to receive medical treatment or for religious or family reasons. The 1999 Act provided an appeal against refusal or withdrawal of support, but no legal aid. A network of law centres, refugee and community groups providing free advice and representation at asylum support appeals created the Asylum Support Appeals Project (ASAP) in 2003. The legal challenges and successful appeals (the success rate on appeal was 40 per cent)[66] resulted in some improvements: NASS was forced to respond with policies on issues such as domestic violence, medical needs or racist incidents which could prevent dispersal.[67] But the central features of NASS – compulsory dispersal to slum housing and sub-subsistence support – remained untouched, surviving the abolition of NASS as a separate agency in 2007. In a further tightening of the screw in October 2009, the level of asylum support for single claimants was reduced to just over half of income support, the level set as a minimum for subsistence.

RETURN OF THE SOUP KITCHEN

These conditions did nothing to stop the arrival of asylum seekers, who came in ever-increasing numbers fleeing wars, repression and other threats. The government's response was to adopt the Tories' exclusionary policy, legislating in 2002 to disqualify from all support childless 'late claimants', that is, asylum claimants who did not claim as soon as 'reasonably practicable' after arriving.[68] Groups from Amnesty International to the British Medical Association and the Maternity Alliance expressed alarm, as local refugee support and church groups prepared to open soup kitchens and church halls once more.[69] Blunkett told parliament that 'section 55' targeted abusive claimants, who had been in the country for a while and then claimed asylum just to get support.[70] But when it came into force on a bitter January day in 2003, NASS officials were instructed to refuse support to all childless asylum seekers who failed to claim asylum at the port 'unless there is a very good reason'.[71] The queues stretching out of the door of the Home Office in Croydon and round the corner in the snow in the January days included:

- 'M', a Rwandan woman regularly raped and beaten by Tutsis in a refugee camp, who on arrival had no idea where to claim asylum, no money and nowhere to live. She could not claim the following day as the Home Office was not accepting any more applications that day. The next day, after her asylum interview, she went to Croydon police station, where police allowed her to stay the night sitting on a chair provided she did not fall asleep. After that, she had nowhere to go, and survived only because a stranger took pity on her.
- 'D', a 22-year-old Angolan suffering from trauma after his father was shot dead, his mother and sister raped by soldiers and he was interrogated and beaten. He claimed asylum on the day he arrived, and was found a bed for one night but then had to sleep rough outside the Home Office.
- 'Q', a 20-year-old Iraqi Kurd who arrived in London in a lorry on 8 January at 5 a.m. with no money, speaking no English. An Arabic speaker told him to go to Croydon. He walked for three hours until he reached the Home Office. He had stomach-ache and toothache and felt sick and tired. He slept the night in a tunnel by a phone box.

There was no appeal against refusal of support under section 55, but human rights law required support to be provided if it was necessary to prevent a breach of human rights, and this provision became the focus of mass litigation for destitute asylum seekers. Over 150 judicial review claims were lodged in the first month. The first test case, *Q and others*, featured six claimants including the three above. In February 2003, high court judge Collins held that officials had not properly investigated the reasons for the late claims, and that the refusal of support in each case breached the law of common humanity as well as the claimants' human rights. With no other means of support and a ban on working, asylum seekers refused support would have to 'resort to begging or other more serious criminal activities in order to survive', he observed. Enforced destitution and homelessness with no prospect of alternative support was inhuman and degrading and violated Article 3 of the Human Rights Convention.[72]

Blunkett furiously accused the judge of sabotaging the new law. 'I'm fed up with having to deal with a situation where Parliament debates issues and the judges overturn them', he said.[73] The attorney-general was sent to argue the Home Office appeal, and JCWI and Liberty intervened to support the asylum seekers' arguments. In March, the appeal court upheld Collins' ruling that officials had behaved unfairly and had interpreted the requirement for prompt asylum claims too strictly, and their judgment led to improvements in interviewing procedures and a policy allowing claimants three days to claim asylum.[74] But the appeal judges did not agree that denial of support would breach human rights 'unless and until it is clear that charitable support has not been provided and the individual is incapable of fending for himself'.[75] The point at which enforced destitution and homelessness would breach human rights became the subject of prolonged litigation, with the success of applications depending on the particular judge hearing the application, until the House of Lords ruled in the test case of *Limbuela*, in which housing charity Shelter intervened, that NASS should normally provide support if an applicant was street homeless, seriously hungry or 'unable to satisfy the most basic requirements of hygiene'. Since the point was to avoid a breach of human rights, they ruled, it was not necessary to wait until someone was actually living in inhuman or degrading conditions before providing support.[76]

The judgment was a victory for asylum seekers and their supporters, establishing that the Home Office could not just leave people in the gutter because of a late asylum claim. But these provisions were not the only legal source of misery and destitution; the plight of refused asylum seekers who were denied all support was becoming increasingly visible. Only those with children retained support until removal; otherwise, rejection of an asylum claim and appeal meant loss of support, since refused asylum seekers could by definition safely return to their own country. That was the theory. In practice, as I described in Chapter 2 above, frequently they could not – the risk of torture or death was all too real, despite being disbelieved, so many refugees remain here following rejection of their claims, too frightened to return home. But shelter and means of survival are denied; a refused asylum seeker from Darfur had to leave his NASS accommodation four days after an operation because his claim had been dismissed, although doctors said he needed three months to recover.[77] In 2005, the Red Cross helped 25,000 destitute refused asylum seekers,[78] and the Salvation Army distributed food parcels.[79] Zekria Mohammed, a trainee dentist from Afghanistan, died in a makeshift noose in his Glasgow flat, 'ashamed and broken' according to friends, 'too proud to beg and scavenge for food' after rejection of his claim.[80]

Many of those refused asylum would a decade previously have been granted exceptional leave to remain under policies for nationals of countries ravaged by war or disaster – which gave them rights to work and to claim benefits. But when these policies were discontinued in favour of simple non-removal, Zimbabweans, Somalis, Afghanis and Iraqis were not forcibly removed for years – but neither were they granted any form of leave, or permission to work, or entitlement to support. A Zimbabwean in this limbo brought a legal challenge, arguing that the non-removal policy implicitly conceded that it was impossible to return. The high court said no; the Home Office's 'generosity' in not removing Zimbabweans forcibly did not mean return was impossible.[81] I recall telling a meeting that asylum seekers got £35 a week to live on; a member of the audience corrected me, 'I have to share that among five of us, as my friends have been refused.' One man was so desperate that he smashed a police car headlight to get arrested. He spent a week in jail, commenting later that 'the food was quite good'.[82] Many end up in prison for working illegally in order to survive.

In response to concerns raised in parliament during the passage of the 1999 Act, there were provisions in section 4 of the Act allowing the Home Office to support certain refused asylum seekers.[83] But getting this support was made as difficult as possible. NASS deliberately kept its existence quiet until ordered by the high court to reveal it.[84] Criteria for 'hard cases' support developed on a case-by-case basis into a policy later enshrined in regulations. Section 4 support is now available to refused asylum seekers such as those who are taking steps to return home (like trying to obtain travel documents); or who can't travel owing to illness or late pregnancy. But applications can take months to process,[85] with applicants homeless and utterly destitute in the interim. Leeds-based charity Positive Action for Refugees and Asylum Seekers (PAFRAS) reported an increase in babies born with serious defects and sometimes chronically under-developed because of the lengthy wait for support during their mothers' pregnancy.[86] The section 4 regime is designed to be even harsher than asylum support, with no cash, but a payment card worth £35 per week, only £5 of which can be carried over to the following week – making saving or bulk buying impossible. In 2004, refused asylum seekers accommodated under section 4 were told they would have to do community work for their daily bread – but there was a furore, the parliamentary Joint Committee on Human Rights said the provision might breach the ban on forced labour,[87] and it was never implemented.

When in 2004 it became clear that the government's removal targets were not being met, the government extended the denial of all support to families with children who failed to leave after refusal of asylum, until then protected from utter destitution up to the point of removal (or their failure to report for removal when ordered to). Now, if they failed to leave, all support would cease and the children of the family would be taken into care.[88] This time, the public outcry did not stop the enforced destitution of families.[89]

In opposition, Tony Blair had said, 'If humanitarian treatment of [asylum seekers] provokes racism, the answer is not to crack down on refugees but to crack down on racism.'[90] In government, his policies fed popular racism and created an invisible underclass living in conditions reminiscent of the poor in Victorian England – but in some respects worse, because of the ban on working. The Joint Committee on Human Rights commented:

> [B]y refusing permission for most asylum seekers to work and operating a system of support which results in widespread destitution, the treatment of asylum seekers in a number of cases reaches the ... threshold of inhuman and degrading treatment ... the Government has ... been practising a deliberate policy of destitution [which] falls below the requirements of the common law of humanity and of international human rights law... The policy of enforced destitution must cease.[91]

The degrading system of asylum support-cum-control and destitution for self-deportation was continued by the coalition. In March 2012, UKBA awarded contracts for asylum seeker housing to giant multinational security companies G4S and Serco, which between them manage most immigration detention centres and provide guards for deportation.[92] The move appears to presage a segregated and seamless housing-detention-removal process with ominous echoes.

MEDICAL TREATMENT DENIED

Refused asylum seekers frequently suffer from physical and psychological problems[93] – but hospital treatment and social work support are denied. International law obliges the UK to ensure access to health care on a non-discriminatory basis, but in 2002, the United Nations' Committee on Economic, Social and Cultural Rights criticised '*de facto* discrimination in relation to some marginalised and vulnerable groups', and asked the government to amend national legislation and policy.[94] Yet two years later, the government extended the ban on free non-emergency hospital treatment to most refused asylum seekers,[95] and announced plans to deny them access to free NHS primary care (although this has since been shelved). Treatment classified as 'non-emergency' and so chargeable includes antiretroviral drugs for HIV/AIDS (although treatment already embarked on was continued). People with serious medical conditions including bowel cancer, diabetes and kidney failure, and pregnant women, have been refused free treatment but cannot afford to pay or have become too intimidated to seek treatment.[96] Doctors for Human Rights wrote, 'Health security is one of the core elements of human security ... the denial of access to health care by one of the richest countries on earth is inhumane because it jeopardises ... health and illegal because it violates international law.'[97] In March 2011, the Home Office announced that refused asylum seekers who cooperated with plans to remove them would get free hospital treatment, but not others – and anyone who left the country without paying NHS bills of £1,000 or more would be barred from re-entering.[98]

CAMPAIGNS FOR HEALTH AND WORK RIGHTS

Myriad community and church groups up and down the country, as well as friends, family and charities, provide what support and friendship they can. Collaborations have developed between community and campaigning organisations and law centres and solicitors' firms. Medical professionals work to provide health care for current and refused asylum seekers in organisations such as Doctors for Human Rights, Medact and Doctors without Borders (whose Project London helps asylum seekers obtain registration, provides free medical care and runs educational campaigns). Test cases have been brought on denial of hospital treatment. YA, a Palestinian refused asylum seeker with a serious liver condition, was admitted to hospital when his liver condition deteriorated, but then got a bill for £9,000. The high court held the demand for payment unlawful. But the Court of Appeal reversed the judgment, ruling that hospitals were entitled (although not obliged) to refuse free hospital treatment in non-emergency situations.[99] But campaigning has achieved exemption from hospital charges for separated children and for some refused asylum seekers.

Campaigning and test cases have also fought for the right to work, using human rights and EU law. The high court held in December 2008 that failed asylum seekers unable to return home for a lengthy period should be allowed to work; a blanket ban was 'unlawfully over-broad and unjustifiably detrimental to claimants who have had to wait as long as this claimant has' (seven years).[100] On the Home Office's appeal, the supreme court condemned the work ban as incompatible with the EU Reception Directive, which provides a right of access to the labour market to asylum seekers waiting for a decision for over a year.[101] The Home Office changed the rules following the supreme court's judgment, but restricted asylum seekers' access to the labour market to 'shortage occupations': skilled trades and professions which cannot be fully staffed by British or EU workers.[102] The campaign against the shaming policy of enforced destitution and for the right to work continues, through the Refugee Council, the TUC, *Still Human Still Here* and other coalitions.

6
Migration Management in the Market State

In this chapter, I turn to examine policies on economic migration, affecting workers and students. As the welfare state gives way to the market state, governments are abandoning ideals of job security for the domestic labour force. At the same time, they are adopting an increasingly cavalier approach to labour migration to respond to the ebbs and flows of the all-powerful market. In the globalised economy, capital is shifted between continents electronically in billionths of a second, corporations buy up vast swathes of land in the poor world, build factories and source goods wherever in the world the greatest profit is to be made with the least interference by national authorities – and borders don't interfere with the movements of the super-rich and even the ordinarily well-off from the rich countries. But the more integrated the world economy becomes, the tighter and more precise is the 'migration management' operated by governments at the behest of the neo-liberals, to enable particular gaps in the economy to be filled at particular times, as and when required. The corollary is the power to dispose of surplus labour by ensuring that labour migration remains temporary – a project now in progress. The international student body, too, is being shaped to fit corporate needs while maximising revenue. And we can still see old-fashioned racism at work in policies and their implementation.

These policies rest on the common-sense but legally controversial[1] doctrine of states' absolute right to control their borders – an aspect of state sovereignty which has taken on increasing importance to the government (and to the governments of all the rich countries). The doctrine, frequently invoked in muscular terms at party conferences and by the tabloid press, justifies the imposition of any restriction deemed necessary in pursuit of 'the national interest', and entails the freedom to change policy in response to changed conditions. Implicit in such unfettered freedom is the right to break policy promises when conditions change. Battles in the field of economic migration have raged over governments' use of the doctrine to shift the goalposts, changing policy as they go along, without regard to legal constraints or human realities. The absolutist doctrine has been modified – through campaigning, litigation under the Human Rights Act and the application of common-law doctrines of fairness. But the lordly attitudes which see migrant workers as commodities and international students as revenue streams, whose needs are irrelevant, still inform policy and practice, and can be dangerous when combined with executive power which seeks to avoid the scrutiny of MPs in parliament and to shake off the restraining hand of the courts.

FROM RESTRICTION TO MANAGED MIGRATION

The story of how Britain reneged on promises to subjects and citizens forms the historical backdrop to more recent betrayals, and is well documented, from the first control of Commonwealth immigrants in 1962, through the treatment of the British East African Asians in 1968 to the abandonment of Hong Kong's former UK citizens in 1997.[2] Britain's entry to the Common Market (the European Economic Community, now the European Union), and the 1971 Immigration Act – the cornerstone of modern immigration law – completed the historical turn away from colonies and Commonwealth towards Europe, as Commonwealth citizens became assimilated with aliens for most immigration purposes.[3] As is well known, the 1971 Act, passed on the eve of the first post-war recession, put a stop to large-scale economic migration for settlement. Immigration for work was tightly restricted under the work permit scheme managed by the Department of Employment. Strict skill, qualification and income criteria were applied to the recruitment of non-European workers, each permit had to be justified, and jobs had to be advertised locally, nationally and eventually in Europe too. Students had to leave the UK at the end of their studies to prevent them staying to seek work. Permits were job-specific, and the loss of the job could mean loss of residence rights and eventual deportation. But although restricted, for skilled workers economic migration still led to settlement: those remaining in approved employment could expect 'indefinite leave to remain' after four years.

Unskilled labour was provided for the agricultural sector through the Seasonal Agricultural Workers' Scheme (SAWS), whereby government-approved (but unregulated) gangmasters recruited foreign students for seasonal labour, ruthlessly exploited them and ensured their return home after harvest time. Commonwealth citizens with UK ancestry retained work and settlement rights, and young Commonwealth citizens could come as 'working holiday-makers' for up to two years. Students could work part-time, and their family members, those of migrant workers, and settled immigrants, could work without restriction. Otherwise, for the best part of 30 years, governments and employers relied on Europeans exercising free movement rights – and unofficially, on undocumented migrants, who came in as visitors and overstayed, or entered illegally – to do the low-paid, low-skilled jobs that increasingly affluent Britons disdained.

MORE WORKERS, FEWER RIGHTS

From the mid-1980s, the economy began to grow once more, and work permits were issued somewhat more readily.[4] As the twentieth century ended, the rapid expansion of the economy and the increasingly elderly demographic of the UK and Europe forced the realisation that large numbers of migrant workers were necessary to pay for pensions and to fill skill gaps. The 1999 Tampere summit of EU ministers heard that Europe needed over a million and a half new workers annually to keep the working-age population stable and support the ageing indigenous population. At the same time, an ever more flexible workforce was required to respond to the increasingly frantic booms, dips and surges of the globalising economy. As European competition for skilled migrants heated up, restriction gave way to selective admission through 'managed migration'.[5] The Labour government pushed open the doors for economic migration, cautiously at first, then more confidently, declaring it to be good for Britain. As the Home Office took over responsibility for overseas workers, its research department set out the economic benefits with the zeal of soap powder advertisers: migration 'fills labour market gaps, improves productivity, reduces inflationary pressures ... makes a net fiscal contribution'.[6] An 'innovator' scheme, introduced in 2000, welcomed entrepreneurs with business plans which would significantly benefit the country. (The Tories had already introduced an 'investor' category, in 1994, whose only qualification for entry was having three-quarters of a million pounds to invest.) International students graduating in the UK were now allowed to stay to look for employment. Work permits became easier to obtain, particularly in 'shortage occupations' such as nursing, construction and catering – and in 2003, 175,000 permits were issued, more than double the number granted in 2000.

Opportunities for unskilled workers, though, remained restricted and were soon closed off. The sectors-based scheme, introduced in 2002 to fill areas of the economy where unskilled labour was in short supply, gave workers only twelve months' stay, no prospect of settlement and no rights to bring family. From 2004 sector-based work permits were restricted to Bulgarians and Romanians (who were to join the EU in 2007) working in food manufacturing. Similarly, in 2003 working holidaymakers' rules were relaxed to encourage young Commonwealth citizens 'to provide more of the flexible labour that the economy and business need' (the original aims of the scheme were to widen the horizons of participants). But the resulting increase in applicants from Asia and Africa prompted the introduction of the scheme's first ever quota in June 2004, amid allegations of abuse,[7] and in 2008, the scheme was replaced by a 'youth mobility' scheme open only to young people from Canada, Australia, New Zealand, Japan and Monaco.

The Highly Skilled Migrants Programme (HSMP), introduced in 2002, was the jewel of Labour's managed migration programme, designed 'to maximise the benefits to the UK of high human capital individuals'. With echoes of Harold Wilson's 'white heat of the [technological] revolution',[8] the 2002 White Paper enthused that the programme 'will help eminent scientists to base their research projects here ... encourage the movement of business and financial experts to our centres of commerce [and] facilitate the entry of doctors to work as general practitioners in the UK'.[9] Those meeting the qualifying criteria were admitted for an initial year and then, on proof of economic activity and self-sufficiency, were granted a further three years, leading to the possibility of settlement after four years. An important and novel criterion for these highly skilled migrants was that applicants had to intend to make their home in the UK.

One of those attracted to Britain was Sylvia, who had left her native Sierra Leone when civil war brought her children's education to a halt in 1997, and had served in various African countries as a charity development worker, supporting the three children's studies in the UK from her salary. With her masters' from New York State University and her acknowledged excellence in her field, she had no difficulty obtaining a one-year HSMP visa in 2003. Recruited by a community development charity, she was granted a further three-year stay in 2004 and, with the promise of settlement in three years, sold her land in Sierra Leone, got a mortgage and in 2006, bought a house in London with her 30-year-old electrical engineer son.

However, the new Labour corporate-speak in the white paper boded ill for highly skilled migrants like Sylvia, demonstrating as it did the government's whole-hearted embrace of the values and imperatives of an unregulated, unfettered and unstable market economy. It sucked up as many highly skilled workers as possible from all parts of the world without thought, planning or regulation for the longer term, or for the rapid swings in demand which would leave British and foreign workers alike high and dry. Their plans, needs and lives remained outside any policy equation. During these years, Labour wasted the opportunity it had to resist predatory market capitalism and its inhuman consequences, to ensure tight control of the financial market, and to protect and enhance workers' rights. It could have ensured that migrants' rights were also protected, by adopting the UN Migrant Workers' Convention, which came into force in 2003[10] – a measure which would also have allayed concerns about the undercutting of British workers. (No EU member state has signed or ratified the Convention, despite the cautious and modest commitments it contains.) Instead, while welcoming the benefits economic migrants brought to Britain, Labour sold them down the river when they were no longer needed.

BREAKING PROMISES

In 2005, the economy slowed, and right-wing pressure about 'uncontrolled immigration' grew to a crescendo after several hundred thousand Poles and Romanians came following their countries' accession to the EU. Labour's response was to disown the skilled non-European migrants it had so vigorously recruited. In 2006, complaining that some foreign graduates and highly skilled migrants were unemployed or in low-wage employment and not performing the expected miracles, the Home Office tightened the rules. First, in April, without consultation, it raised the qualifying period for settlement for highly skilled workers to five years. Migrant groups including the North London Chinese Association and the Voice of Britain's Skilled Immigrants led doctors, chefs, architects and NHS workers in protests against the change.[11] Then, in November, the criteria for staying on were drastically tightened, with a new points system which favoured young people on high salaries. There is, of course, nothing wrong with rule changes per se, in response to changing economic conditions – but these changes were retrospective. Many who had expected to qualify for settlement after four years were told that they had not been here for long enough, and worse, that they no longer qualified to stay, and would have to leave at once, on pain of being criminalised as overstayers. The *Times of India* reported that 30,000 Indians were intent on challenging the rule changes,[12] and the HSMP Forum was formed to defend the migrants' interests. The Forum gave evidence to the parliamentary Joint Committee on Human Rights on the impact of the changes, estimating that nearly 40,000 skilled migrants faced deportation, and the Committee described the changes as 'so contrary to basic notions of fairness, that the case for immediately revisiting the changes to the rules in Parliament is in our view overwhelming'.[13] HSMP Forum also launched a high court challenge.

Meanwhile Sylvia, oblivious to the rule changes, applied for settlement after four years, in 2007. Although she was still in the same job, she was refused – not only did she now need five years, not four, before qualifying for settlement, but she did not earn enough to qualify under the new rules – even though her earnings matched the projected salary she had indicated in her original, approved application. Her sister, brother and children were all in the UK, and she had recently become a grandmother. But she was told to leave the country which she had previously been told to make her home.

We won Sylvia's appeal because of her family ties here, but the grotesque unfairness she had suffered at the hands of the Home Office was not then acknowledged. Later, however, she was to receive compensation for her treatment. In January 2008, the HSMP Forum won its legal challenge against the retrospective application of the rule changes. The judge observed that: 'The policy was designed to target a particular group of migrants and to encourage them to come to the UK to assist the UK economy ... once a migrant had embarked on the scheme it was intended that he should carry the expectation of attaining settlement.' Good administration and straightforward dealing with the public required the promise to be honoured; to allow the Home Office to apply the new rules to those who had come under the original scheme would, he said, 'give rise to conspicuous unfairness and an abuse of power'.[14]

The Home Office decided not to appeal, but instead issued a policy which claimed to apply the judgment but retained the five-year qualifying period for the affected group, arguing that the judge had not condemned this and the claimants suffered no prejudice from having to wait an extra year. To members of HSMP Forum, this was a further betrayal. The Forum went back to court, pointing out that settled status was often needed to get a mortgage, a decent job or promotion, to run a business, to travel and for many other purposes, that further uncertainty was debilitating and psychologically damaging and that members had a right to be treated in accordance with the rules under which they had been admitted. The second judge agreed. She observed in the Home Office a 'developing pattern of refusal to acknowledge the clear evidence of hardship and disadvantage' caused by its rule and policy changes.[15] Finally, people in Sylvia's position got their settlement rights back.

For some affected by the retrospective policy changes, it was too late. Dr Imran Yousaf, devastated at being told he had to leave the country, took his own life in January 2007. He was one of thousands of international medical students encouraged to come to the UK when junior hospital doctors were scarce, and discarded when demand waned with the rise in graduates from British medical schools. Rule changes in April 2006 restricted postgraduate medical training (junior doctor posts in hospitals) to graduates of UK medical schools, and limited their stay to three years, while Department of Health guidance warned hospitals not to appoint international medical graduates to training posts unless there were no suitable UK-trained candidates. Once again, the changes were applied to doctors already recruited to the UK with the promise of settled status after four years. The expectations of doctors like Imran Yousaf that they could continue to live and work in the UK, fuelled by the requirement to make the UK their home, were dashed. The British Association of Physicians of Indian Origin (BAPIO) began a legal challenge, arguing that doctors who had been attracted to the UK by the promise of work and the prospect of settlement had a legitimate expectation that the promise would be honoured,[16] and Dr Yousaf joined it. Eventually, after rejection in the high court, the challenge succeeded on appeal; the law lords held that the government had behaved unfairly to those already in the country, who should have been given the benefit of the old rules.[17] But Dr Yousaf did not live to see the victory; he had become increasingly anxious, according to friends, and although he did not leave a suicide note, the notice from UKBA refusing his application for a visa extension was beside him when he was found dead.

AUSTERITY AND NATIVISM

The Right and the tabloids meanwhile kept up a constant chorus of disapproval at the numbers of foreign workers being admitted, and the government found itself torn between the demands for 'British jobs for British workers' and the economic imperative of keeping the door open to migrants to maintain growth. In September 2007, Tory leader David Cameron stirred the pot, warning that 'the scale of recent immigration from within and outside the EU has damaged the country', leading Gordon Brown to promise at the TUC conference that half a million new jobs would be created for Britons[18] (he had reportedly already promised his union backers in June that Britons would get 'first refusal' on jobs under his premiership).[19] His gesture towards nativism defied the evidence that, as PriceWaterhouseCoopers had shown, migrant workers had boosted economic growth without undermining the jobs of British workers.[20] It was also foolish, since EU free movement law made it illegal to close jobs to EU nationals, and to EU firms employing non-EU labour. Brown's promise was quoted back at him during mass picketing at Lindsey and other oil refineries in 2009 by workers refused jobs by companies which brought in a workforce from Spain, Italy or Portugal to build new power stations. Although the BNP attempted to infiltrate some protests, union leaders such as Unite's Derek Simpson worked hard to ensure the protests were not about race but about class – 'a battle for jobs in a deepening recession and a backlash against the deregulated, race-to-the-bottom neoliberal model'.[21]

By this time, economic migration was being reorganised once again, when the points-based system, announced in 2006,[22] was phased in from 2008. Based on the Australian model, PBS simplified the 80 or so routes to economic migration and made the criteria more transparent and objective. Work visas were organised into tiers, with professionals and highly skilled migrants, investors and entrepreneurs in Tier 1, able to come without a specific job offer; skilled workers in Tier 2, needing a job offer and sponsorship to enter; and temporary workers, including the youth mobility scheme which replaced 'working holidays', in Tier 5. The schemes which formerly brought in around 12,000 non-EU workers to fill unskilled jobs were ended (although an unskilled category, Tier 3, was created, it has never been activated), and students were brought into the PBS as Tier 4.

The changes were designed to enable the immigration system to respond more quickly and proactively to changes in labour market needs. Entrepreneurs and professionals would be attracted by the lack of any requirement to have a job waiting, while the criteria and the occupations for which skilled (Tier 2) visas would be granted could be changed quickly and easily. Employers had to register as sponsors to obtain licenses to recruit, and applicants had to achieve the points specified by the rules – for qualifications, previous and prospective earnings, age and English language proficiency – to get a visa. Companies could be granted licences for a certain number of employees in specified occupations and could use them to bring in the workers they needed, instead of having to apply for individual permits. The Migration Advisory Committee (MAC) was set up to prepare lists of 'shortage occupations' to which skilled migrant workers would be recruited – a list which is revised regularly. With the PBS in place, it was much easier to fine-tune economic migration; so while social workers and senior care workers remained on the 'shortage' list to be recruited from outside Europe, along with engineers, psychiatrists, maths teachers and a variety of specialists,[23] doctors, other secondary school teachers and nurses were generally barred as posts were filled from within the EU.

But the Right still kept up a relentless anti-immigration campaign, blaming Labour for recklessly allowing mass immigration – and as Labour gave way to the coalition in May 2010, the emphasis shifted back to restriction. The Tories had pledged to cut net migration from over 200,000 to just tens of thousands a year, although a Confederation of British Industry (CBI) survey had showed that restriction would hit business hard; companies believed cuts to skilled migration would lose them 50 British workers on average, or force them to relocate abroad.[24] But these concerns were largely ignored; cutting economic migration was a Tory manifesto promise, sending a message, no matter how duplicitous, to British workers that they came first. Jobs would be restored to British workers and unemployment would fall, the message went, as employers would take (and train) British school-leavers and graduates, rather than relying on better-skilled foreigners. Encouraging workplace training is clearly beneficial – but training to the high skill levels needed to replace skilled migrants takes many years, and the government had no answer to the pressing needs of employers.

CAPPING ECONOMIC MIGRATION

In June 2010, home secretary Theresa May announced the government's intention to impose a cap on skilled migration the following April. To prevent a surge in applications, she announced an interim cap, to be imposed imminently, without the normal consultation. New immigration rules were brought in announcing the cap – but the actual numbers were not in the rules which went to parliament, but on UKBA's website. The number of workers admitted for skilled employment was to be capped at 5 per cent fewer than those admitted the previous year – by ministerial diktat, with no parliamentary scrutiny or debate, contrary to the requirements both of good governance and of the Immigration Act 1971.[25]

Even without the manner of its imposition, a cap is an arbitrary and unfair way of cutting migration. The social work and care sectors expressed particular concern; the shortage of senior care workers meant non-Europeans were needed to fill posts, but the interim cap invalidated previously issued certificates of sponsorship, and UKBA now refused to re-issue them on the basis that the salary, at under £20,000, was too low.[26] The English Community Care Association (which represents independent care providers) joined JCWI in a challenge to the interim cap, arguing that its imposition without parliamentary scrutiny was illegal. UKBA protested that it was important to be able to impose and alter limits at will, bypassing parliament, to respond to economic needs with the maximum flexibility. The judge condemned the Home Office's 'deliberate evasion of the statutory purpose' and 'attempt to place the exercise of ministerial discretion beyond the bounds of Parliamentary scrutiny'.[27] The Court of Appeal had already that year warned UKBA that ministers could not unilaterally make law or change it, after hundreds of graduates were refused permission to stay despite satisfying all the criteria for a post-study work visa, because additional requirements were imposed by policy.[28] These cases were of constitutional significance for their reminder that the separation of powers is integral to the rule of law.[29]

Five days after the high court's rejection of the interim cap as illegally imposed, the UKBA put rules before parliament which re-imposed it. Parliament could have voted the rules down, but didn't.[30] Despite further expressions of concern from (among others) the CBI and senior executives from large companies including Honda, Toyota and Nissan,[31] the government introduced a permanent cap in April 2011. For the following year, skilled work visas were capped at 20,700, a reduction of a quarter, and employers had to apply for a certificate of sponsorship for each job vacancy, instead of getting an annual allocation. Visas for professionals and highly skilled migrants were limited to a thousand individuals of 'exceptional talent', while chefs, senior care workers and other non-graduate jobs were reserved to Bulgarian and Romanian workers or deleted. But bankers, lawyers and other high earners (on over £150,000 a year) were exempted, together with senior corporate transfers.[32]

The rationale for restriction is that 'unlimited migration' placed 'unacceptable pressure on public services, school places and the provision of housing'. The image of complete, anarchic lack of controls and of public services being overwhelmed is false and misleading. Non-EEA (European Economic Area) migration had remained carefully regulated, and the requirement of economic self-sufficiency precluded access to welfare benefits or public housing. Only schools and NHS treatment are freely available to non-EU economic migrant workers and their families; but migrant workers fund these services just as British citizens do, through taxes and national insurance contributions.[33]

STUDENTS – FROM CONTROL TO RESTRICTION

Students, like workers, have been buffeted by shifting policies, from expansion and control under Labour, to severe restriction under the Tories. They too have been subject to frequent rule changes, to the PBS, and to illegal policy changes by ministers seeking to avoid parliamentary scrutiny – changes brought about often in the teeth of opposition from education providers.

The Labour government worked to increase international student numbers, alive to the economic benefits they brought. The income from their fees subsidised home students at many British universities and supported hundreds of small colleges round the country teaching languages, business and law.[34] In 2002, as part of the liberalisation of economic migration, international students graduating from UK universities were permitted to stay to seek work, making the UK an attractive destination for study. With expansion came increasing control, with monitoring and accreditation of education providers, and crackdowns which could cause hardship and injustice. Rashid Anwar was one of three students who challenged their attempted removal from the UK for 'deception' after their college was taken off the 'approved' list. Lord Justice Sedley accused the Home Office of 'a serious abuse of power ... to prevent the exposure of a shameful decision – the effective criminalising and enforced removal of an innocent person without either worthwhile evidence or the opportunity to answer'.[35] And the UKBA adopted the sledgehammer approach to suspected abuse in January 2010, when it stopped issuing visas to students from North India, Bangladesh and Nepal in response to a 'surge' in applications from these countries. Would-be students had no recourse save political protest.

The points-based system was applied to students in March 2009. As with workers, the claim was that the PBS would create transparent and objective criteria for entry. And as with workers, what it achieved was far greater flexibility in terms of numbers admitted and to which institutions, as well as a move away from micro-control of individual students by visa and immigration officers – who now had to check only that students had a 'confirmation of acceptance for studies' from an accredited institution and sufficient funds[36] – to macro-control through a licensing system for universities and colleges.

Students, too, were subjected to illegal policy changes. To cut 'abuse', UKBA significantly raised the standard of English required of students seeking entry to learn the language, making it impossible to come to learn basic or intermediate English. Again, the change was set out, not in the immigration rules, but in revised guidance to sponsors. UKBA's renewed attempt to impose extra criteria for entry without parliamentary approval took it back to court, in a challenge brought by English UK, whose 441 member bodies taught English to around 400,000 international students annually. English UK pointed out that parliamentary debate on the policy changes had been denied despite the impact on the half-million or so English language students, who brought in £1.5 billion in revenue annually, and the colleges they attended. The judge agreed, holding that the opportunity for proper debate within the legislature could not be bypassed.[37] Once again, UKBA put the changes into rules, giving parliament the opportunity to vote them down – an opportunity again missed.[38] Other rule changes capped student numbers enrolling at colleges outside the ranks of the 'highly trusted sponsor' institutions,[39] as a prelude to ending enrolment in such colleges altogether by April 2012.[40] But the rule change which, more than any other, is predicted to devastate student numbers and the colleges which depend on them is the halving of non-degree students' entitlement to work from July 2011 (to ten hours per week during term-time), and the complete ban on work for students attending private colleges.[41] The ability to work – part-time during term-time and full-time in vacations – has been the key which has enabled most of the half-million international students – all except the very rich – to afford the fees and living expenses of studying in the UK. Sending a son or daughter to study here represents a huge investment for the students' families; life savings have been used, family land and jewellery sold to enable the student to get a British qualification. And many international students send remittances home from their earnings. Removing this ability to work for those at private colleges may well fulfil government targets of cutting student numbers, as students look to more hospitable countries for their study. But in the process, many students already here are likely to find themselves destitute, dropping out of college for inability to pay fees and sinking into illegality, ashamed to return home without the all-important qualification. Colleges will close, destroying livelihoods of those running and teaching in them – and all those attending the affected colleges will be subject to summary removal. An exodus of students from private colleges seems likely.

The package of measures was designed to cut the number of student visas issued by a quarter,[42] and by 360,000 (including dependants) by May 2015.[43] A belated impact assessment foresaw a loss in tuition fee income of around £170 million and total indirect costs at around £3.2 billion over the four years it covered. As ILPA commented, 'these are very large sums to sacrifice on the altar of reducing net migration'.[44] Universities described the restrictions as a serious error which would adversely affect not just would-be students but the whole higher education sector and the economy; the cuts might hit private language schools hardest, but many who study English go on to British universities.[45] Permission for a judicial review of the cuts was granted.[46]

However, restriction alone was not the name of the game. As the cuts were announced, a deal was being struck by the universities minister to bring 10,000 Brazilian students to British universities at a cost to the Brazilian government of up to £18,700 per student, to help fill over 20,000 university places withdrawn from British and EEA students following funding cuts.[47] As major British universities, including Durham and Exeter, planned to expand their international intake to make up for the government squeeze on their funding, with international student fees running at up to £26,000 a year, coalition policy seemed to be to sell university places to the highest bidder while decimating the small language schools and the privately run colleges set up to provide good teaching at an affordable cost.

BUREAUCRATIC MINEFIELD

Rules which are supposed to provide a clear, predictable and reliable guide to those planning to work or study in the UK and for the institutions planning to receive them, have now become so complex, and are changed so frequently and with so little notice,[48] that even immigration lawyers can hardly follow them. Colleges found all the confirmations of acceptance for studies issued by UKBA retro-spectively invalidated by rule changes made following the *English UK* judgment. Performers and artists seeking visas under Tier 5, the temporary worker category, to fulfil engagements in the UK, face 'daily nightmares'.[49] Artists coming for a few days to perform must travel to an application centre to supply biometric details, prove they have £800 in a bank account and have a sponsor who would pay the £400 fee. None of the five featured Iraqi artists could attend a Contemporary Art Iraq exhibition in Manchester because they could not supply bank statements.[50] The directors of the National Theatre, the Tate, the Royal Academy and the Royal Opera House, and dozens of authors, playwrights and performers were among the 120 arts luminaries who signed an open letter to the *Daily Telegraph* complaining that the 'needlessly bureaucratic and intrusive' PBS and the poor treatment from immigration officials were leading to an unofficial artistic boycott of Britain.[51]

'GUEST' AND DOMESTIC WORKERS

In February 2012, following a public consultation in the summer of 2011,[52] rule changes were announced to bar most workers earning under £35,000 a year from settlement.[53] 'High net worth individuals' – investors and entrepreneurs – and 'exceptionally talented individuals' retain routes to settlement, but most other workers, other than the 'brightest and best', can stay only six years, with no settlement prospects.[54] Making migrants leave jobs, home and adopted country, forcing employers to replace them with new staff, uprooting children from school, seems counter-productive and cruel, and was condemned as 'incredibly disruptive to companies of all sizes and to the UK's economic recovery' by the British Chambers of Commerce.[55] Proposals to make the measures operate retrospec-tively, to deny workers already here the possibility of permanent settlement, were dropped following the consultation.

Domestic workers are the group potentially worst affected by the rule changes, a group massively expanded since the 1970s as the globalised market economy has led to greater inequality and new forms of exploitation. Working in private homes, domestic workers – mostly women, who send earnings home to the Philippines, south Asia and Africa to support families – often endure slave-like conditions and physical and sexual abuse.[56] They have fought tenaciously for decades for recognition, for the right to switch employer and for a route to settlement, in the face of political betrayals.

Visas for domestic workers were abolished in 1979. Thereafter, the law treated them as virtual chattels of their employers,[57] and no matter how exploited, mistreated or brutalised they were, leaving their employer rendered them illegal. The Commission for Filipino Migrant Workers (CFMW) set up a group, Waling-Waling, in the early 1980s in response to the numbers of runaway domestic workers needing help, and in 1987 Kalayaan was formed to fight for justice for overseas domestic workers. The organisation campaigned to secure a status which would allow domestic workers to switch employers without risking deportation. Having secured the support of unions including the TGWU, rights groups, MPs and peers, in 1997, with the change in government, it achieved a change in policy (incorporated into the immigration rules in 2002) which recognised domestic workers as workers and included provisions for switching employers and a route to settlement.[58] Around 16,000 visas in this category were issued annually, and domestic workers' security of status finally enabled them to access workplace rights such as payment of wages, time off and employment tribunal remedies for abuses.[59]

In 2006, the Labour government proposed reverting to a six-month 'business visit: domestic assistant' visa, with no right to change employer and no route to settlement. The proposal would wipe out all the gains achieved by the domestic workers. Kalayaan, with support from the TUC, Unite (formerly the TGWU), Oxfam, the Anti-Slavery Society and others, launched a campaign to fight the rule changes, reminding parliament and the public of the inherent vulnerability of domestic workers and the importance of security of status to accessing workplace rights.[60] The campaign was successful: the government did not press ahead with the rule change, and immigration minister Liam Byrne promised that no changes would be made to the protections for migrant domestic workers unless 'an appropriate package of safeguards against abuse and exploitation is in place'.[61] Domestic workers were left outside the PBS, with their own route to settlement. But the coalition revived Labour's retrogressive and abandoned proposal.[62] In September 2011, hundreds of migrant domestic workers demonstrated outside parliament to protest the proposed destruction of secure status.[63] But in February 2012 the government announced its intention to go ahead with the rule changes.[64]

The coalition's proposals to abolish domestic workers' visas were published just as organising in this sector had been gathering pace. In June 2011, the long campaign of unions and migrants' rights groups to protect the rights of the estimated fifty to a hundred million domestic workers worldwide, bore fruit with the adoption of the Convention on Domestic Workers at the one hundredth conference of the International Labour Organisation (ILO). The Convention ensures for domestic workers basic labour rights such as reasonable hours of work and weekly rest of at least 24 consecutive hours. But the British government argued against some of its provisions – including those providing special protection to child workers[65] – and abstained on the vote, conduct met with shock and anger by campaigners who accused it of betraying Britain's 200-year-old history in the fight against slavery. The Department for Business, Innovation and Skills said it would not be ratifying the Convention in the foreseeable future.[66] The market-obsessed coalition government is even less interested in a decent and dignified life for workers – British and migrant – than its predecessor.

7
The Fight for Family Life

Human beings are social animals. They depend on others. Their family, or extended family, is the group on which many people most heavily depend, socially, emotionally, and often financially. There comes a point at which, for some, prolonged and unavoidable separation from this group seriously inhibits their ability to live full and fulfilling lives.[1]

So said Lord Bingham in 2007. But the immigration rules were never devised to protect the family life of migrants. They had not done so for Mrs Huang, a 60-year-old separated woman refused permission to live with her daughter, son-in-law and grandchild in the UK. Although there was no question of her becoming a burden on the state, the rules said she could stay only if she would otherwise be 'living alone in the most exceptional compassionate circumstances'. Simply wanting to stay with her family as a mother and grandmother was not enough.

Politicians extol the family, and the importance of family life is reflected in rules for the entry of family members of EEA nationals.[2] In EU law, it is accepted that the right to live and work in another country must, to be fully effective, provide for the entry of family members. Children, grandchildren, parents and grandparents as well as spouses and civil partners have clear and definite rights of entry, while dependent adult siblings, uncles and aunts are to have their admission facilitated.[3]

But for non-EU migrants, and for British citizens trying to bring in non-European relatives, family reunion is not a right, but a struggle against ever tighter restrictions and conditions. For government, family members are migrants first and foremost, whose entry is to be strictly controlled, and its right to reject spouses or partners as unsuitable through age, earning power or linguistic limitation is widely assumed. If someone living and working in the UK seeks to bring in a non-EU husband, wife or civil partner, both of them must be over 18, and the incoming partner must pass an English language test (unless he or she comes from an English-speaking country, or has a degree taught in English).[4] The couple must not only be able to prove that their relationship is genuine and that they can support and house themselves with no state assistance, but must, if government proposals go through, have a minimum household income of between £18,600 and £25,700. A partner who seeks permanent settlement must undergo a probationary period of two years (soon to be raised to five years), during which time the relationship must not break down (unless the applicant can prove domestic violence). Another, tougher language test must be passed, and a 'life in the UK' test, and the applicant must not have any 'unspent' criminal convictions, even for a driving offence. Short-term students cannot bring any family members at all.

Husbands, wives and partners of British citizens and those settled here account for most of the family reunion visas issued – four-fifths in 2010[5] – and so it is not surprising that they have been the primary target of restrictive rules. But children, particularly those seeking to join single or divorced parents, can also face severe difficulties, and it gets even worse for others trying to join relatives here. The restrictions are not motivated by concern about migrant families living on benefits, although this is often presented as a justification.[6] Family reunion has for decades been conditional on proof of economic self-sufficiency; all 'sponsors', whether British or settled migrants, except for refugees, have had to prove that they have the resources to house and fully support incoming relatives. Breach of the rules on 'no recourse to public funds' can lead to removal. And legislation in 1999 and 2002 excluded non-settled migrants from eligibility from means-tested benefits and social housing anyway (unless they come from the EU) – meaning that for most migrants, welfare benefits and public housing are simply unavailable. In my practice I had to instruct sponsors in low-paid jobs to bring detailed accounts to court showing income and expenditure to the last penny, to prove to sceptical immigration judges just how cheaply they could live. British sponsors on disability benefits must prove that a one-person benefit can be stretched to cover two, or must bring along a credible job offer for an incoming spouse.

The exclusionary mentality meant refusal to allow offers of support from more affluent relatives and friends, on the basis that the rules didn't allow support from anyone but the sponsor. In the 1990s officials refused visas for the six children of Arman Ali. He was in regular employment but could not house all the children in his house, so his uncle agreed to house the two oldest boys. This was not acceptable to the Home Office: Mr Ali must house his own children. The high court overruled the refusal: why should willing third parties not provide long-term support or accommodation?[7] The Home Office responded by changing the wording of the rules to remove what they saw as the 'loophole' of third-party support, making it virtually impossible for poor or disabled sponsors to have their children join them even if better-off relatives were willing to help. Then, in 2009, the supreme court settled the issue, ruling that it was always open to parents and other sponsoring relatives to accept support from others in discharging their duty of housing and supporting their incoming family members.[8]

Since that decision, the coalition has targeted poorer migrant families more directly by proposing a minimum income threshold for family reunion. Families will be debarred from joining their parents and partners in the UK under the proposals, even if they are used to living on low incomes, unless better-off relatives or friends can make up the shortfall. The justification is 'integration', although the notion that wealth makes for better social integration is daily disproved.[9] But migrant families are a convenient scapegoat, particularly in a recession when jobs are scarce and benefits are being cut for British families. Apart from the welfare scroungers myth, restrictions on family reunion have also been justified by the need to stop migrant family members taking 'British jobs' (although studies show that migration grows the economy, creating rather than reducing jobs for British workers), or putting pressure on other public services (although migrants have historically provided much of the labour power to run them), or simply by the political imperative dressed up as a need to 'cut immigration'. Cultural stereotypes have been deployed to justify denial of family rights; Caribbean men have been portrayed as feckless and promiscuous (and therefore not genuine husbands), Asian men as wife-beaters and cheats who use marriage as a passport for entry. Asian women have been painted both as submissive victims of male domination and oppressive customs such as forced marriage, and as complicit in sham or immigration marriages, in fraudulent applications to enter by 'bogus children' (children who are not biological children of the sponsoring 'parents'), or party to sham adoptions. Such stereotypes have been deployed to justify heightened scrutiny of marriages and of the genuineness of claimed parent–child relationships.

The most notorious measure taken to check the veracity of claimed relationships was the virginity testing of fiancées from the Indian sub-continent referred to in Chapter 2. Less well-known were the examinations of skulls, teeth and pubic hair carried out well into the 1980s by male doctors on women applicants at British posts in Bangladesh, ostensibly to check age.[10] These 'examinations' were the culmination of contemptuous and degrading treatment of applicants who travelled from distant villages to be herded into packed waiting rooms and interrogated like criminal suspects.

CHILDREN'S CLAIMS DENIED

Children applying to join parents in the UK were not exempt from the culture of exclusion or from hazardous and degrading tests. The 1970s and 1980s saw widespread targeting of children from the Indian sub-continent for refusal of entry to join fathers here. Children were subjected to X-ray 'bone age' tests in British posts in Dhaka and Islamabad to check their claimed age. The tests were as unreliable as they were harmful, but it took years to get them stopped.[11] It was not just children's age that was routinely disbelieved, but also their claimed relationship with a UK-based parent. Asian immigrants were 'liars' – a *Sun* headline of 1986 said just that, 'The Liars', over a story of Bangladeshi migrants arriving in the UK before more restrictions were imposed,[12] and allegations abounded that men from the Indian sub-continent were getting tax credits for non-existent children. This was the background to the routine rejection of children's applications to join fathers in the UK, based on disbelief that they were 'related as claimed', using the 'discrepancy-counting' approach I described in Chapter 2. The disbelief was sharpened by the myth that immigrants were pouring in to live on benefits, as Commonwealth citizens could at that time bring family members in without proof that they could support and house them, in a concession reflecting their historical freedom of entry and repealed in 1988.

DNA testing, which became widely available in the late 1980s, proved the vast majority of the relationships genuine (as well as proving just how unreliable the 'discrepancy-counting' approach was). But by then, most of the children concerned were over 18, too old to qualify to join parents. Families like that of Kalpesh P were permanently separated and lives blighted through the wrongful application of the 'related as claimed' rule, and the government's refusal to remedy its officials' mistakes compounded the wrong.[13] Kalpesh, his parents' only child, was refused entry to join them in 1986, when he was 15, and then barred as over-age ten years later after proving the family relationship. The refusal of his settlement applications also condemned him to repeated refusal of visit visas, as officials argued he would not return home. They maintained their stance even after his father's third stroke in 2001, when the old man was distraught at not being able to see his son, perhaps ever again. Kalpesh's appeal against refusal of a visit visa was allowed, but the Home Office appealed to the Tribunal – fortunately unsuccessfully.[14]

There were other cruel rules which kept children from joining parents in the UK. The 'sole responsibility' rule has caused despair to countless migrant worker single parents, generally mothers from the Caribbean or south-east Asia, who worked for years in low-paid jobs, sending earnings home to support and house families, educate children and pay medical bills, and saving to provide a home for their children here, only to see the children refused visas. Officials were 'not satisfied' that the UK-based parent had, as well as providing financial support, made all the important decisions about the children's lives, their education, religion, health, discipline and morals. Shared decision-making disqualified lone parents from bringing children here. The rule allowed officious and judgmental Home Office officials to vent their ignorance and arrogance on single parents. At the appeal of Filipina Lydia C against refusal of her daughter's visa, the Home Office representative asked Lydia why she had not visited her daughter more often, or had longer phone conversations with her. As a domestic worker, Lydia had been paid £150 per month, most of which went for the child's support. The adjudicator, who was unusually compassionate and understanding, condemned the Home Office representative's crass questioning as 'demeaning to yourself and to the witness', pointing out that 'she has limited funds and her daughter is thousands of miles away'. That appeal was allowed; many were not.[15]

Children who did not otherwise quality to join parents or other relatives had to demonstrate 'serious and compelling family or other considerations' to be admitted. You might think that an eleven-year-old who had been subjected to a machete attack leaving him with serious head injuries, in the course of a massacre in which his young sister was killed and which left his parents suffering mental illness and unable to care for him, had 'serious and compelling' reasons for being brought from Algeria to be looked after by his uncle's family in the UK. But the ingrained suspicion in the Home Office that the child was being brought in as an economic migrant defeated the application – although the child's appeal was allowed by an outraged adjudicator before I could say a word.[16] And Somali orphan children stuck in refugee camps in Ethiopia or Kenya were frequently refused entry to join siblings or uncles here under this rule.[17]

COUNTERING 'MARRIAGE MIGRATION'

However, it is marriage migration in particular which successive governments have sought to curb, through a variety of measures. From the late 1960s to the late 1990s, strenuous efforts were made to restrict the entry of the husbands of new Commonwealth migrants, who were seen as threatening the jobs of British workers. (Women coming to join husbands were seen as 'dependants' and not a threat, as well as following the natural, male-ordained order of things.) In the early days the entry of foreign husbands was banned completely (unless there were special circumstances); then from 1982 British, but not migrant, women could bring their husbands – but they had to prove not just that the marriage was genuine but also that its 'primary purpose' was not settlement for the husband.[18] The rules went way beyond the detection of sham marriages, and gave officials huge scope for indulging racist assumptions – particularly in relation to arranged marriages, which hostile politicians and press lumped with forced marriages. By 1984, around 60 per cent of husbands applying to join their wives in the UK were refused.[19] The Immigration Widows Campaign and JCWI challenged the rules in the European Court of Human Rights for race and sex discrimination in family life rights.

Although they did not win an unqualified victory, their case became the foundation of migrants' family rights. The court ruled that the government's entitlement to regulate the admission of migrants was not absolute, as the Home Office argued, but subject to rights to family life, which had to be weighed against economic or social policy aims. Protection of the domestic labour market, the judges ruled, although a legitimate aim, did not justify the explicit sex discrimination which kept husbands out.[20] The government was forced to lift the ban on the entry of husbands of settled migrant women. But the women's challenge to the rules as racially discriminatory failed – so the 'primary purpose' rule, far from being abolished, was extended to wives seeking to join UK-resident husbands. With the 'discrepancy-counting' approach to a couple's responses on the dates and circumstances of their meetings and marriage, it proved a very effective tool to keep numbers down, and the scourge of tens if not hundreds of thousands of couples, until its abolition in 1997. The implicit starting point for officials was that the marriage was an immigration marriage, a particularly easy assumption if the marriage was arranged, and one shared by many adjudicators and senior judges.[21] By its very nature, the primary purpose rule encouraged humiliating questioning, even more so if the wife was older than her husband, or not attractive, or divorced, with the husband being cross-examined on why he would marry such a woman if not for her passport. Couples' letters to each other were scrutinised by officials, lawyers and adjudicators for affection or lack of it.[22] On appeal, the virtually impossible burden of proving that the husband was not using his wife as a passport to settlement fell on the sponsoring wife (the husband being stuck abroad), and many times I had to intervene to put a stop to appallingly crass questioning. Even after the birth of one or two children, conceived on wives' yearly visits, husbands were still refused on 'primary purpose' grounds. No wonder the authors of a leading textbook described the primary purpose rule as having 'generated more anger and anguish than perhaps any other immigration rule'.[23]

NEW LABOUR FACING BOTH WAYS

When the Labour government came to power in 1997, it quickly abolished the primary purpose rule, delighting campaigners.[24] From over half of all husbands being refused entry in 1996, refusals fell to a third immediately.[25] But the rule's demise did not spell an end to all the difficulties faced by couples seeking reunion in the UK, as officials primed to curb abuse now directed their inquisitions to the genuineness of the couple's intention to live together. The government too was determined to outflank the Right in combating 'immigration abuse'. But it sought to use persuasion to get British Asians to find spouses who were settled here in preference to bringing in partners from the sub-continent,[26] at the same time making it more difficult for temporary migrants to marry here and acquire settlement rights.

Labour also provided routes to entry and settlement for gay partners, responding to decades-long campaigning by groups such as Stonewall. Veteran right-winger Anne Widdecombe was up in arms: 'If you allow people to come in on the basis that they have a same-sex relationship', she expostulated, 'you have no real means of testing it.'[27] The new provisions transformed the prospects for gay couples to stay together in the UK without having to resort to ploys such as immigration marriages with UK residents, repeated visit visas or perpetual studenthood. A legal route was also provided for spouses and partners whose relationship had broken down through domestic violence perpetrated by the sponsoring partner, in response to demands by groups such as Southall Black Sisters, who had long campaigned on the issue,[28] and for ex-partners who wanted to stay for access to their children. But the strict rules impeding the entry of other relatives remained. Other than spouses and children, relatives continued to be disqualified if they had 'close relatives to turn to'; so the 45-year-old severely disabled sister of a Pakistani settled in the UK, unable to do anything for herself and cared for by her brother until his departure for the UK, was refused permission to join him after officials claimed that other, unwilling relatives in Pakistan would help her,[29] and I could not persuade the adjudicator or the Tribunal to reverse the decision. Relatives had to be 'living alone in the most exceptional compassionate circumstances' in their country of origin – so a widow was refused a visa to join her son in the UK because her other son, a violent drug addict from whom she was seeking to escape, lived with her in Pakistan.[30] And when the courts gave a broad and generous interpretation of the rules, the response of the Home Office, too often, was to re-draft the rules to 'close the loophole'.

THE IMPACT OF THE HUMAN RIGHTS ACT

Immigration lawyers welcomed Labour's Human Rights Act, which allowed us to seek protection in the domestic courts for the human rights protected by the 1950 European Human Rights Convention. In 1986, the women denied the right to have their husbands with them in the UK had had to go to the European Court in Strasbourg for vindication of their right to respect for family life, protected by Article 8 of the Convention. Now, we could call on the immigration tribunal and the courts to protect family life in cases where the strict, exclusionary rules worked injustice, such as Mrs Huang's case. The Singh family, with my colleague Stephanie Harrison, used the Human Rights Act to bring their adopted child to the UK when the Home Office and the rules said no – although ironically they had to go to Strasbourg before they could win their case in the UK. They, like many adopters from the Indian sub-continent, adopted a relative's child, because they wanted another child but could not have more of their own. The boy was two months old when they adopted him and applied for a visa for him to live with them in the UK. But the rules allow in adopted children only if the birth parents were unable to care for the child and all ties with them had been severed. The battle for the child's visa took seven years, during which time the child only saw his adoptive parents when they could visit India. Eventually, after the European Court intervened, the appeal court accepted that the adoption had had 'the most profound emotional, personal, social, cultural, religious and … legal significance' for the child and the adoptive parents, and the high commission had to give the boy a visa.[31]

Ever since the Act was passed, right-wing politicians have campaigned for its repeal, and the *Daily Mail* and the *Daily Telegraph* would have you believe there are thousands of illegal immigrants' and 'foreign criminals' cynically using this new weapon of 'family life' rights to avoid their just deserts of deportation.[32] The reality is quite different. For those facing removal or deportation, the Human Rights Act was not so revolutionary an advance. For decades beforehand, immigration rules had acknowledged that family ties (among other factors) had to be taken into account before deportation, and relationships formed here could protect overstayers and offenders from removal. A secret Home Office policy, drawn up in 1993 to comply with human rights obligations, told officials not normally to remove overstayers or illegal entrants in a lasting relationship with a UK resident.[33] When the policy was revealed, high court judges told the Home Office that officials could not ignore it.[34] Another policy protected families with children who had lived undocumented in the UK for ten years (reduced to seven years in 1999) from removal, in recognition of the roots put down by children.[35]

But when the Act came into force in October 2000, the government was determined to prevent its 'abuse' by 'undeserving' migrants. Particular targets were refused asylum seekers who had married or entered relationships and had children here during the years of waiting for their claims to be decided, as well as irregular migrants and offenders married to British citizens or with British-born children. Pressured by the tabloids for its supposed laxity, Labour was obsessed with what ministers called 'the integrity of immigration control' – which meant forcing such migrants to go home and wait in a queue abroad for a family reunion visa. The courts, too, expected an avalanche of cases from 'undeserving' migrants using the Act to stay, and decided to pre-empt it. In the first week of the Act, my clients Mr and Mrs Mahmood and I were the unlucky victims of their ambush. Mr Mahmood had a British wife and two children by the time he faced removal as a refused asylum seeker. It was clear that he satisfied all the requirements for a marriage visa – he was in a genuine, lasting marriage, supported the family and without him, his wife would have to claim benefits – so what was the point, I asked the appeal court judges rhetorically, of making him go home, disrupting the family's life together? The judges came down like a ton of bricks on me, my argument and my clients. The point was nothing less, they reminded me sternly, than the integrity of immigration control itself. You couldn't have people jumping the queue; it brought the whole system into disrepute.[36] So for the sake of the integrity of immigration control, Mr Mahmood was ordered back to Pakistan to wait in the queue to get his visa to come back to his British wife and children, who in the meantime would have to struggle along without him.

The arguments against making the spouse or partner of a UK resident go home to get a marriage visa met with more success following battles inside and outside the courts. In a case in which the Home Office had done nothing for five years either to remove a British citizen's Nigerian husband or to let him stay, ignoring solicitors' and MPs' letters, the Court of Appeal declared its neglect a 'public disgrace', and vetoed his enforced removal to Nigeria to apply for a visa to rejoin his wife. The authorities should realise, the judges said, that they are dealing with human beings whose lives go on, whatever the administrative basis for them.[37] And in 2008, the House of Lords said a Zimbabwean refused asylum seeker should be allowed to stay in Britain with the refugee she had married six years earlier and their four-year-old British-born daughter, rather than undergo the costs and hazards of returning home to apply for a marriage visa. Lord Scott said, 'What on earth is the point of sending her back? Why cannot her application simply be made here? The only answer given on behalf of the Secretary of State is that government policy requires that she return and make her application from Zimbabwe. This is elevating policy to dogma. Kafka would have enjoyed it.'[38] 'It will rarely be proportionate', the judicial committee said in a third case, 'to uphold an order for removal of a spouse if there is a close and genuine bond with the other spouse and that spouse cannot reasonably be expected to follow the removed spouse to the country of removal, or if the effect of the order is to sever a genuine and subsisting relationship between parent and child.'[39] Common sense prevailed – but the government was furious.

FORCED MARRIAGE AND THE COHESION AGENDA

Meanwhile, in 2003, Labour increased the probationary period for foreign spouses and partners from one to two years, and raised the minimum age for sponsorship of a foreign spouse from 16 to 18. The following year the minimum age of entry for a spouse was raised in line. At the time, the government was turning away from policies of multiculturalism to embrace more assimilationist policies under the banner of 'community cohesion' and promotion of 'British values', and the justification for the changes was said to be concern over forced marriage.[40] But they were viewed with deep suspicion in south Asian communities and by political commentators; the alleged concern for women's rights looked like Victorian-style paternalism married with colonial-style policing, and a pretext for more restriction. Critics pointed to the cuts in provision for women's refuges and to legal aid, which restricted access to physical and legal protection, and to the Home Office's battles in the immigration courts to deny and deport women complaining of sexual and domestic violence abroad. Ignoring all these issues to take up in such a high-profile way the rarer problem of forced marriage, which south Asian women's groups were working to combat in their own communities anyway, was widely perceived as smacking of hypocrisy, and feeding into and perpetuating anti-Asian and particularly anti-Muslim racism.[41]

Ignoring these criticisms, the Home Office raised the minimum age for entry and sponsorship of foreign spouses again in 2008, from 18 to 21, again using the prevention of forced marriage as justification.[42] A group of organisations including JCWI, Southall Black Sisters and the Henna Foundation launched a challenge, arguing that the new rules took a sledgehammer approach which penalised large numbers of innocent couples, and that forced marriage was being used 'in a cynical way to create a moral panic to justify the government's immigration agenda'.[43] The test cases involved a young British-Chilean couple who fell in love but had to go abroad to be together, and a Pakistani couple who had had an arranged marriage. In October 2011, the supreme court ruled that the veto on under-21s obtaining marriage visas was unlawful. It had been brought in hastily, there was no evidence of its efficacy, and the Home Office had not thought about the 'colossal interference' with the family life of the thousands of couples affected by the change.[44] Another success for campaigners, another irritant for the politicians.

PERMISSION TO MARRY

A third area where the government clashed with the courts was the 'certificate of approval' scheme introduced by Labour in 2004,[45] which meant that no non-EU migrant without a fiancé(e) visa or settled status could marry or enter a civil partnership here without

Home Office permission, unless the marriage was to take place in an Anglican church. Permission was refused to those without secure status. The scheme went much further than the no-switching rule preventing visitors who married from staying on as spouses, or the duty imposed on registrars to report 'suspicious' marriages. It so obviously combined blatant unlawful discrimination against non-Anglicans with denial of the right to marry protected by article 12 of the Human Rights Convention, that when refused couples began legal challenges, the Home Office often backed down, even when the migrants seeking to marry had no legal status. But three couples insisted on continuing with their judicial review of the scheme, a challenge upheld by the high court, the Court of Appeal and in 2008 by the House of Lords. There was nothing wrong with a scheme which allowed the Home Office to check that proposed marriages in the UK were not sham marriages undertaken purely for immigration purposes, the judges said, but this law enforced religious discrimination, and the high fees and the criteria for the grant of approval prevented genuine marriages, and so made it unlawful.[46] The Home Office continued with a modified scheme for a couple of years, before announcing its abolition in July 2010, which finally took effect in May 2011.[47]

THE CHILDREN'S RIGHTS CONVENTION

A development which changed the landscape for irregular migrants with UK-born children was the incorporation of the UN Children's Rights Convention (CRC) into the UK's immigration law and practice in 2009.[48] Lengthy and sustained campaigning by children's rights groups forced the government to withdraw the 'immigration reservation' to the Convention which subsumed children's welfare to immigration control,[49] and the new law, reflecting the CRC, makes the best interests of children central to officials' decisions.[50] The supreme court showed how radically this changes the balance for parents of British children who are irregular migrants when the UKBA sought to remove a long-term Tanzanian overstayer. Her children, who lived with her, were British citizens through their father, whom they saw regularly. The Tribunal, in a decision as punitive as it was routine, blamed the children's situation on their mother, who had given birth to them knowing her precarious status in the UK, and said the children could go with her to Tanzania, where their father could visit them. But the Children's Convention made this routine denial of children's rights no longer feasible, and the supreme court vetoed it; the best interests of the children required that they and their mother stay in the UK. Finally, recognition came that a mother is a mother first, and then a migrant.[51]

These rulings from the higher courts upholding family life between spouses and partners, parents and children have vindicated campaigners' emphasis on human realities over rigid controls – and by the same token have provoked the anger of politicians, who argue that the courts are subverting their attempts to clamp down on irregular migration. In recent years, the area of family life has seen some of the fiercest clashes between governments determined to assert sovereign power and a judiciary determinedly reminding them of their obligations in domestic and international human rights law.

THE COALITION'S ASSAULT ON FAMILY LIFE

The coalition's policies on family migration are designed to cut numbers in line with Cameron's pledge on taking office. They promote an unashamedly marketised approach to migration, while appealing to a xenophobic nationalism. For home secretary Theresa May, coming to the UK to join a partner working here is 'a privilege … I am committed to raising the bar for migrants and ensuring that those who benefit from being in Britain contribute to our society', she said, announcing the populist measure of demanding that spouses and partners seeking visas speak English.[52] In vain, Jeremy Corbyn MP protested that the language requirement 'will discriminate against South Asians, women, those in conflict zones and poor people in developing countries who will struggle to access English teaching before coming to the UK'. The requirement was introduced in November 2010.[53]

The coalition's stance is clear: rights are for governments, not migrants. Governments have the right to restrict migration, including family migration, while for migrants, family unity in the UK is a privilege to be earned or withheld. Senior judges, in the European Court and in British courts, are accused of putting migrants' rights before British sovereignty. The prime minister, the justice minister and the home secretary have all pledged to 'rebalance' the relationship with the ECtHR in order to regain the right to exclude and deport those they wish to without outside interference – although the rights upheld by the Court are enshrined in domestic legislation.[54] If their plans are implemented, families will have to fight to stay together in the UK in an even bleaker legal environment.

8
Prisoners of Immigration Control

When an Algerian deported to Algeria in 2006 was detained incommunicado for twelve days, his lawyer went to the judge to complain. 'How can you complain of twelve days' detention', the judge remarked, 'when in England, he was held for three years without charge?'[1] In 2004, the appellate committee of the House of Lords condemned the indefinite imprisonment of undeportable foreign suspected terrorists as arbitrary and discriminatory.[2] But immigration laws allow the incarceration of asylum seekers and migrants awaiting removal or deportation – including children, torture victims, people who are vulnerable, mentally ill, suicidal – for weeks, months, even years. The right to liberty is (along with free speech) perhaps the right most frequently invoked by British judges, along with politicians, as distinguishing our country from the undemocratic and repressive states which asylum seekers have fled;[3] but a large and increasing proportion of them know the UK only from the back of a caged van and the inside of a detention centre.

The administrative detention of asylum seekers and migrants is one of the worst and most shocking aspects of their treatment, and has perhaps generated more protests, campaigns, reports and litigation than any other migration-related issue. Over the past three decades, fierce political and legal battles have been fought over who can be detained, for how long, on what grounds and under what conditions. Unlike criminal prisoners, immigration prisoners have no date of release towards which the days and weeks can be counted off; the law imposes no time limit on immigration detention, and when, in 2008, the EU adopted a Directive stipulating an absolute limit of 18 months, the UK opted out, complaining it wasn't long enough. With no idea for how long they will remain locked up, they are more like hostages, waiting daily for news of their fate. Detention is extremely costly, yet the numbers in detention have risen from about 200 each day in 1990 to around 3,500 each day in 2010. Over two-thirds of those held in detention have claimed asylum at some point.

ASYLUM DETENTION

Asylum seekers are incarcerated, not on criminal charges but on their claim of persecution.[4] Locking someone up is a strange response to a claim for protection. It is permitted by the law which allows the Secretary of State, acting through immigration officers, to detain anyone arriving in the country 'for examination', to find out who they are and whether they qualify for entry. Detention is a last resort, according to UNHCR, the UN Working Group on Arbitrary Detention, the Council of Europe and the Home Office's own policy. But in practice, ever since asylum seekers began arriving in larger numbers in the mid-1980s, it has too often been the first resort. The relentless message that asylum seekers were 'bogus' produced the idea that their cell was 'three-sided': detention could be ended by their leaving the country. This was the comment of the coroner at the inquest of 24-year-old Zairean Kimpua Nsimba, who in June 1990 hanged himself in the toilets at Harmondsworth detention centre, where he had been detained on seeking asylum four days earlier because he could not be interviewed for want of a Lingala interpreter. No one had spoken to him for the whole time he had been detained.[5]

In 1987, an obsolete car ferry docked at Harwich, the Earl William, was used as a floating asylum prison until it broke free from its moorings and came perilously close to sinking in the October hurricane and its hundred or so prisoners, mostly Tamils, had to be quickly landed.[6] It had been brought into service because of the rapid filling up of the remand wings of prisons, where in the 1980s and 1990s most asylum prisoners were held, and many were subjected to racism and violence. Omasese Lumumba, the great-nephew of Zaire's first president Patrice Lumumba, was killed in Pentonville prison in September 1991 by six or seven guards using wrist and ankle locks on him and stripping him with scissors. A fellow prisoner saw officers standing on him, kicking him and jumping up and down on him. The coroner refused to allow the inquest jury to consider a verdict of unlawful killing, but the family successfully challenged his ruling in the high court, and the jury decided he had been unlawfully killed. But the CPS decided not to prosecute.[7] According to the Campaign Against Immigration Act Detentions (CAIAD), by 1993 there had been 80 suicide attempts by immigration prisoners at Pentonville.[8]

From the beginning, immigration detention had been met with protests. As more asylum seekers were detained in prisons around the country, so protests had spread. From the late 1980s the hunger strike became the commonest form of protest by detained asylum seekers, the weapon for those who had nothing but their bodies with which to protest.[9] They swept through prisons where asylum seekers were detained. A Zairean hunger striker said in 1992: 'We go on hunger strike to remind the Home Office that we don't want food but freedom.'[10] Refugee groups representing Iranians, Zaireans, Ugandans, Tamils and Kurds organised solidarity actions with supporters. A National Day of Action against detention was organised by Refugee Forum and Hackney Anti-Deportation Campaign in September 1987, with pickets outside 20 prisons and detention centres and a march from Southall to Harmondsworth.[11] And local support groups sprang up wherever asylum seekers were held. The Winchester Action Group for Asylum Seekers (WAGAS), for example, was formed in July 1989 during the first hunger strike at the prison. Members organised visits to the men, stood surety for them in bail applications, provided them with clothing, produced and distributed leaflets to attract more support and organised vigils.[12] Soon every prison and detention centre had its own asylum support group.

Holding asylum seekers in prison was attracting widespread condemnation by the 1990s.[13] At the same time, powerful interests were pushing for expansion of private detention facilities. Harmondsworth detention centre had been privately run from the 1970s on, and as ministers sought more immigration detention places, American corporations such as Wackenhut and Corrections Corporation of America saw opportunities to expand their operations into the UK. There were close relations between the security industry, right-wing think tanks such as the Adam Smith Institute and Conservative MPs – including influential members of the Home Affairs Committee (whose brief included immigration detention).[14] In 1991, Group 4 was awarded the contract to run Campsfield House, a former young offenders' institution at Kidlington, near Oxford, which opened in November 1993 as a dedicated immigration detention centre. The largest in the country, with 200 beds, it was described as a 'secure hostel', but with 20-foot fences, barbed wire and electronically opened gates, was the first of many new immigration prisons. Trades unionists, refugee and migrant support and anti-racist groups greeted its opening with banners saying 'Refugees are not criminals', 'Close down Campsfield'. Opposition spread to Oxford dons, 86 of whom wrote to the prime minister urging him to respect the spirit of the Refugee

Convention by not detaining asylum seekers. The Campaign to Close Campsfield has held monthly pickets of the detention centre ever since it opened.

A major disturbance at Campsfield in August 1997 resulted in the first criminal trial of immigration detainees for protest. An attempted transfer of a detainee to prison sparked the disturbance, in which over 40 detainees took control of part of the centre. Among detainees' complaints were that guards watched pornographic films during Muslim prayers, failed to register complaints and had those who complained transferred to prisons. Nine detainees, all West Africans, two of whom were only 17, were charged with riot and violent disorder. A defence campaign was formed and over 100 Oxford professors and college heads wrote to prime minister Tony Blair demanding the dropping of the charges.[15] Four of the defendants held on remand, including a 17-year-old, attempted suicide, and detainees who were to give evidence for the defence were deported. At the trial, security guards were shown to have lied in their testimony, including their accusation that detainees smashed phones which they themselves had broken. The prosecutor was forced to withdraw the case from the jury, saying that 'on this evidence, no proper prosecution could invite a jury to convict'.[16]

Although 186 MPs signed an Early Day Motion in 1997 expressing concern about detaining asylum seekers,[17] and hopes were raised by the new Labour government's decision to review procedures for asylum detention, Labour massively expanded immigration detention. UNHCR's London representative condemned Britain for detaining more asylum seekers than any other country in Europe[18] – but Labour, determined to get rid of more asylum seekers than arrived, trashed the 'detention as a last resort' policy in favour of routine detention and accelerated processing of asylum seekers with 'straightforward' claims' (see Chapter 3). From March 2000 they were dispatched to Oakington, a former RAF barracks, for around ten days while their claims were processed, not because of any risk that they might abscond, but solely for administrative convenience; holding them made it easier to process their claims quickly. This, said Dr Saadi and other Iraqi Kurdish asylum seekers held at Oakington, was unlawful: human rights law only allowed detention of migrants to prevent their unauthorised entry, or for deportation. Dr Saadi had claimed asylum on arrival and was not seeking to enter illegally, nor was he being deported. The high court agreed that the detention was unlawful, but the Court of Appeal and the House of Lords saw no problem with locking up asylum seekers to process their claims.[19] By weasel words the law lords interpreted this as 'preventing unauthorised entry', putting asylum seekers at a stroke outside the normal legal protections against arbitrary detention. The European Court of Human Rights upheld the law lords' decision.[20]

The 2002 White Paper contained plans to detain nearly a third of asylum seekers in the fast track, in an expanded detention estate of 4,000 places. Immigration detention centres were re-branded immigration 'removal centres' (IRCs) – a term calculated to destroy any confidence asylum seekers had left in the likely success of their asylum claims. Ministers realised that, if asylum seekers were detained 'end to end' – from making the claim through appeal to departure – removal would be speedier, the holy grail of the Blair government. In 2003 the newly refurbished and expanded Harmondsworth became the setting for the new procedure, designed for single men, and in 2005, it was extended to women detainees at Yarl's Wood detention centre in Bedfordshire. Yarl's Wood had opened in November 2001 as a mixed-sex centre, designed for 400 inmates (later expanded to house 900), with five metre fences and triple barbed wire-topped secure walls, pan and tilt dome cameras and microwave detection systems – but no sprinklers, despite the wooden structure of the centre and against the strong advice of the fire service, and a whole wing burned down in disturbances just three months later.[21] It became notorious for self-harm, hunger strikes and suicides,[22] and has been named a 'Bleak House' for our time.[23]

WHY DETAIN?

Why are so many vulnerable people detained? What on earth possesses ministers and officials to deny people's liberty, to jeopardise their health, sanity and even their lives? According to Wackenhut's religious affairs officer, detainees at Tinsley House were 'detained as a result of having acted against the will of God'.[24] Deterrence (to stop asylum seekers coming),[25] isolation (to prevent the growth of solidarity),[26] administrative expediency (to make processing claims and removal easier), have all been cited. Another policy rationale is the preservation of order: asylum seekers and migrants are seen as somehow embodying illegality and disorder.[27] The burgeoning private security industry, whose lobbyists swarm in Westminster and whose directors have often come through the revolving door of politics, has also influenced policy. Governments are increasingly reliant on the global security firms for more and more functions, and the influence of lobbyists and the 'locking in' of administrations to contracts made by their predecessors adds to the pressure to keep increasing detention rather than trying alternatives. A confluence of private and public interests demands more and more incarceration.[28]

Political and media pressure forced Charles Clarke's resignation as home secretary in 2006 when it was revealed that foreign prisoners were being released at the end of their sentence without consideration of deportation. As a result of the furore, the Home Office secretly decided to detain all foreign ex-offenders for deportation, in complete contradiction to the published policy of detention as a last resort. Thousands of decent, long-settled people who had committed minor offences many years ago found themselves rounded up and held for many months pending deportation. In one detention centre where I visited a client (a Jamaican who had been in the country for over 30 years and had four generations of his family here), a British citizen had also been swept up and detained for two months. It took five years for the secret policy to come to light and for the supreme court to rule that detention under it was unlawful.[29]

REGULATIONS MADE – AND BROKEN

In the rush to build more immigration prisons, basic safeguards such as written reasons for detention, rules for staff, standards of care or criteria for or regulation of the use of force had been ignored. In 1998, HM prisons inspector Sir David Ramsbotham had condemned the detention of asylum seekers as a 'complete and utter shambles', with 'no rhyme or reason for the decision to detain',[30] and the UN Working Group on Arbitrary Detention found detention to be arbitrary, depending on the availability of space rather than on proper legal criteria, with no judicial oversight, no written rules or statutory procedures and no effective remedy for those detained.[31] In the Campsfield trial, the chief immigration officer said he had no idea whether those detained there had suffered torture or were mentally ill as he was not concerned with their welfare.[32]

In 1998, Labour published criteria for detention, indicating that torture survivors, unaccompanied minors, families, pregnant women and those suffering from serious medical conditions, mental illness or severe disabilities should not normally be detained.[33] Rules promulgated in 2001 defined staff powers and duties, and required written reasons to be given for detention, and regular monthly reviews for so long as someone was detained, as well as safeguards for torture survivors.[34] All new arrivals were to be medically screened within 24 hours for signs of torture or serious illness, to ensure that torture survivors were not inadvertently detained, in recognition of the profound distress, terror, suicide attempts or self-harm that can result.[35] But a test case in 2006 brought by two torture survivors revealed that for years the private medical services provider in detention centres had not done routine screening – because the Home Office regarded it as unnecessary and inappropriate and refused to pay for it.[36]

The rules also required medical staff to report concerns that detention was harming a detainee's health, fears of suicide or self-harm, and any evidence of a history of torture, and for immigration officials to respond with appropriate action within 48 hours. A 2009 audit by the UKBA – three years after the failures of protection for torture survivors were revealed – showed that in only a third of cases did officials respond within the 48-hour timeframe; there was no response at all in a third of cases, and reports resulted in release in fewer than 10 per cent of cases.[37] And in some cases, officials have authorised the detention of severely ill people in the teeth of medical advice, and sometimes despite court orders. Two cases which came before the courts in 2011 revealed how immigration detention fosters a culture of inhumanity, in which suicide attempts, self-harm and hunger strikes are dismissed as 'attention-seeking'.

S, an Indian Sikh, suffered severe post-traumatic stress disorder and psychosis after being raped as a 14-year-old by four masked gunmen who murdered his parents. In prison for assault, he regularly self-harmed and attempted suicide, but at the end of his sentence UKBA decided to detain him for deportation, recording that he seemed 'in good health' and that there were no 'compelling or compassionate circumstances' preventing his detention or deportation. They never revised this opinion, despite his relapse into psychosis, hallucinations, repeated wrist-slashing, an escape attempt, an interim hospital order and numerous psychiatric reports confirming that his continued detention was literally driving him mad and he should not be detained. So far as UKBA officials were concerned, there was 'no evidence' of mental illness, and the evidence of torture had been 'considered when the order for detention was made'.[38]

BA became psychotic while serving a prison sentence as a drugs courier. He began starving himself, and was transferred to hospital under the Mental Health Act. On his discharge he was detained in Harmondsworth despite medical advice that it would cause a relapse, which it did. Private medical care providers did not monitor his health for two months; then, it took them seven weeks to arrange for him to see a psychiatrist; and he was handcuffed for hospital visits, making him unwilling to go. After five months, a consultant psychiatrist and Harmondsworth's own medical staff warned that he could die 'imminently' unless released. The response was to continue detention while making plans to manage press coverage in the event of his death (a response described by the judge as 'chilling'). Even after a court order, when there were signs of lasting physical damage, it took nearly two more weeks to transfer BA to Hillingdon hospital. As soon as the hospital discharged him, two months later, UKBA sent him back to Harmondsworth, despite medical warnings and in breach of another order, having assessed his condition as 'self-inflicted'.[39]

High court judges found that the detention of both men was not only unlawful, it amounted to inhuman or degrading treatment. It occurred more than 15 years after the Medical Foundation had warned of the impact of detention on torture survivors.[40] These cases are the tip of a large iceberg. In July 2010, a plan to move a mentally ill, suicidal detainee out of Chelmsford prison and into immigration detention failed – there was no space, because of the large number of mentally ill detainees in immigration detention. But instead of ensuring that people suffering from mental illness were no longer detained in the wake of these cases, UKBA changed its policy so as to legitimise the detention of mentally ill and other vulnerable people.[41]

A DANGEROUS PLACE TO BE

Detention fosters inhuman treatment. A culture of casual racism, brutality and neglect has been consistently documented – from allegations of being spat on, given time-expired food and sedated for control at Walton prison in Liverpool in 2001, the 'subculture of racism, casual violence and abuse' revealed in 2005 by the BBC documentary, *Detention undercover*,[42] to the broken limbs described in the report *Outsourcing abuse*,[43] in 2008 – a report which forced the government to hold its own inquiry.[44] The attitudes of underpaid, under-trained private security guards, shaped by the anti-immigrant consensus of politicians and press, are encapsulated by the use of the term 'dog kennels' to refer to the cells in one short-term holding centre at the Channel Tunnel.[45]

Detainees seem caught in a vicious cycle of punishment and protest. An attempt by staff at Harmondsworth to prevent detainees hearing of a damning inspection report provoked a major disturbance: tornado teams (riot-trained guards) were called in and detainees were crammed into airless, sometimes flooded, smoke- and gas-filled cells with bare electrical wires and no toilet, for up to 40 hours, without food or water, or evacuated to courtyards to wait in the cold with no proper clothes. Helicopter news teams filmed them with bed sheets spelling out the letters 'SOS'.[46] The violent removal of a detainee for deportation led to another serious disturbance at Campsfield in 2007.[47] At Yarl's Wood, women reported racist abuse and sexual intimidation by guards,[48] and in February 2010 hunger strikers were punished by being 'kettled' for over five hours in a hallway, denied access to toilets and water, locked out in the freezing cold, and 'ringleaders' transferred to prison – the invariable response to complaints or protest, however polite and peaceful.[49]

And when detention is privately managed, the line of accountability is broken and redress more difficult. In 1995 the UN's Human Rights Committee expressed concern that 'the practice of contracting out to the private commercial sector core state activities which involve the use of force and the detention of persons weakens the protection of rights under the Covenant'.[50] This concern was borne out by the failure of a claim for malicious prosecution brought by a defendant against the Home Office and Group 4 after guards' evidence was exposed as fabricated in the 1998 Campsfield trial. The judge ruled that the Home Office had no duty to have regard to the welfare of detainees once contractors were appointed to run detention centres, and so was not responsible for Group 4 staff's misdemeanours.[51]

HEALTH NEGLECTED

Despite ministers' claims that primary health care in detention centres, provided by private companies, is equivalent to NHS provision, the HMCIP and other official bodies have been consistently critical of the standard of health care there.[52] When the Joint Committee on Human Rights visited Yarl's Wood, members were surprised that despite nearly all detainees being women, the only doctor there was male. The HMCIP, the Bail Circle of the Churches' Commission for Racial Justice and BID were among the many organisations complaining to the committee about the 'institutional failure to address health concerns' and 'institutional resistance to evidence of torture' in immigration detention,[53] and the committee expressed concern that the quality of health care in detention did not comply with the UK's obligation to prevent inhuman or degrading treatment and to provide adequate mental and physical health care.[54]

Because detention companies are paid a fixed sum per detainee and the maximisation of profit is their raison d'être, campaign groups battle constantly to hold the line against declining service provision. One study found the hourly basic pay of private prison staff 43 per cent less than that of public sector equivalents (except for directors, who were paid much more); there were 17 per cent fewer staff per prisoner – hence greater reliance on security, CCTV and tagging – and staff turnover in private prisons was between twice and seven times the public sector average.[55] Cost-cutting logic applies to the subcontracting of medical services too. Dr Frank Arnold, former clinical director of Medical Justice, blames privatisation for the routine lack of essential medication for serious illnesses including HIV and diabetes, routine failures of investigation, examination and treatment of detainees' medical conditions, even when torture is alleged, routine handcuffing of male detainees for outpatient consultations and inpatient treatment in hospitals, and routine cancellation of hospital visits when UKBA refuses to bear transport and escort costs – a state he describes as 'institutional medical abuse'.[56]

ROUTINE ILLEGALITY

In 2009–10 UKBA paid out £12 million in compensation and legal costs for unlawful detention.[57] Rules requiring detention to be regularly reviewed were generally honoured in the breach. Shepherd Kambadzi's case was typical; following a twelve-month sentence for assault from which he should have been released in April 2006, he was detained for deportation to Zimbabwe, although no one was being deported there because of the risks. The high court ordered his release two years later. For the first ten months of detention there were no reviews at all, and the high court judge found 'casual mendacity' in UKBA reports justifying continued detention. But the courts' refusal to hold detention unlawful for failure to give proper reasons or to perform the regular review, encouraged officials' laxity. Only in 2011 did the supreme court finally rule that these failures rendered Kambadzi's detention unlawful.[58]

The only apparent reason for the detention of Abdillaahi Muuse, a Dutch national of Somali origin, was his colour. As an EU citizen, he could not be deported for an offence of common assault, and so could not be detained for deportation – but his repeated protests that he was Dutch, and production of his Dutch passport and driving licence were met with 'Look at you, you're African!' by UKBA officials, who held him for nearly four months and told him they were sending him back to Africa. Fortunately, he was able to challenge his detention, but government lawyers redacted officials' names from the documentation produced to the court. The Court of Appeal said there was evidence of 'reckless indifference to legality', and upheld an award of exemplary damages for Mr Muuse's 'arbitrary detention by unidentified persons who have been accorded the cloak of anonymity and immunity from explanation of their unlawful conduct'.[59]

In Mr Muuse's case, as in many others, the Home Office treated the court with contempt, hardly bothering to put in witness statements to explain officials' actions, or complying with requests for evidence only at the very last moment. Sometimes, it simply ignores requests or even orders from the courts. This happened in February 2009, when home secretary Jacqui Smith decided to re-detain five Algerians and Jordanians who had previously been granted bail on stringent conditions by the Special Immigration Appeals Commission (SIAC, which hears appeals against decisions involving national security) pending their appeals against deportation. After UKBA lawyers' arguments for revocation of bail failed, officials illegally took the men to Belmarsh maximum security prison. The judges ordered the release of four of the men in an emergency hearing the following day. Instead of apology for flouting the court's order, there was defiance from Smith, who said she was 'extremely disappointed that the courts have allowed these individuals to be released'.[60]

SCANT JUDICIAL OVERSIGHT

The ancient remedy of *habeas corpus* is not much use in the context of immigration because of the breadth of the statutory powers to detain and the lack of any time limit. Legality of detention is more often challenged by judicial review. In 1984, the high court ruled Hardial Singh's five-month detention unlawful as there was no imminent prospect of deporting him.[61] Singh's case established that there were implied limits to immigration detention: it had to be for its statutory purpose, in this case removal, and limited to the period reasonably necessary for that purpose. Yet now, a quarter of detainees awaiting deportation are held for over a year.[62] The UKBA blames detainees' 'failure to cooperate' for lengthy detention, but even those who want to go back remain locked up while travel documents are obtained, a process which can take years. And a challenge to the length of detention has become something of a lottery, depending on different judges' interpretation of a 'reasonable' period and whether removal is 'reasonably foreseeable'. In 2011, detention of a Somali ex-offender for three and a half years pending deportation – the equivalent of an additional seven-year sentence – was upheld as lawful.[63] In opposition, Liberal Democrats opposed indefinite immigration detention. But since coming to power they have disavowed any intention to push for a statutory time limit.[64]

Immigration judges can grant bail to detainees without deciding whether their detention is lawful. In 1999, in response to criticism from the UN Working Group on Arbitrary Detention, the Labour government legislated for automatic bail hearings at regular intervals during detention.[65] But the provision was never brought into force, and in 2002 it was quietly repealed. So detainees must apply for bail. They must first find out about their right to apply, then, if possible, they must find a lawyer to help them. With legal provision in detention centres cut to the bone, these prerequisites to getting bail are hard to come by.[66] BID, a charity set up in 1998, produces materials and trains detainees to make their own bail applications.[67] But the success rate, poor even for represented applicants, is minuscule for those without legal representation. Detainees are rarely even brought to court; to save costs and delays most hearings are now by video link. Home Office reasons for detention, often riddled with factual errors or dubious assumptions, are rarely questioned by immigration judges who place the burden squarely on the detainee to justify bail. Sureties are often demanded when none are necessary.[68] The proportion of successful bail applications in the Tribunal fell from a quarter in 2006 to less than a fifth in 2010, as fewer immigration judges were prepared to take the risk of releasing ex-offenders or refused asylum seekers.

The impatience and contempt with which some immigration judges treat detainees and their families and friends in refusing bail is legendary.[69] One occasion stands out for me, when I applied for bail for a Sudanese refugee facing deportation. As his young wife, bereft and distraught, described trying to cope with a new baby in a strange land without him, and others from his community testified to the man's kindness and public-spiritedness, the immigration judge didn't bother to hide his impatience, and refused bail without pausing for breath. His refusal to engage with the human realities, his effortless assumption of superiority as he began reciting the standard formula for refusing bail infuriated me so much that I walked out, not allowing him my presence to legitimate the empty exercise.

CAMPAIGNING: FAILURES AND SUCCESSES

A huge network of organisations has built up since the 1980s, befriending and supporting detainees, providing legal advice and campaigning against immigration detention. It has forced governments to regulate detention – criteria, reasons, length and conditions – through rules, published policies, official monitoring and high court supervision. But the increased transparency over detention forced on the Home Office by litigation and campaigning has not stopped the relentless increase in detention to manage, control and isolate asylum seekers and foreign national ex-offenders, and the essential injustice of detention has not really caught the public's imagination. In one area, however, campaigners can claim success, and that is over the immigration detention of children.[70]

The fact that two of the defendants in the 1998 Campsfield trial were 17 showed the scandal of lone children who 'looked' over 18 being routinely detained as adults by immigration officers who believed that adults were posing as children to get better treatment and to avoid detention.[71] The assessment of children as adults was also rife in social services departments for the same reason.[72] A legal campaign resulted in an award of £1 million to 40 children unlawfully detained as adults[73] and forced the adoption of proper age assessment procedures[74] resulting in far fewer age-disputed minors being detained.[75]

More children were detained in families. In the interests of immigration control, in 2003 the Ay family from Turkey, a mother and her four children aged from seven to 13, were detained for 13 months, mostly in one room in Dungavel. Their case attracted a huge campaign and raised awareness of children's detention, and in 2012 the family were awarded compensation.[76] A one-year-old born in the UK to a French father and Ivorian refused asylum seeker mother was detained for removal with her mother for six months, although the nationality of her father meant neither mother nor daughter could be removed.[77] In 2005, Save the Children reported that 2,000 children were detained annually.[78]

The No Place for a Child campaign brought asylum, human rights and children's groups together,[79] and UN and European bodies condemned children's detention. Children's Commissioner Sir Al Aynsley-Green described the bewilderment and distress of children, many of whom believed themselves British, woken in their homes by loud knocking and shouted orders, pushed and harried by uniformed strangers who sometimes followed them into the toilet, given no time to collect belongings or medication, seeing parents manhandled and handcuffed, shoved into caged urine-smelling vans, not told where they were going, and held for weeks, sometimes months behind up to ten locked doors.[80] Children were wetting, soiling and harming themselves, he reported.[81] The campaign continued to build, as the government legislated for children's welfare to feature in immigration decisions in 2009,[82] but continued detaining children, and celebrities and authors became involved, more reports described the impact on children[83] and even the *Daily Mail* referred to 'innocent children behind bars at Christmas'.[84] In May 2010, the coalition government announced that it would end the immigration detention of children. Rejoicing among campaigners was muted by the further announcement that families with children could still face up to seven days in 'pre-departure accommodation', billed as child-friendly with Barnardo's staff working there, but with all the familiar security features.[85] And the pledge did not stop 700 children in four months being detained on arrival at Britain's south-eastern ports, many unaccompanied, with no record kept of how long they were held or why.[86] But although the campaign to end children's detention has not yet been won, its success is measured by the headlines such detention now attracts.[87]

The campaign to end immigration detention for all, meanwhile, has gone global, making links not only with campaigns working to end the detention of migrants and refugees across Europe and worldwide, but also with other campaigns making the links between immigration detention, the massive growth of the private security industry and other aspects of globalisation.

Part Three

Departure: Resisting Total Controls and Mass Removal

9
The Growth of the Internal Border Force

Through legislation in 1999, 2002 and 2004, the immigration service was transformed into a fully-fledged police force, with all the powers of arrest, use of force, entry to premises, search and seizure of evidence that the regular police have, with few of the democratic safeguards against abuse. Immigration officers already had powers to arrest illegal entrants, but the new powers allowed them to enter and search homes and business premises on suspicion of immigration-related offences including unlawful employment or asylum support fraud, acting independently of police.[1] Internal immigration policing was again transformed in 2008 when the Immigration Service became the UK Border Agency,[2] with 7,500 enforcement officers organised into over 70 local immigration teams (LITs) in six regions, each with its own command structure and website.

INFORMATION INFRASTRUCTURE

In parallel with the increase in powers and structural changes, the information infrastructure of immigration policing was transformed. An information exchange network between the Home Office, the police, crime databases and customs, replacing *ad hoc* cooperation, was enabled by legislation in 1999.[3] The Home Office was given powers to demand information from property owners and managers on occupants of their premises.[4] Marriage registrars were required by law to report 'suspicious' marriages between British or EU and non-EU citizens to the Home Office.[5] In 2002 the Home Office was empowered to demand information from the Inland Revenue, local authorities and employers and other state agencies to trace suspected unauthorised residents and migrant workers,[6] and to compel banks and building societies to provide financial information about account holders suspected of asylum support offences.[7] Some of these information-gathering powers were backed up with criminal offences of non-compliance, just in case a bank employee, an employer or former employer was tempted to say

'Mind your own business'.[8] Information exchange now crosses Europe and beyond; the Schengen Information System (SIS) has over half a million terminals located in the security services of the member states, and contains over 30 million alerts;[9] and in April 2009, UKBA announced plans to develop appropriate data sharing protocols with the US, Canada and Australia. It cannot be long before someone falling foul of immigration law in one country, in no matter how minor a way, is *persona non grata* and inadmissible in much of the world. And no one knows the incidence of 'false positives' – errors in data systems leading to wrongful refusals, which are impossible to challenge.

BIOMETRIC CONTROL

In opposition, Labour had opposed Tory proposals for a compulsory identity card,[10] but in the wake of the 9/11 attacks and in the media panic around asylum cheats and scroungers, home secretary David Blunkett revived the idea. In 2003, the government announced plans for universal biometric identity cards as a tool against identity theft, illegal working, benefit fraud and terrorism. Powers to forcibly fingerprint asylum seekers, taken in 1993, had already been extended to suspected overstayers and illegal entrants in 1999 and to all other migrants in 2002.[11] A Bill introduced in 2004 provided for a national identity register which would collate 50 categories of information about holders, provoking the information commissioner to worry publicly about 'sleepwalk[ing] into a surveillance society'.[12] The Joint Committee on Human Rights said the proposals would violate rights to privacy and non-discrimination,[13] and an LSE study in 2005 concluded that the proposed scheme was 'a potential danger to the public interest and to the legal rights of individuals'.[14] Despite strong opposition from civil liberties groups and the House of Lords, in 2006 the Identity Cards Act was passed, although the scheme was to be voluntary to begin with. But not for foreign nationals: from 2008, all non-EEA citizens in the UK for more than six months for work, study or on marriage or partner visas have been required to attend one of the dozen or so 'biometric enrolment centres' in the UK to have a digital photograph and ten digital finger scans taken, and must pay for and carry a biometric immigration document (BID, also known as a biometric residence permit, BRP), which contains not only the digitised photo and fingerprint scans but also details of the person's conditions of stay and other information.[15] Failure to obtain a card carries a £1,000 penalty, but it doesn't stop there; the holders are under a legal duty to notify the authorities when they change their name, their gender, their nationality or their facial appearance, on pain of a fine and curtailment of their permission to stay.

A lengthy and hard-fought campaign by groups such as No2ID, and equally vociferous arguments from the Conservative libertarian right wing, meant that one of the coalition's first announcements on coming to power in May 2010, waving its civil liberties credentials, was the scrapping of the ID cards project. But civil liberties were not to apply to non-EEA nationals, for whom ID cards remained firmly in place. In February 2012 the requirement for biometric residence permits was extended to refugees and settled migrants.[16]

CONTROLLING ASYLUM SEEKERS

Asylum seekers, the main focus of popular racism in the 1990s and early 2000s, were the first group to be subjected to intensive controls. In 1999, a new Home Office agency, the National Asylum Support Service (NASS), was formed to fuse welfare with control of the asylum seekers it supported and housed.[17] Asylum seekers who refused dispersal or were away from their allotted accommodation for more than a few days could lose support, immigration officers were empowered to search accommodation for unauthorised occupants or activities, and a whole raft of regulations and criminal offences were created to deal with 'abuses' of asylum support. Even the Post Office was co-opted, compelled to provide, on demand, information about redirection of mail by asylum seekers suspected of not living where they should.[18] Then in 2002, legislation was passed to house vast numbers of asylum seekers in huge 'accommodation centres' to be built on the sites of old airfields and in one case, where the diseased carcasses of tens of thousands of sick cattle had been incinerated. The idea was to prevent families from integrating into local communities, which made it 'virtually impossible' to remove them.[19] The centres attracted hostility both from anti-asylum campaigners who did not want their villages threatened by alien hordes, and from asylum rights groups angered by the attempt at segregation, and none were ever built.

Accommodation centres were meant as part of a system of 'end-to-end' control of non-detained asylum seekers, which began with screening and the issue of the Standard Acknowledgement Letter (SAL),[20] establishing entitlement to be in the UK and to obtain asylum support, health care, education and other purposes. Labour replaced the SAL by an electronic Application Registration Card (ARC), containing the holder's fingerprints as well as a photographic image, information about employment status, eligibility for asylum support, languages spoken and other personal information, some unknown to the holder. From 2002, non-detained asylum seekers were required to attend induction centres for two weeks, and to report at intervals at reporting centres. In 2004, new laws allowed asylum seekers (among others) to be electronically monitored through tagging, telephone reporting with voice recognition, and tracking. Of these methods of so-called 'contact management', tagging proved the most popular with the Home Office, and despite a commitment that it would be voluntary when it was introduced, in January 2006 tags began to be fitted without consent to monitor the whereabouts of asylum seekers.[21]

TARGETING STUDENTS AND COLLEGES

As asylum numbers dropped off from the mid-2000s, international (non-EEA) students joined irregular migrants as a new target for politicians and media, suspected not only of being 'bogus students', economic migrants, but also of being terrorists, in the wake of the 2005 London bombs and the failed car-bomb attempts in London and Glasgow.[22] Up till then, Home Office officials had policed students after entry – attendance and progress were checked before extensions of stay were granted, students could be refused if they repeatedly failed examinations, and were sometimes arrested for working in excess of the permitted 20 hours per week. Immigration officers occasionally visited colleges to check that they existed and were providing courses, and very occasionally a 'bogus' college was closed down. But controls were not systematic or continuous.

All this changed in 2009, when the Labour government extended the PBS to students and outsourced their policing to the colleges and universities they attended, which were required to perform the necessary controls as part of the price of enrolling the students. The new measures put in place end-to-end control of students, sub-contracted to colleges – who are forced to pay for the privilege. In the process, colleges have found themselves subjected to increasingly heavy policing – and it is here that immigration policing has gone furthest in terms of the technology and the degree of surveillance and control demanded by UKBA of its unwilling educational 'partners'.

Education providers – schools, colleges and universities – must obtain a licence from the UKBA to 'sponsor' international students. The licence enables them to issue visa letters or 'confirmation of acceptance for study' (CAS) on the strength of which visas are issued. To get and keep their sponsor licence, colleges must demonstrate that they have rigorously tested students for their genuineness and intention to follow the course as well as their ability. They must also sign up to policing of their international students and reporting regularly on them to UKBA via a computerised 'Sponsor Management System', which records students' personal and contact details, academic background, English language proficiency, progress and attendance on the course, sickness and unauthorised absence, their immigration status, the college's dealings with them (warning letters etc.) and its continuing assessment of their genuineness and intention to study. Sponsors must track all the students to whom they issue a CAS from arrival in the UK to departure, reporting if students fail to enrol, are absent from the course for 'a significant period', leave the course or exhibit 'suspicious behaviour', and must be prepared to drop everything to respond to the queries of officials, who make unannounced visits to check compliance.

Guidance for sponsors on what they need to do to get and keep a sponsor licence changes frequently – it was revised nine times in its first year of operation, and the threshold for suspension or revocation of a licence was repeatedly lowered. Education providers are ranked not according to the excellence of their teaching under this system, but according to the efficiency of their procedures for policing their students. In April 2010 'highly trusted sponsor' status was introduced for colleges with the strongest procedures, and the coalition announced that by March 2012 all educational institutions had to achieve 'highly trusted sponsor' status in order to continue to teach non-EEA students. The costs involved in obtaining and setting up the necessary computer systems, training staff and administering the system are formidable for small colleges. Some universities and colleges have issued biometric swipe cards to staff and students to keep track of them; others have invested in fingerprint scanners for recording attendance. External examiners are increasingly being asked to submit their passports. And according to a *Manifesto Club* report, universities are over-complying through fear of losing their licence, sending some 1500 reports a month to the UKBA.[23]

Small ethnic minority-run colleges in particular complain that they come up against the old culture of suspicion, that the worst possible construction is put on recording failures or errors, that

UKBA suspends and revokes licences too readily and often without warning, or without giving them a chance to improve their systems, destroying teachers' livelihoods and jeopardising students' study and their right to remain. The London Reading College introduced fingerprint scanning to check students' attendance following an inspection in which its attendance records were criticised, but it still had its sponsor licence revoked and had to refund all its students' fees. Officials said the poor English of some of the students had been behind revocation of the licence – a new criticism which the college had had no chance to deal with. The high court quashed the revocation of the licence as unfair – but by then, the college's inability to operate without a licence had led to withdrawal of its educational accreditation.[24] UKBA emailed Westech college in Plaistow requesting detailed information about the college's students and their work placements, to be sent within five days, and a week later, claiming the requested information had not arrived within the deadline, it stopped further enrolments, then suspended and later revoked the sponsor licence, saying the college had not obtained planning permission, and had made mistakes recording students' placements. The college was given no chance to improve its recording systems.[25] Little wonder that small colleges feel they are being policed to extinction. Four hundred and fifty colleges had reportedly withdrawn from the market by autumn 2011, 11,000 fewer students had registered and Universities UK was warning of damage to Britain's reputation for providing education.[26] English language colleges threatened to sue the Home Office for suggesting that they were 'bogus' colleges which had been unable or unwilling to comply with the strict conditions for licences.[27]

Judges have held that UKBA officials 'are entitled to maintain a fairly high index of suspicion as they go about overseeing colleges and a light trigger in deciding when and with what level of firmness they should act'. But as Judge Kaye said in quashing a slipshod and unfair decision to refuse a licence based on an uninvestigated allegation of dishonesty, 'that does not mean that they can disregard established laws of natural justice or ride roughshod over a person's reasonable expectations'.[28]

There has been political resistance to the imposition of policing duties on colleges and universities. Sixty-eight academics signed a letter to the *Times Educational Supplement* urging fellow academics to 'resist collusion with the creeping surveillance mentality being introduced into institutions ... The only reason for monitoring student activity or achievement should be to inform best pedagogic, pastoral and ethical practices'.[29] Reporting on students 'betrays the trust and destroys the openness on which academic freedoms and ethics depend', said a further statement.[30] The Universities and Colleges Union (UCU) resolved in May 2009 to support members who refused to comply with the policing obligations. At one university, UCU succeeded in stopping plans for international students to report weekly with identity documents, and the campaign group Students not Suspects achieved a tenfold reduction in the number of international students reported to UKBA at Goldsmiths College. Many academic staff refused to show passports for external examinations. But lacking the cooperation of the UK's biggest and most prestigious universities, the campaign was unable to stop the 'creeping surveillance' of international students.

THE POLICING OF EMPLOYMENT

If the policing of students and colleges is the most advanced in terms of the technology and the demands made of sponsors, the policing of employment, with its raids to find unauthorised workers and undocumented migrants, has become the most public face of immigration policing, and the most violent. It started in 1996, when the Tory government introduced fines for employers who took on migrants unauthorised to work,[31] ostensibly to protect British workers from unfair competition and undocumented migrant workers from exploitation. It had previously shown little concern for workers' rights, abolishing wages councils (which set minimum wages) in 1993, deregulating employment agencies, diluting workplace protections and restricting the right to strike, creating job insecurity and exacerbating inequality in the name of labour flexibility; and its concern for undocumented workers was belied by the rush to expel those found working illegally. It turned a deaf ear to trade unions' counter-arguments that the measure would exacerbate race discrimination in the workplace, and that regularisation was the best protection for both British and migrant workers.[32] Ten thousand marched in February 1996 against the new provisions, but they became law anyway.

Labour consolidated the Tories' embrace of employers' liability, tightening the law in 2002 to require employers to perform more rigorous document checking of recruits,[33] but until 2006 it did little by way of enforcement. In the decade since the coming into force of the 1996 employers' liability measures, there were only a handful of prosecutions. But as large numbers of eastern Europeans from the ten new EU member states flocked to British fields, building sites and factories following accession in May 2004, and the tabloids foamed at the new 'invasion', the government saw the political necessity of cracking down on the old bogeyman, the (non-EU) illegal immigrant who was 'taking our jobs'. In 2006, tough new employers' liability laws required employers to check migrant employees' right to work not just on recruitment but every year, to avoid liability for employing unauthorised workers. It doubled the maximum penalty to £10,000, and created a new offence of knowingly employing unauthorised migrants, which could result in a prison sentence and an unlimited fine.[34] And from 2008, under the points-based scheme for economic migrants, to get and keep sponsors' licenses employers also had to report to UKBA when employees left their employment.

However, more important than the new laws were their enforcement. In the year 2007–8 alone, the new regional enforcement teams of immigration officers carried out over 15,500 raids, resulting in 10,750 arrests.[35] In the same year, there were only 30 employment standards inspectors to cover the whole country and only 100 minimum wage inspectors at HM Revenue and Customs (5 per cent of the numbers investigating benefit fraud), while health and safety inspectors' numbers had been cut by 200 in the previous four years.[36] Monitoring workplace compliance now meant overwhelmingly policing of immigration status rather than workers' protection.

Squads of immigration officers, sometimes with police, often wearing body armour, now descend daily on homes and (more often) workplaces, generally small, ethnic minority run High Street businesses – Indian, Chinese and Turkish restaurants and takeaways, Vietnamese nail bars and ethnic supermarkets – sealing exits and storming in to demand that residents or staff prove their right to be living or working in the UK. Sometimes all the ethnic minority restaurants in a particular street or village are raided in one day. Officers often carry mobile fingerprint terminals to perform instant identity checks, and cart off those who can't prove their entitlement, for further checks, possible prosecution and detention or summary removal from the country. Police dogs and helicopters have been used to pursue workers who have fled the premises. Employers are served with penalty notices for up to £10,000 per irregular worker, which can wipe them out financially, and face 'naming and shaming' on the UKBA website. The owner of an Exmouth restaurant and chair of the Devon and Cornwall Chinese Association complained that during a raid he and his staff were treated like terrorists, and a Kent Indian restaurant manager whose two restaurants were raided by 18 uniformed officers on Friday and Saturday evenings was moved to protest, 'We're not drug dealing, we're selling curry.'[37] And a Scottish hotelier, Helalul Islam, who gave money, food and accommodation to two overstaying waiters and a kitchen hand to help them out was sentenced to 16 months' imprisonment, although on appeal the sentence was quashed and he was admonished.[38]

The over-policing of immigration, the use of body armour, dogs, police helicopters and paramilitary tactics, reinforced the message that migrants are dangerous, that unauthorised living or working in the UK is a serious crime. And the development of employer sanctions drew employers inexorably into immigration control functions; to avoid penalties they were forced to police their workers and exclude those not entitled to work. The increase in workplace checks by employers to comply with the law has led to wrongful dismissal and withholding of wages of migrants and black and minority ethnic workers entitled to work; to employers simply not hiring 'foreign-looking' staff; and to an atmosphere of suspicion and hostility, and a climate in which undocumented workers are treated as thieves of 'British' jobs.

Prison for Undocumented Workers

In the 1980s and 1990s, those I represented on charges of illegal working[39] were often commended for their initiative by the magistrates who dealt with them, and given token punishments. But the barrage of policing and enforcement measures of the past two decades has changed the climate inside as well as outside the courts, and judges now treat illegal working as a serious crime, particularly where there is resort to false documents to obtain work. This is so even though it is often Home Office delays in deciding asylum claims, or the creation of a rightless limbo of non-acceptance and non-removal, which has caused the resort to illegal working. So 49-year-old Zimbabwean paramedic Thomas Mvemve waited four years for his asylum claim to be decided before, desperate to provide for his family, he got work with a care agency using a fake Home Office letter. His asylum claim was finally accepted, but by then he had spent nearly three months on remand for obtaining a pecuniary advantage (the chance to work) by deception. Another Zimbabwean, Florida Ziki, overstayed with her husband after being refused asylum. When she was arrested for using false Home Office documents to get work in a care home, she broke down and said,

'What was I supposed to do? I can't live or work here without these papers'. It was accepted that Florida, a former member of an opposition party in Zimbabwe, could not go back there, but as a refused asylum seeker, she could not legally work or obtain benefits. But she was still jailed for eight months. The sentences handed down to migrants who use false documents to work are similar to those imposed on people who use theft or fraud to enrich themselves, and do not take account of the fact that falsely documented migrant workers actually do the work for which they are (usually poorly) paid. Sometimes, adding insult to injury, workers find their hard-earned pay treated as 'proceeds of crime'. This happened to Liberian failed asylum seeker, Masdan Kamara, who was jailed for 15 months for using false documents to obtain employment through nursing agencies in Staffordshire, and was told that her earnings would be confiscated.[40]

Exploitation Intensified

All this enforcement leads to more exploitation. Academics, journalists and undocumented migrants themselves have described life in the shadows.[41] The TUC's Commission on Vulnerable Employment (CoVE), set up to investigate conditions of employment in sectors such as hospitality, care, construction, cleaning and security, found widespread, open law-breaking by employers and employment agencies. It met 'workers who had spent 70-hour weeks on around £2 an hour, and had been sacked immediately they challenged their employer; hotel chambermaids who had to be available to work from 8am, but who were not paid for the extra hours if rooms were vacated in late morning; migrant domestic workers who had been beaten or sexually assaulted, but lived in too much fear of deportation to report these serious crimes; and security guards who had worked for months but had never been paid'.[42]

The Labour administrations of 1997 to 2010 missed the historic opportunity to humanise the debate around unauthorised working. Although Labour signed up to the EU's Social Chapter and introduced a national minimum wage, its obsession with enforcement led to betrayal of the most vulnerable workers. It retained the exclusion of undocumented workers from enforcement of basic workplace rights (payment of wages, limited working hours) – an exclusion which perpetuated exploitation and undercut its own minimum wage and protection measures. The drowning of 23 Chinese cockle pickers in Morecambe Bay in February 2004 shone a light on the desperate and dangerous world of undocumented workers, ruled by gangmasters,[43] and forced the government into regulation of gangmasters in certain sectors.[44] But with no mechanism for enforcement of undocumented workers' rights, raids on gangmasters have resulted not in protection for those found living and working in slave-like conditions, but in their detention and removal.[45] Unions' activities in support of migrant workers, such as Unison's campaigns, Unite's work with Kalayaan, the organisation of and for migrant domestic workers, and the GMB's 'Know your rights' scheme, have made real gains – but for undocumented workers the big problem of status remains. The Justice for Cleaners and London Living Wage campaigns succeeded in forcing large multinational cleaning companies to pay a living wage to their workers in the City and Canary Wharf, but shortly after cleaners at London's School for Oriental and African Studies (SOAS) won their battle with the help of the students there, the undocumented workers among them were arrested and deported. The TUC Commission supported regularisation of undocumented workers and the separation of immigration control from employment protection.

CAMPAIGNS FOR THE UNDOCUMENTED

It took years for campaigners to realise that the new Labour government was intensifying controls and immigration policing and entrenching the exclusion and criminalisation they had fought against during the 1980s and 1990s. In Europe, the *sans-papiers* movement was taking hold, with huge sit-ins and protests under the banner 'Undocumented but not illegal'. But in the UK, after the mid-1990s, the campaign against internal controls was largely quiescent, and it was another decade before a large-scale regularisation movement was to appear.

Labour did perform 'stealth' regularisations – of domestic workers in 1998–99,[46] following the campaign by Kalayaan; the 'one-off exercise' involving refused asylum seeking families in 2003–6; and of so-called 'legacy' cases ('backlog clearance' of asylum seekers and other migrants whose cases had been in the system for a long time) in 2006–11 (the latter two undertaken in the spirit of fiddling the numbers on waiting lists rather than for benevolent purposes) – but even as these amnesties (in effect) were carried out, ministers banged the drum for more control, more enforcement.

There has been resistance to criminalisation by migrant communities. A Chinatown protest against immigration raids in October 2007 was followed by a rally in April 2008 uniting thousands of catering staff and restaurant owners from the Indian sub-continent, China and Turkey. As protests spread, Zimbabweans protested outside Downing Street demanding the right to legal work. There was widespread support for the 'earned regularisation' campaign launched in 2006 by churches, trade unions such as the TGWU, the Refugee Council, JCWI, Strangers into Citizens and the Institute for Public Policy Research (IPPR). Studies by some of these groups concurred that enforcement of internal controls exacerbates popular racism and that regularisation would benefit the economy and restore a sense of proportion.[47] Lib Dem leader Nick Clegg endorsed the campaign, London's Tory mayor Boris Johnson supported it, as did a number of local councils. Ninety-three MPs signed a supportive parliamentary motion in 2007,[48] and opinion polls showed support from a majority of the public.[49] But regularisation was an early casualty of the coalition: to retain the support of Tory backwoodsmen, David Cameron forced Clegg to ditch the policy, and later the IPPR withdrew its support, saying the demand was unrealistic in the new political climate.[50] But it is a far more realistic solution to irregular migration than the inhuman and prohibitively expensive escalation of immigration policing of the past two decades.

SURVEILLANCE CULTURE

The growth of immigration policing forms part of an encroaching surveillance culture in which CCTV cameras monitor all our movements in public places; the electronic traces left by certain 'suspect' communities, generally Muslims, are analysed as they shop, use the internet and mobile phones, travel, draw cash and donate to charity; and university staff are expected to report Muslim students (home and international) who show signs of 'radicalisation'. Yet trafficked children go missing from care homes every week, vanishing without trace into the sex trade, and attempts to find them are desultory.[51] The contrast between the resources going into policing migrants and on finding missing trafficked children gives an unedifying picture of government priorities.

More and more parts of the public and private sectors have been drawn in to immigration control functions. The systematic exclusion of non-settled migrants from mainstream welfare benefits, public housing and social services assistance was complete by 2002, and Department of Work and Pensions (DWP) and local authority officials now routinely question applicants and check immigration documents to ascertain eligibility. Hospital staff must do the same by further restrictions in 2004 on eligibility for free NHS hospital treatment. In February 2012, plans were unveiled for an online checking service which will enable employers and local authorities to run real-time checks on eligibility to work or access services.[52] Checking passports and eligibility, denying access to health care, housing and employment on immigration status grounds, picking up the phone to inform or check on someone with the Home Office has become a natural and normal part of the job, permeating most sectors and areas of life, and there are few areas where immigration status is seen as irrelevant. While universalism has been rejected as a basis of access to basic essentials of life such as livelihood and shelter, controls have become universalised, fostering an atmosphere of suspicion, hostility and exclusion.

In this atmosphere, migrant and refugee children attending school for the first time have been asked to produce papers, although children are entitled to a school place regardless of immigration status.[53] Many GP practices refuse registration or demand proof of lawful residence, according to charity Doctors without Borders, although primary health care remains (for the time being) freely available regardless of status. A woman housed in temporary accommodation days before giving birth needed a doctor a few days after the birth. 'The receptionist ... wanted my passport, national insurance number, bank statement, baby's birth certificate and red book, everything. I said to her "I do not have these things; I just moved house, just gave birth! My baby is only four days old, my wound is weeping, I can't walk properly and I'm in so much pain." But she just told me to go to accident and emergency, and hung up on me.'[54]

Members of the public are encouraged to join in the witch hunt; we are all border enforcers now. Following a proposal in the 2002 White Paper, a confidential phone and email service was provided for members of the public to report their suspicions, and in October 2011 David Cameron called on the public to 'shop an illegal immigrant' by reporting those they suspected of being in the country unlawfully to the Crimestoppers phone line or through the Border Agency website. 'Together we will reclaim our borders and send illegal immigrants home', he said.[55] It is left to organisations such as No One is Illegal to point to the absurdity of describing a person, rather than an action, as illegal, and to defend 'immigration outlaws'.[56]

10
The Deportation Drive

It was only in the late 1990s that serious efforts began to enforce the large-scale removal of undocumented migrants – illegal entrants, overstayers and refused asylum seekers – and the deportation (removal with a ban on re-entry) of foreign offenders. The statistics tell their own story. In 1997, about 7,000 refused asylum seekers and around 3,500 overstayers, illegal entrants and offenders were removed or deported. The budget of the Enforcement Directorate and its staff complement was doubled in size in the financial year 2000–1.[1] By 2005, the numbers of refused asylum seekers removed had doubled, and removals of irregular migrants and offenders had quadrupled. The enforcement budget was massively expanded again in 2006,[2] and by 2010, while the number of refused asylum seekers removed had fallen to around 10,000, the number of offenders and irregular migrants removed had jumped to 31,500 – nearly ten times the 1997 total.[3]

Why the deportation drive? Perhaps because a 'reserve army' of irregular migrant labour is surplus to requirements in our post-industrial society; the requisite flexible, mobile and cheap labour can now be supplied from eastern Europe and from the de-skilled British workforce.[4] Tough enforcement policies are good for the global security corporations, ever hungry for contracts; they delight the nationalist Right and the media, for whom politicians' ability to remove as many 'foreign criminals, illegals and terrorists' as possible is a political virility test. When the Home Office was described as not 'fit for purpose' in 2006, the 'purpose' was the deportation of foreign ex-offenders. Economic and political imperatives, public and private interests converge in deportation.

The setting of targets for deportation has created its own impetus.[5] Home Office enforcement units proliferate, with Orwellian names like DEPMU (Detainee Escorting and Population Management Unit), which 'tasks contractors with escorting detainees', ReSCU (an inapt acronym for the Removals Support and Coordination Unit), which manages the removals budget, arranges charter flights and liaises with scheduled carriers, and RGDU (Returns Group

Documentation Unit), which liaises with embassies to obtain travel documents for deportees. The security companies are awarded contracts for escorts, airline companies for chartering aircraft, charities for 'voluntary removals'.[6] And as removal has become central to immigration policy, ever higher targets are devised, mass removals are routinised, laws changed, appeal rights hollowed out or removed, and procedures devised to deny access to legal help and judicial intervention.

HUMAN RIGHTS AND THE NARROWING OF DEPORTATION APPEALS

The mass deportation of irregular migrants and offenders was an unexpected by-product of the Human Rights Act. As the Home Office sought to prevent the 'undeserving' from using the Act to stop deportation, the removal of these groups became easier as the grounds for legal resistance narrowed. The old rules promulgated from 1972 onwards[7] had emphasised the discretionary nature of deportation of overstayers[8] and offenders, requiring officials (and judges on appeal) to consider their situation in the round, taking into account 'every relevant factor' – age, length of residence, family ties, character, employment record and so on. Some long-resident Commonwealth citizens were exempt from deportation altogether, and for the rest, deportation was by no means automatic. It was extremely unusual to deport even a persistent offender or long-term overstayer who had been in the country for many years and had put down roots in the community. Policies allowed long-term overstayers and illegal entrants to stay after ten years (later 14). Deportation was recognised as an extreme measure, particularly for offenders with settlement rights, British spouses and children. In 1980 the Court of Appeal, giving guidance for criminal judges on recommending foreign offenders for deportation when passing sentence, enjoined them to consider carefully the effect of deportation on family members: 'the courts have no wish to break up families or to impose hardship on innocent people'.[9]

The care which had to be taken in weighing the factors for and against could make deportation appeal hearings lengthy, and community members were often involved as witnesses. Bakhtaur Singh, a Sikh priest and musician originally admitted for two weeks, had overstayed for several years, but was greatly valued by his community for his musical and religious services, and when I arrived to represent him on his deportation appeal in 1983, I found dozens of supporters at the court, several of whom testified for him. The level of support impressed the adjudicator, who, however, regretfully dismissed the appeal on the ground that he could not legally take into account the man's value to the community. The adjudicator's positive findings enabled us to take his case further, and after a three-year legal battle, the House of Lords' appellate committee confirmed that the value to the community of a proposed deportee's presence and activities was relevant to deportation.[10] However in 1988, the Tory government drastically curtailed the grounds on which alleged overstayers could appeal.[11]

EARLY ANTI-DEPORTATION CAMPAIGNS

Many of those around whom campaigns formed in the 1980s and 1990s were overstayers: Muhammad Idrish, a Bangladeshi social worker whose marriage to a British woman had broken down;[12] Viraj Mendis, whose two and a half years in the Church of the Ascension in Hulme, Manchester following the dismissal of his appeal against deportation to Sri Lanka put the UK sanctuary movement on the map;[13] Kulvinder Kaur, Hemlata Patel and Mamta Chopra, threatened with deportation after leaving violent husbands, and many more. Local anti-deportation campaigns mushroomed and came together to form a national anti-deportation movement. The Campaign against Double Punishment held its first annual conference in 1992, and the NCADC was formed in 1995 to support community-led anti-deportation campaigns. NALGO (the local government officers' union, now Unison) lent its support to many of these campaigns, which achieved significant results, not just winning individual cases, but also resulting in legal and policy changes which protected irregular migrants with UK-resident partners and children.[14]

On the face of it, the Human Rights Act granted a new, higher level of protection for migrants, by preventing deportation or removal which would breach the person's human rights. No one could be removed to a situation where there was a real risk of torture or inhuman or degrading treatment. No such absolute ban prevented family separation through deportation, but private[15] or family life[16] ties were to be weighed against the public interest in deportation. But as the executive and the courts clamped down on so-called 'abuse' of human rights by the 'undeserving', the floor of human rights protection became an ever lower ceiling. The harsher climate for refused asylum seekers, undocumented migrants and ex-offenders post-2000 encouraged the Right and the tabloid press to raise its demands for even more enforcement.

REFUSED ASYLUM SEEKERS RETURNED TO DANGER

In the early years of the Labour administration, the government focused on preventing and deterring the arrival of asylum seekers, rather than on their removal. The Home Affairs Committee accused the Home Office in 2001 of being dilatory in sending them home,[17] but the focus had already shifted to removal, with prime minister Blair's pledge to remove more refused asylum seekers than the number of new ones, although he failed in his bid to increase removals to 30,000 by 2001–2. When in 2002 home secretary David Blunkett introduced legislation allowing for instant removal of refused asylum seekers whose claims the Home Office deemed 'clearly unfounded' (the 'white list' described in Chapter 3), even the *Daily Telegraph* criticised him – although only for hypocrisy. As the paper pointed out, Labour had described similar legislation as 'nasty', 'deserving of contempt' and 'an abdication by the government of its responsibilities under international law' when Michael Howard introduced it in 1996 – even though Howard's law had merely curtailed pre-removal appeal rights, not abolished them.[18] That summer, Blunkett announced his plan for TV crews to film removals to deter asylum seekers, slammed a Lottery Fund grant to anti-deportation campaigners and had the Ahmadi family's sanctuary in a mosque destroyed by a battering ram.[19] The Blunkett template of ruthlessness in the removal of asylum seekers has been followed by home secretaries ever since.

Forced removals to Somalia, Iraq and Afghanistan, Eritrea, Iran and Sudan proceeded in the teeth of UN condemnation of British returns to war zones.[20] Barely a year after the 2003 invasion of Iraq, Blunkett was threatening to defy UNHCR advice and return Iraqis 'to maintain the integrity of the asylum system',[21] and the following August, the first Iraqis were being rounded up for removal to the Kurdish-controlled north. Removals to the lawless and violent centre and south of the country resumed in October 2009, after the Tribunal ruled that the violence was not sufficiently intense to endanger ordinary returnees, although the Court of Appeal quashed the decision for applying too high a threshold of risk.[22] The first return flight to Baghdad ended in fiasco, with Iraqi immigration officers refusing to guarantee the safety of the 44 mainly Kurdish involuntary passengers, and returning 33 of them to the UK. This did not prevent the Home Office describing the operation as a 'success' when embarking on the next such flight, a joint charter flight with Sweden in March 2010,[23] and although the European Court stopped deportations to Iraq after the Campaign to Stop Deportations to Iraq and the International Federation of Iraqi Refugees documented beatings and detention of deportees on arrival,[24] they resumed despite warnings from UNHCR.[25]

Legal battles over forced returns to Zimbabwe, where Mugabe supporters were terrorising anyone suspected of 'disloyalty', led to a moratorium in 2002, but removals resumed in 2004, only to be suspended again following hunger strikes (Zimbabwean women at Yarl's Wood went on a month's hunger strike), press reports of ill-treatment on return and a high court stay. Following years of litigation over the safety of returnees,[26] immigration minister Damian Green announced a resumption of forced removals in 2010.[27] And as the world condemned Sudanese ethnic cleansing in Darfur, the Home Office was returning Darfuri refugees to at best, a life of misery and squalor in displaced persons' camps around Khartoum – a returns policy upheld by the Tribunal and by the House of Lords,[28] then suspended after interrogation and torture on return was confirmed. Returns to Khartoum resumed in 2008 and were abandoned once again following the execution of a returned activist in 2009.[29]

Similarly, forced returns to Somalia, suspended since the fall of Barré and the all-out civil war in 1991, were quietly resumed in 2004 although Somalia was then seen as 'the most dangerous country in the world' – and were suspended again only because Daallo Airlines, contracted to fly deportees from Dubai to Mogadishu, refused to take them.[30] When removals resumed, the Tribunal saw nothing wrong with refused asylum seekers having to hire armed militias to protect them on the dangerous route from the airport, and the Court of Appeal upheld its decision.[31] In 2011 the European Court ruled that decisions like these ignored or downplayed a mass of evidence of indiscriminate warfare, pervasive violence and human rights violations of such intensity as to jeopardise the lives of all civilians. The government has appealed the decision to the court's Grand Chamber.[32]

The European Court was forced to intervene to stop hundreds of deportations to Sri Lanka, which it ruled unsafe for Tamil refused asylum seekers in 2008.[33] Returns there resumed after the defeat of the Liberation Tigers of Tamil Eelam (LTTE), despite a UN report accusing the government of war crimes,[34] and allegations of torture from human rights groups.[35] MP Siobhain McDonagh's attempt to secure an emergency parliamentary debate on the deportations in June 2011 was overruled by the speaker.[36]

Despite attempts by campaigners, the government has always refused to monitor what happens to those returned to their countries of origin, even when allegations persist of ill-treatment of returnees. For years, campaigners have claimed that asylum seekers returned to the DRC are detained, interrogated and sometimes brutally ill-treated, allegations brushed aside by the Home Office and by the Tribunal. NGOs and small groups such as Justice First record the consistent testimony of returned asylum seekers trapped in a vicious circle of disbelief, their evidence dismissed as 'unreliable' because of their status as refused asylum seekers.[37] Even the concurring evidence of Congolese former immigration officials was rejected by the Tribunal in a 2008 'country guidance' decision which appears a model of wilful disbelief.[38]

... AND CHILDREN TOO

The inhuman logic of removal has not exempted children. Children on their own used to be protected from removal to their own country until their eighteenth birthday, because of the difficulty of finding anyone to receive or care for them on return. But for the past few years the government, with other European governments, has been seeking ways round this difficulty. In 2005 the Home Office proposed return and 'reintegration' of unaccompanied children to Vietnam.[39] Campaigners and lawyers demonstrated how threadbare such 'reintegration' would be. But in December 2009 the government announced it was conducting a 'feasibility project' on the return of lone children to 'a small number of Asian countries in the first instance'.[40] And a 'reintegration centre' was designed for teenage boys in Kabul, to enable them to be returned at 16 or earlier, despite the concerns of children's organisations. Human Rights Watch feared that the UK was 'developing a model of institutional care in an unstable country', without regard to children's best interests, 'for export' to other EU member states.[41]

Children travelling alone should not be redirected around Europe like parcels, and the Dublin regulation, which allots responsibility for processing asylum claims in the EU,[42] accepts this, saying their asylum claims should be decided where they are made. That has not stopped lone children being returned to European states where they had previously claimed asylum.[43] Thus, at four o'clock one morning in December 2009, a 16-year-old Eritrean girl was 'descended on by a posse of enforcement officers [and] bundled out',[44] taken to the airport and put on a plane to Italy, where she had previously been sexually assaulted and forced to work as a prostitute. In February a 15-year-old girl, also Eritrean, had been arrested and handcuffed at her foster-parents' home in the early hours and taken to the airport for removal to Italy. She successfully resisted removal. Neither girl was given any notice of their impending removal, something which provoked strong condemnation from the high court judge who, in February 2010, ordered the Home Office to bring the first girl back and suspended the policy allowing 'no-notice' removal of children.[45] In December 2011, Court of Appeal judges asked the ECJ to decide whether removal of children to the member state where they made an earlier asylum claim is lawful. Meanwhile, a 'gentlemen's agreement' going back to 1995 was revealed in November 2011 whereby children who failed to apply for asylum immediately after arriving in lorries at Dover docks or through the Channel Tunnel were sent straight back to France or Belgium, with no contact with social services or child protection staff. Children's commissioner Maggie Atkinson, who unearthed the agreement during an investigation into the treatment of child migrants, said the children included some who were being trafficked for exploitation and others fleeing war or persecution.[46]

DEPORTATION, FOREIGN OFFENDERS AND HUMAN RIGHTS

In April 2006, the Home Office revealed that in the seven years from 1999, over 1,000 foreign offenders had been released from prison after serving their sentence without being considered for deportation. The admission provoked a massive media and political furore which resulted in home secretary Charles Clarke's resignation.[47] Before he left, he changed the rules to create a presumption in favour of deportation of foreign offenders, and the following year a new law made deportation compulsory whenever a foreign offender was sentenced to 12 months (whether in one sentence or cumulatively), unless human rights considerations prevented it.[48] Many long-estab-lished and generally law-abiding residents were rounded up for deportation because of an offence committed years before. Ernesto Leal, a Chilean refugee who came to the UK with his family in 1977 at the age of 13, was one of them. On 1 May 2006, 30 police officers arrived at Leal's home to serve him with a deportation decision, and took him to Belmarsh maximum security prison. Four years earlier,

Leal had been sentenced to 42 months for grievous bodily harm with intent, following a brawl in a bar. He had served 18 months, mostly in an open prison, and on release had complied meticulously with the conditions of his licence. But after 29 years in the UK, he faced deportation for a one-off, out-of-character offence in an otherwise law-abiding and productive life.[49] Following a strong campaign the deportation threat facing Leal was lifted.

However, public opinion had been shifted so far to the right that it became axiomatic that 'foreign criminals' represented such a threat that they should be deported regardless of long residence or family ties, even though most were not the serious villains and dangerous sexual predators of modern folklore, but more often arrested for immigration crimes such as travelling on false documents, working illegally or even refusing to cooperate in their own removal.[50] The number of offenders deported more than doubled to 2,400 in 2006, and doubled again to 5,400 by 2008.[51]

Those who committed more serious crimes were frequently young adults who came as child refugees from Sudan, Somalia, Rwanda or the former Yugoslavia and, given no support to deal with their experiences of horror, exile and urban poverty, fell into a life of delinquency or vagrancy. One of those I represented on deportation appeals was a Rwandan teenager who had arrived aged ten with his mother and siblings. Traumatised, hating his cold new surroundings, mocked at school for his funny accent and not given any help to cope – his mother was suffering from post-traumatic stress – he began truanting, got involved in a street gang and committed several robberies. A four-year sentence in a young offenders' institution brought him the help he needed to rehabilitate and settle down, and at his appeal, neighbours and others formerly terrorised by him described his transformation into a respectful young man. But despite this evidence of rehabilitation, the Tribunal upheld his deportation at the age of 20 to Rwanda.[52] This young man, like many other damaged youngsters, was not given a second chance, but was instead treated as some kind of toxic waste, to be disposed of by deportation.

The Refugee Convention allows refugees to be sent home if they commit particularly serious offences and are a danger to the community.[53] UNHCR and refugee law commentators note that this is meant to apply only to the truly dangerous. But a law passed in 2002 ruled that any offence attracting a sentence of two years' imprisonment, or specified in regulations, was thereby 'particularly serious' and the offender was deemed a danger to the community.[54] The regulations listed hundreds of offences, from genocide and chemical warfare to shoplifting and criminal damage, as 'particularly serious crimes', and the new law gave offenders no room for argument. The parliamentary Joint Human Rights Committee said the regulations were incompatible with the Convention.[55] The law cried out to be challenged. In 2008, I was bawled out of court for suggesting to the Court of Appeal that holding a small quantity of drugs for a dealer was not a 'particularly serious crime' and the offender not necessarily a danger to the community. But the legal fight against the deportation of refugees for minor offences bore fruit the following year, when the appeal court accepted a legal challenge brought by a colleague for a Serbian former child refugee. He faced deportation following twelve months in a young offenders' institution for burglary. The court declared the regulations unlawful for authorising the deportation of refugees for relatively minor offences.[56]

The 'foreign prisoners scandal' fuelled the expansion of the prison estate, and led to the concentration of foreign offenders in a small number of prisons to serve their sentence so that deportation would be easier. In the process, family ties and access to legal help were ignored. Some prisons, designated 'hub prisons', would thenceforth contain only foreign offenders, institutionalising their segregation from the mainstream prison population. The plan was implemented in 2009 through a service agreement between the ministry of justice, UKBA and the National Offenders Management Service (NOMS), with no race equality impact assessment (a legal requirement), without consulting the prisons inspector[57] and in defiance of her criticism in 2006 that 'a national strategy for managing foreign national prisoners should not begin and end with the question of ... deportation' at the expense of welfare needs.[58] Despite these flaws, a high court challenged failed.[59]

The anti-human rights campaign by right-wing politicians and media has gained impetus under the coalition. Such is the hysteria engendered over foreign offenders and human rights that it has become increasingly difficult to argue for their rights to stay. The European Court's ban on the deportation of two Somali offenders because of the dangers they would face in Somalia caused media outrage.[60] Judges who allow deportation appeals on human rights grounds have been subjected to a barrage of ministerial criticism and media abuse. Home secretary Theresa May accused judges of being 'over-zealous' in their protection of the human rights of offenders and overstayers,[61] and, to the acclaim of right-wing Tories at the

2011 party conference, derided the judge who refused to authorise the removal of a Bolivian overstayer because of his pet cat. The story, which first appeared in the *Daily Telegraph* and *Daily Mail* months before, was a fabrication,[62] but undaunted, immigration minister Damian Green joined in, accusing the courts of distorting 'beyond all measure' the use of human rights, in particular family rights, against deportation.[63] Pronouncements from ministers, and from conservative lawyers such as Jonathan Sumption QC, a recent supreme court appointee who accused law lords of trespassing on parliamentary functions in human rights interventions,[64] add to the pressure on judges to back off.

Political pronouncements and media 'moral panics' signal legislative changes, such as the 'rebalancing' of family rights and deportation promised by May and Green in December 2011. Meanwhile, justice secretary Kenneth Clarke initiated a Council of Europe move to raise the threshold for intervention in deportation cases by the European Court.[65] The anti-human rights crusade is so strong that the British presiding judge Sir Nicholas Bratza complained of senior members of government fostering 'vitriolic' and 'xenophobic fury' against the Court, and the Council of Europe's Human Rights Commissioner warned the UK that weakening human rights protection would 'send a powerful signal to other states about what they can do tomorrow'.[66]

THE END OF 'COMPASSIONATE CIRCUMSTANCES'

The immigration minister has always had the power to allow people to stay for humanitarian or compassionate reasons, waiving the strict criteria of the immigration rules, in response to terminal or incurable illness or disability or compelling family circumstances. Hundreds of anti-deportation campaigns were built around this power, many of which succeeded. But the punitive climate which encourages the sweeping-up of the undocumented and offenders for deportation has had a dramatic impact on vulnerable people seeking to stay in the UK for life-saving medical treatment. With the advent of the Human Rights Act, exercise of the power became limited to cases where applicants' human rights – to dignity, freedom from inhuman or degrading treatment, and physical or psychological integrity – would be violated by removing them. In 1996, the European Court had given a landmark ruling, banning as inhuman treatment the deportation of a terminally ill AIDS sufferer to die on the streets of his native St Kitts, without support or comfort.[67] And in a 2000 case involving the deportation of an Algerian who suffered from schizophrenia, the Court accepted the principle that deportation to conditions which would exacerbate illness and cause acute anguish could breach the ban on inhuman or degrading treatment.[68] In response, the Home Office formulated a policy that removal would not be enforced where credible evidence indicated that, because of the medical facilities in the home country, return would shorten life expectancy and cause acute mental or physical suffering, where the UK had assumed responsibility for the person's care. The policy was tightened in 2001, and 'a complete absence of medical treatment' in the home country had to be shown. N's case tested this policy – to destruction.

N arrived in the UK in March 1998 seeking asylum after years of terror including kidnap and rape by the Lord's Resistance Army and the Ugandan authorities. She was very ill on arrival and was admitted to hospital, where she was diagnosed with aggressive cancer, tuberculosis, liver problems and advanced HIV/AIDS which had virtually destroyed her immune system. With chemotherapy and antiretroviral treatment, the virus was suppressed and eventually, by 2002, she was reasonably well, although she would continue to need antiretroviral drugs for life. By this time, HIV/ AIDS had been transformed, in the rich countries, from a death sentence to a chronic but manageable disease by the combination antiretroviral therapy N was receiving. The death rate was a fraction of what it had been in the early to mid-1990s. But with the large pharmaceutical companies charging around £10,000 per person per year for triple combination therapy, it was completely unaffordable in the countries of the south to all except the very wealthy. In Africa, as the infection took hold, death rates soared and average life expectancy plummeted – in some countries, to under 40. The production of generic versions of the branded drugs in India and elsewhere dramatically forced down the price of treatment, but big drug companies responded by prosecution for breach of intellectual property rights.[69] Although a global campaign by AIDS activist groups eventually shamed the companies into dropping such tactics, antiretroviral treatment remained unaffordable for most in the poor world, and even by 2009, fewer than half of Africans needing treatment were receiving it.[70]

N's asylum claim was refused and the adjudicator, while accepting the truth of her account, upheld the refusal, saying that the ill-treatment she had suffered was by 'rogue elements' and would not happen again. She argued that it would be inhuman to return her: the treatment she needed was not accessible in Uganda and without it, she would die within a matter of months in acute suffering as the illnesses she had suffered before treatment would re-emerge to overwhelm her damaged immune system. To remove her now would be like rescuing someone from drowning, drying them off, warming them up and then throwing them back into the sea. The adjudicator accepted that her return to Uganda contradicted Home Office policy and was inhuman, contravening Article 3 of the Human Rights Convention.

The Tribunal allowed the Home Office appeal, saying that treatment 'was available' in Uganda – an irrational conclusion on the evidence. N appealed, and I was instructed to represent the Terrence Higgins Trust (THT), a charity providing help to HIV/AIDS sufferers, as an intervener in the Court of Appeal. The court accepted that the Tribunal's conclusion was wrong, but ruled that the UK was not obliged to allow an HIV/AIDS sufferer, refused asylum, to stay to continue treatment, even if her removal would kill her. For the House of Lords' judicial committee, senior barrister Nick Blake QC and I lodged further evidence about the impact of HIV/AIDS in Africa. N herself had lost five of her six siblings to the disease. The judges wanted to know how many African HIV/AIDS sufferers THT was assisting in the UK. The answer was somewhere in the low thousands. But our figure was not quoted in the judgments – it was the Home Office barrister's reference to twenty-five million HIV/AIDS sufferers in Africa which the judges cited, as if every AIDS sufferer in that continent would flock to Britain if N's appeal was allowed. In their judgments, the law lords adopted the numbers-driven, fearful approach of the government. 'The Convention gives no right to stay in order to continue to benefit from medical treatment', they said. Removal of HIV/AIDS sufferers would only breach the Human Rights Convention in 'exceptional' circumstances (when someone was on the point of death), so the prospect of a fatal relapse some months later in the home country, and a painful and distressing death caused by lack of treatment, was not enough to prevent removal.[71]

The decision in N's case, subsequently upheld by the European Court,[72] stunned migrant groups, human rights lawyers and AIDS activists. Many AIDS sufferers who had previously been allowed to stay received notice of removal. The case put paid to most appeals based on compassionate circumstances. If it would not breach someone's human rights to send them back to conditions which would kill them, it was hard to imagine circumstances when a claim based on illness could succeed. We kept trying. I recall bitter arguments with hard-faced immigration judges over the removal of mothers whose death would leave their young children orphans with no obvious means of support. We had many clients from Zimbabwe, where, amid political violence and rampant corruption, inflation running at 100,000 per cent, a raging cholera epidemic, townships in Harare bulldozed to disperse government opponents, a near-total collapse of the health system and a massive food shortage, there was evidence that what food and medicines there were went to ZANU-PF members only. This evidence of discriminatory denial of medication meant success for one claimant,[73] but the Tribunal later found that the evidence of discrimination was not strong enough to allow other Zimbabwean HIV/AIDS sufferers to stay.[74] Generally, it was only in cases where children had the virus or were otherwise in danger of dying that appeals could be won[75] – and not without a fight, even in these cases. When an immigration judge allowed the appeal of a Ghanaian HIV-positive woman with two UK-born infant children, both of whom had serious health problems, the Home Office appealed, saying he should not have considered the human rights of the appellant's children.[76] Another low point was reached when in January 2008, mother-of-two Ama Sumani was taken from her hospital bed in Cardiff, where she was receiving cancer treatment, and deported to Ghana, where she died three months later.[77]

THE MECHANICS OF REMOVAL

The despair felt by many refused asylum seekers, overstayers and ex-offenders facing involuntary return is often exacerbated by the manner of their removal. In some cases it involves offensive and racist, sometimes violent treatment. It can start with a sudden irruption of uniformed men into a home in the early hours of the morning; it can mean losing possessions and having no chance to say goodbye to friends. Frequently it involves detention, and almost always involves sitting in the back of a caged van for hours. I describe below some of these manifestations of institutionalised inhumanity, and some legal and extra-legal responses.

Suicide as 'Manipulation'

Traumatised and vulnerable individuals, told that they are to be removed, are sometimes so distressed that they attempt suicide. The IRR documented 28 suicides between 2006 and 2010 by those receiving notice of deportation. Hundreds more injure themselves: in 2009 alone, 215 people needed hospital treatment for self-injury, including a ten-year-old girl held at Tinsley House removal centre at Gatwick, a 19-year-old who set fire to himself outside the UKBA office in Leeds, a Congolese man who slit his throat in Campsfield, a 51-year-old Algerian who doused his clothes with petrol intending to set fire to himself outside his local MP's office and a 34-year-old Afghan who banged his head repeatedly on the wall of his cell, breaking three vertebrae in his neck.[78] Occasionally, the distress is such that mothers have threatened to harm their children. But these desperate acts evoke no compassion or comprehension; they are treated instead as manipulative behaviour. In a case involving the removal of a suicidal Ivorian woman to France, the Home Office barrister argued that 'to create a *de facto* rule that anyone attempting suicide will not be removed would be to encourage asylum seekers to make suicide attempts'.[79] The risk of suicide could, he said, be averted by physically restraining her. This argument won the day, the judge ruling that the woman could be removed. The Court of Appeal accepted in that case that the increased risk of suicide prevented her removal.[80] But in later cases, the courts accepted the Home Office approach of managing the risk by medication or physical constraints.[81]

'No-notice' Removal

Ever since the home secretary was held to be in contempt of court in 1993 for removing a failed asylum seeker in breach of an undertaking to the court,[82] senior judges have watched Home Office conduct of removals carefully. In 2007, the Home Office curtailed the normal 72-hour notice of removal (the minimum period necessary for legal advice and assistance to be obtained) for people who might react to the notice by attempting suicide or self-harm. In January 2010 the policy of abridging notice of removal was extended to parents who might react by threatening to harm their children, lone children who might abscond, or detainees who might disrupt 'good order and discipline'. Immigration officers were swooping late at night or first thing in the morning and taking people direct to the airport, effectively denying them access to justice.

There had already been severe judicial criticism of Home Office conduct towards refused asylum seekers, particularly those who made fresh claims based on fresh evidence or changed circumstances. It was common Home Office practice in the early 2000s to fail to respond for years to these new claims, and then to swoop at night or at the weekend, serve a document refusing the claim (which could be challenged only by judicial review in the high court) and simultaneously notify claimants of their imminent removal and take them to an airport removal centre. This process appeared calculated to deprive those concerned of any possibility of legal advice or assistance to challenge the decision.[83] It happened to Mr Karas, who waited for three years for a response to his fresh claim, reporting weekly to the Home Office in the meantime. He and his pregnant wife were explicitly prevented from contacting their solicitor when seven immigration officers came for them at 8.30 one night, telling them the claim had been refused and that they were booked onto a flight for Croatia the following morning.[84] The judge found officials' actions were for the 'improper purpose [of] spiriting away of the claimants from the jurisdiction before there was likely to be time for them to obtain and act upon legal advice or apply to the court'.[85] In another context law lord Johann Steyn had described a Kafkaesque state as one of 'hole and corner decisions or knocks on doors in the early hours'. 'That is not our system', he said.[86] But it was an apt description of Mr Karas' case, and those like it. The judge found 'at best an unacceptable disregard by the Home Office of the rule of law, at worst an unacceptable disdain by the Home Office for the rule of law, which is as depressing as it ought to be concerning'.[87]

In Mr Karas' case, 'no thanks to the Secretary of State or his minions',[88] the couple managed to contact their solicitor from the airport at 1.30 a.m., and the solicitor stopped the removal. But in many cases, removal has gone ahead; people have been sent back to fearsome situations because they have been denied a meaningful opportunity to challenge it, and the high court has had to issue an increasing number of orders requiring the Home Office to bring people back to the country. Some have disappeared and cannot be brought back.

Campaigns to demand the end of dawn raids on families for removal included local neighbourhood patrols in Scotland to protect families from raids, and a 'dawn raid' on a Glasgow UKBA office.[89] These actions, and the judicial condemnation of Home Office conduct, led to the policy of 72 hours' notice of removal. So the curtailment of this minimum period in 2007 and 2010 meant effective denial of access to a court for those affected. In July 2010, in a challenge brought by Medical Justice, the high court ruled that any curtailment of the 72-hour notice was unlawful, as it failed to ensure access to justice.[90] Former home secretary David Blunkett accused judges of 'colluding in creating new technical loopholes'.[91]

Judges, he said, had 'no answers' and should leave immigration matters to parliament.

Use of Force

The death of Jimmy Mubenga on a British Airways flight about to leave Heathrow for Angola in October 2010 made front-page news. Mubenga had lived in the UK lawfully for 20 years, working as a fork-lift driver; he had a wife and five children here, four of whom were born here, but a nightclub brawl led to a 24-month sentence for actual bodily harm, and a decision to deport him. Passengers said he was heavily restrained by the G4S guards escorting him, and repeated 'They're going to kill me' and 'I can't breathe' before collapsing.[92] But for campaigners, and for concerned employees of the huge contractor, the routine use of dangerous restraints, the lack of training and the culture of force made death – someone's death – inevitable sooner or later. Months before, the *Independent* newspaper had uncovered a variety of painful techniques authorised to restrain deportees, including 'nose control', 'head control' and 'goose neck' wrist lock, the use of 'rigid bar', 'chain link' and double-locked handcuffs and of leg restraints.[93] Positions such as 'carpet karaoke' – pushing a deportee's head down between his legs as he was strapped in to his seat, were commonly used despite the risk of suffocation, because they were effective in shutting deportees up – if they made too much noise, pilots might refuse to fly, removal could be aborted and escorts would lose pay. Staff were thus under financial pressure to ensure successful removals by any means necessary.[94] Following the death, many other allegations of excessive force were made against G4S,[95] and it lost the removals contract to Reliance, another huge security company.

Yet brutality is endemic to deportation. Until the death in 1993 of Jamaican Joy Gardner, bound and gagged with 13 feet of sticky tape, the police had carried out most deportations.[96] After the arrest and (unsuccessful) prosecution of the three officers involved, the police sought to hand over responsibilities for deportation to the immigration service, which subcontracted them to private companies. But allegations of brutality multiplied. A Medical Foundation study in 2004 found gratuitous force used in 12 of 14 attempted removals, and called for automatic medical examination of all individuals subject to failed deportation attempts and for the investigation and prosecution of perpetrators.[97] Neither recommendation was followed. A 2005 BBC film showed degrading treatment of people en route to and at the airport, and led to the installation of CCTV cameras in escorts' vans.[98] A 2008 report by lawyers and doctors described 'systematic' physical and racial abuse.[99] And a prisons inspectorate report on Tinsley House removal centre in July 2009 referred to force being used on children during removal of a family.[100]

And still, no lessons appeared to have been learned from Mubenga's death. When prisons inspector Nick Hardwick inspected removals to Jamaica and Nigeria in March and April 2011, his findings included use of forceful restraint for longer than necessary, and the use by some staff of 'highly offensive and sometimes racist language between themselves'. Hardwick expressed disappointment that he needed to 'call on UKBA to ensure that detainees are treated decently at all times, with no physical or verbal abuse, throughout their journey and when they arrive'.[101] The call appears to have fallen on deaf ears: in July 2011 Amnesty International found continuing use of excessive force, including deportees being dropped down aircraft steps, strangled and beaten, causing broken limbs and other injuries.[102] In October 2011, a Nigerian woman claimed she was beaten on her chest and legs, had her hair pulled, her hand twisted and her throat seized during an attempted so-called 'family friendly' removal with her three young children following a 5.30 a.m. raid by ten or twelve officials.[103]

Passengers on commercial flights sometimes try to intervene. A journalist complained when deportation guards held a girl round the neck and paraded a handcuffed woman dressed in only her underwear. She was threatened and told she was 'obstructing government business'.[104] Other passengers who have complained about the treatment of deportees have said they were thrown off a flight.[105]

Charter Flights

Some campaigners believe that specially chartered deportation flights were introduced so that force could be used on deportees without interference from members of the public. Their use certainly increased when violent deportations were in the news and deportees and campaigners were achieving some success in disrupting flights and putting pressure on commercial airlines to stop taking deportees. In 2007, home secretary John Reid complained that nearly 1,200 deportations had been aborted in the previous two years because of 'disruption', leading to pilots refusing to take them.[106]

Charter flights not only confer invisibility on deportations, but also enable mass expulsion, as they can carry as many as 60 deportees, with two or more guards per deportee. Military aircraft from air bases such as Brize Norton in Oxfordshire are sometimes used, but more often, it is commercial charters such as Inflite, operating from civilian airports (although deportees are not treated to the executive frills such companies advertise). The Home Office refuses to publish a list of its removal and escort contractors, citing commercial confidentiality. Mass deportation, like mass detention, is becoming big business, providing large profits for the main corporate players, and employing thousands in low-paid 'escort' jobs. In 2010, UKBA organised 67 charter flights, at a total cost of £10.3 million (£4,800 per passenger), removing people to Iraq, Afghanistan, Sri Lanka, Nigeria, DRC and other destinations. Deportees from the UK are picked up on joint EU deportation flights too, since the adoption of an EU Council Decision in April 2004. In 2010, the EU's border management agency Frontex organised 38 joint charter flights involving returns from several EU states to Africa (mainly Nigeria), Iraq and elsewhere.

When charter flights are announced, refugee and solidarity groups converge in protests and sometimes in direct action, risking arrest as they blockade removal centres to stop the vehicles which take deportees to the airport. Like the Tamils who stripped off to prevent their removal in 1987 to make time for a legal challenge, direct action sometimes goes hand in hand with legal challenges to removals, which have multiplied. Although they can be brought only on behalf of individuals, not whole groups of passengers, many succeed and deportees are taken off the flights for their claims to be reconsidered. UKBA's strategies to ensure that charter flights leave as planned, with all seats full, have included writing to the high court a few days beforehand to dissuade judges from intervening, and taking 'reserve deportees' to the airport to replace any whose challenges to removal succeeded. The latter practice was condemned by the prisons inspector as 'objectionable and distressing'.[107]

11
Enemies of the State

In some parts of the world national security has on occasions been used as an excuse for all sorts of infringements of individual liberty. But not in England. (Lord Denning)[1]

In 1976, a young American investigative journalist, Mark Hosenball, found himself facing deportation for 'obtaining for publication information harmful to the security of the United Kingdom'. Particulars of the allegation were not forthcoming. Appearing before an advisory panel, dubbed the 'three wise men', who reviewed the decision but whose findings did not bind the Home Office, he had no idea what information they had, so could not rebut it. Hosenball challenged the subsequent deportation order on grounds of denial of natural justice – the right to know details of the allegation against him so as to be able to challenge it effectively. The Court of Appeal rejected his claim, holding that rights to natural justice had to take second place to the security of the realm. 'We cannot allow our men's lives to be endangered by foreigners', said Lord Denning.[2]

Over 35 years later, with the 'three wise men' replaced by the Special Immigration Appeals Commission, national security deportees, nearly all Muslim men,[3] still face a system where fundamental principles of justice – including the presumption of innocence, equality of arms, the right to know what is said against them – are routinely violated. The secrecy that shrouds the intelligence services has been breached in places, but not for those facing deportation, exclusion or denial of citizenship on national security grounds. Worse, there does not have to be any specific allegation; it might just be their associations or their reading matter which makes them a 'danger' to national security. And what constitutes such a danger has been stretched beyond imagining.

It should not have been like this. In 1967, the Wilson committee had advised that national security cases need not be excluded from the immigration appeal system it recommended be set up.[4] 'Special arrangements' could be made for such cases, but there was 'no question of withholding from the appellant particulars of what is alleged against him'. So appeals against national security deportation (in technical parlance, on the ground that the person's 'presence in the UK is not conducive to the public good for reasons of national security') were heard in the Immigration Appeal Tribunal. But secret evidence was adduced in a 1969 case, and in 1971, the Tribunal's jurisdiction to hear these appeals was abolished and the advisory panel set up. It was described by former US attorney-general Ramsey Clark as 'utterly lawless'.[5] In 1991, the shibboleth of national security was used to deny justice to over a hundred Iraqis and Palestinians, detained for deportation during the first war against Iraq on standardised grounds reciting that 'your known links and activities in connection with the Iraqi regime make your presence in the UK an unacceptable security risk'. Later it transpired that the MI5 files on which the arrests were founded were inaccurate and outdated. Abbas Cheblak, a Palestinian moderate with a public history of opposition to Saddam Hussein, sought judicial review of his deportation, only to be told that 'the court cannot interfere in matters of national security', and besides, he could appeal to the panel.[6] At these 'appeal' hearings, lawyers were denied the necessary time to prepare their cases and were not permitted to see their clients before the hearings or to speak to the panel on their behalf – and of course no particulars of the allegation were given, and no Home Office witnesses called. The hearings lasted 40 minutes on average, and Cheblak's six witnesses were allowed two minutes each.[7]

'DEMOCRACIES DIE BEHIND CLOSED DOORS'[8]

The 'three wise men' system was abolished in 1997 following condemnation from the European Court in a case brought by Karamjit Singh Chahal. Chahal was a Sikh activist settled in the UK who was detained in Bedford prison for over six years while he fought deportation as a 'terrorist' on allegations of funding Punjabi militants. The ECtHR ruled that the advisory panel lacked the essentials of a court and failed to provide protection for national security deportees.[9] SIAC came into being in 1998 as a response to that ruling. It was headed by a high court judge and its other two members were a senior immigration judge and a lay member (generally with security services experience). Its decisions bound the Secretary of State. But from the start its priority – the protection of state secrecy – hobbled it as a vehicle for justice. Its location in a gloomy basement off Chancery Lane, claustrophobic and with no natural light, seems to symbolise its role and function.

In SIAC appeals, neither the men facing deportation nor their lawyers see evidence or allegations deemed not disclosable for national security reasons. Instead, a government-appointed 'special advocate' represents the appellant's interests in 'closed' sessions. But the requirement for secrecy means that the special advocate – the only person, apart from Home Office lawyers and the judges, who knows the allegations in detail – cannot put them to the appellant to ask for his comments.[10] And ignorance of why he has been assessed as a threat means the appellant cannot clear himself.

This lack of disclosure was condemned by the supreme court as unfair and in breach of basic rights to fair trial in the parallel system of control orders, devised in 2005 as an alternative to internment for those perceived as threatening national security but who, either because they are British or because of the risk of torture in their home country, cannot be deported.[11] As a result, the system of appeals against control orders was modified to ensure that appellants are given the gist of the allegations, enough to be able to rebut them.[12] But those facing deportation are deemed not entitled to fair trial rights.[13] And the secrecy is not limited to evidence and allegations whose disclosure is said to harm national security. The use of secret evidence about the risks of torture for returnees to Algeria was upheld by the House of Lords, even though it breached an explicit ministerial assurance given when the Bill creating SIAC was going through parliament. The law lords accepted the Home Office argument that disclosure to appellants of British government assessments might harm the relationship between the UK and Algeria (or other torturing states).[14] But the lords' later acceptance that appellants' witnesses fearing reprisals for testimony of torture could be given a guarantee of total confidentiality was fiercely resisted by the Home Office, which argued for its right to check such evidence with the relevant authorities.[15] Recently, the battle for disclosure has resulted in partial success; appellants seeking bail must be told the gist of reasons for security services' objections, so they can argue for their release.[16] But detailed reasons and evidence underlying deportation decisions may still be withheld.

DEFERENCE AND RISK

The regime of secret allegations and secret evidence in SIAC is rendered even more grotesquely unfair by the untrammeled power of the home secretary to make 'national security' mean anything he or she wants it to mean. SIAC allowed its very first appeal, by

Shafiq ur Rehman, who was alleged to have provided support for insurgents in Kashmir. Even if he had done so, which the SIAC judges doubted, they ruled that it had nothing to do with the UK's national security. The Court of Appeal and the House of Lords' appellate committee slapped SIAC down hard. They ruled that SIAC 'is not entitled to differ from the opinion of the Secretary of State' on whether specified activities were contrary to the interests of national security, which might include actions directed against a third state.[17] So raising money for the liberation struggle in Kashmir or Palestine may be construed as a threat to the UK's national security, since the targeted country might retaliate against British interests, and if the Home Office chose to treat it as such, SIAC could not disagree. This was not only a massive extension of the common-sense meaning of 'national security', as Brian Barder, the lay member who brought security service expertise to SIAC explained when he resigned,[18] but also represented a huge abdication of judicial functions in favour of executive power. The lords' further ruling that someone might *be a danger* to national security despite having committed *no actions which endangered* national security completed the judicial abdication.[19]

The judgment in Rehman's case was a body blow to SIAC's independence. Barder commented: 'It is difficult to see what functions are left for SIAC ... These rulings give [the Secretary of State] such wide discretion as to make his powers virtually unaccountable.'[20] A number of senior lawyers appointed as special advocates resigned over the next couple of years, stating they did not want to legitimise a system designed solely to rubber-stamp unfair decisions,[21] and the feistiness and independence of SIAC under its first chair, Sir Andrew Collins, gave way to a more risk-averse, executive-minded culture with his successors. In very few appeals since *Rehman* has SIAC rejected the security services' assessment.[22]

MOSAICS OF SUSPICION

The difficulties for those seeking to establish their innocence were demonstrated in SIAC's 2003 judgment on several Algerian 'suspected international terrorists' alleged to have connections with Al Qaeda.[23] Al Qaeda was, they ruled, 'a loose-knit body', which 'makes it the more difficult to identify its members and supporters'. Extremists included 'those who are lying dormant for specific tasking from bin Laden as well as those who have been instructed to establish themselves in the country against a future occasion when they are needed'. And support for terrorism can include provision of false documents or accommodation. So a Muslim going to the mosque, participating in nothing at all, could be a terrorist 'sleeper', while one offering hospitality or worse, a false document, or giving money to Palestinian, Chechnyan or Algerian resistance movements could be actively encouraging terrorism.[24] SIAC decided that Home Office suspicions of the men were justified. But as their solicitor Gareth Peirce pointed out (the quote is SIAC's summary of her evidence):

> [T]he provision of financial help ... was a primary duty of Islam ... The ordinary activities involved in fundraising and sending money to contacts in Chechnya was a worthy cause ... The possession and production of false documentation was an inherent part of the existence of being a refugee and assisting others to become refugees ... The provision of shelter and assistance in travel are necessary parts of everyone's life.[25]

Home Office lawyers have said that national security decisions tend to be based on a 'mosaic' of fragments of intelligence and information, which might relate to travel, acquaintance, study and financial transactions. Some Algerians I represented on deportation appeals had been arrested by anti-terrorist police because they played football with a man who was convicted of terrorist fundraising. One man's friendships with men who travelled to Somalia formed the basis for his deportation in the open case against him.[26] Another was put under a control order after living in Syria for a year, where he studied at the university of Damascus,[27] and others were picked up for attending the same mosque as known or suspected extremists. For the Libyans who fought deportation and ended up with control orders, it seemed that mere membership of or connection with the Libyan Islamic Fighting Group sufficed. Perhaps membership of any group with 'Islamic' in the title is enough for a file to be opened.

In these 'mosaics', pieces are arranged to fit a pattern based on preconception, prejudice and the familiar 'culture of disbelief'. Taking photographs of London landmarks, correspondence about arranged marriages, going from one telephone box to another and driving the wrong way home have all been seen as evidence of terrorism-related activity. The SIAC judges believed that one man, who went to Pakistan to do work on his family home, booked but cancelled another trip to Pakistan the following year and did an overland trip to Turkey two years later, was trying to get to a terrorist training camp in Afghanistan, although they accepted he had never been to the country.[28] Everything he did, including undertaking a TEFL course and keeping in touch with classmates, was seen through the distorting lens of suspicion.

It was this distorting lens that led to Husein Al Samamara's arrest for deportation and his six-year fight in the appeal courts. A Jordanian Palestinian, he was arrested by anti-terrorist police in 2004, questioned for four days about the somewhat bloodthirsty terms of a will pinned up in his kitchen, and a CD-Rom containing a widely available 'terrorist handbook', and released without charge. Two years later (and three days after his wife had given birth by caesarian to the couple's first child) he was arrested again, this time for deportation. I applied for bail for him a couple of months later, and the judges showed sympathy for his bereft wife, coping alone with the baby, but said they could not release him, nor could they tell us why. He spent the next two years in HMP Long Lartin, where he learned to make model sailing ships and mosques from matchsticks to pass the time,[29] and at the time of writing had been on bail for another nearly four years while his appeal against deportation wended its way through the courts – but the only 'open' evidence against him remained the will and the CD-Rom that he had been questioned about seven years before.[30]

The replacement of objective evidence of criminal conduct by the subjective assessment of risk led to men who had been acquitted by the criminal courts being re-arrested for deportation. A group of Algerians, dramatically arrested in January 2003 for a conspiracy to produce ricin, a strong poison made from castor oil beans, to commit a 'bio-terrorist' outrage, were acquitted or had all charges dropped when it transpired two years later that there was no trace of ricin on any of the items seized (a fact known to government departments within days of the men's arrest).[31] The allegations turned out to have come from statements under torture in Algeria by an alleged co-conspirator, and were rejected as unreliable by the criminal court. But the acquittals meant nothing to the Home Office, or to SIAC, who dismissed the appeals of all but one of them. The jury's verdict simply meant that the allegations had not been proved, not that the suspicions of the security services were unreasonable – and SIAC did not need proof, only reasonable suspicion.

But the *Rehman* judgment, given in the immediate aftermath of 9/11, also gave the green light to the Secretary of State and the security services to broaden their territorial focus – which justified working closely with intelligence services of repressive 'friendly' states, exchanging intelligence on individuals and, as we subsequently learned, cooperating with rendition and on occasion organising delivery of the regime's enemies to them.[32] The use of evidence obtained by torture abroad became inevitable, despite violating international obligations under the UN Convention Against Torture. In 2003 SIAC refused to exclude the use of torture evidence in its assessment of appellants' danger to national security,[33] and the Court of Appeal agreed. The House of Lords' appellate committee outlawed its use – but only on proof that it was so obtained, the majority held, which as Lord Bingham pointed out, was virtually impossible, since torturers 'do not boast of their trade'.[34] Another dissenter, Lord Nicholls, complained that the majority were merely paying lip service to the principle of exclusion of torture evidence. And years later, the Lords upheld the return of Islamist cleric Omar Othman (known as Abu Qatada) to face trial in Jordan on evidence obtained by the torture of others.[35] When its judgment (overruling the Court of Appeal) was in turn overruled by the European Court as violating both fair trial and anti-torture provisions of international law, prime minister David Cameron told the ECtHR to stop behaving like a 'small claims court', as if adherence to the most important international legal obligations of all was of minor importance compared with the sovereign right to deport undesirables.[36]

DEPORTATION TO TORTURING STATES

Back in 1996, in Mr Chahal's case, the European Court vetoed the deportation of terrorist suspects to a real risk of torture; it would, the court ruled, breach Article 3 of the Human Rights Convention, no matter what danger they presented to national security.[37] The judgment infuriated the government, which has constantly sought to overturn it, arguing (so far unsuccessfully) that the right not to be returned to torture should be conditional, not absolute.[38] After the demise of internment as a way of managing undeportable foreign terror suspects, the Blair government embarked on the conjuring trick of diplomatic assurances, which opened the way to deportation of the men who couldn't be deported because of the serious risk of torture.[39] The assurances rendered 'safe' the most unsafe of deportations – even as bail was refused on the grounds that the men's fear of torture on return made them likely to abscond.[40] SIAC – and the higher courts – were content with the flimsiest of assurances from torturing states. With the exception of Libya; even

SIAC balked at returning alleged members of the Libyan Islamic Fighting Group to such fragile protection.[41] But even the European Court of Human Rights bowed to their use in Abu Qatada's case.[42]

EXPANSION OF SECRECY

Both Labour and Tory governments have sought to extend secret evidence procedures – to parole board hearings,[43] inquests into 'sensitive' deaths[44] and to civil actions. Government lawyers argued that disclosure of evidence revealing Binyam Mohamed's torture and British security officials' knowledge of it would endanger Britain's relationship with 'friendly' states and thus the flow of information vital to the fight against terror, but were overruled by the Court of Appeal.[45] They argued for a secret procedure in the civil claim for damages brought by the Guantánamo detainees, to avoid disclosure, and when the court ruled against them, settled the claim by paying the men.[46] Even the Cameron government's official inquiry into complicity with torture, headed by retired judge Sir Peter Gibson and abruptly called off in January 2012, was to have been conducted largely in secret, leading ten human rights and detainee groups to boycott the proceedings for their lack of credibility.[47] And a green paper of October 2011 proposed extension of the 'closed material procedure' of SIAC to any civil action.[48] Lawyers, including many who act as 'special advocates' in SIAC, overwhelmingly opposed the plans as an unnecessary denial of fundamental rights of natural justice.[49]

DEPRIVATION OF CITIZENSHIP – BY STEALTH[50]

At the same time, citizenship has become harder to get – but much easier to lose. In 2002, the so-called 'Hamza amendment'[51] changed the law so as to allow dual-national British citizens to be stripped of their British citizenship 'if the Secretary of State is satisfied that the person has done anything seriously prejudicial to the vital interests of the United Kingdom'.[52] Not only did these provisions apply to citizens by birth, who could not previously be deprived of citizenship, but the grounds for deprivation were both broader and fuzzier than the old provisions which required 'act or speech ... disloyal or disaffected towards her Majesty', or trading with the enemy.[53]

However, there was worse to come for British Muslims suspected of support for terrorism or radicalism. In 2004, a tiny, undebated amendment to the British Nationality Act of 1981, tucked away in a schedule of another Act, removed vital protection against injustice. The amendment read 'omit subsections (6) to (8)' of section 40A'. Few, if any, took the trouble to find out what it meant – until British Muslims notified of a decision to strip them of citizenship found their British passports cancelled immediately. Previously, the implementation of such decisions had always been suspended pending appeal. The practical effect of this change has been hugely exacerbated by the Secretary of State's practice of waiting until someone targeted for removal of citizenship goes abroad. Once out of the country, he is served with notice of intention to deprive him of citizenship, and immediately afterwards, with notice that he is no longer a British citizen.[54] An exclusion order bans him from returning to the UK. The Home Office simultaneously notifies ports and airports that the person is not to be readmitted if he tries to return. Sometimes notices have been sent to the home address in the UK, and those affected have known nothing until they try to come back. Exclusion from the country makes exercise of appeal rights virtually impossible, while the impact on families, in particular children who have spent their lives in the UK, and wives who must choose exile with husbands or separation from them – can only be imagined.

Between 2007 and the end of 2010, eight people had their British passports cancelled in this way,[55] and lawyers know of at least four more in 2011. Meanwhile in 2006, the threshold for deprivation was dramatically lowered. No longer was it necessary to show that the UK's vital interests had been seriously prejudiced; removal of citizenship merely had to be 'conducive to the public good' – the same test as for deportation. The combination of the two measures enabled the government to strip Australian Guantánamo detainee David Hicks of his British citizenship the day after its grant, ordered by a court on grounds of his mother's British citizenship.[56] Needless to say, the secret evidence regime applies here too, as it does for those refused naturalisation on national security grounds.[57] The ease and lack of accountability with which citizenship can be removed means that British Muslims with dual nationality can never feel secure in their British citizenship. And in 2012, in a horrific development, Bilal el-Berjawi, a London Muslim stripped of his citizenship while abroad, was killed by a US drone – extrajudicially executed – in Mogadishu, hours after a call from his wife in London telling him she had given birth to his son. The family believe the call pinpointed his location for the drone attack.[58]

FIGHTING FOR THE RULE OF LAW

Deportation, denial or deprivation of citizenship on national security grounds require no more than suspicion of undesirable activity or associations, and none allows its subject a fair trial where the evidence can be properly challenged. In the past decade, the rule of law has taken a severe battering, as time and time again the executive has pushed the boundaries of permissible conduct. Parliament has been supine for the most part, allowing draconian intrusions and the removal of safeguards without blinking. Lord Steyn, an upholder of human rights as a law lord, reminded us that 'even totalitarian states mostly act according to the laws of their countries'.[59] 'The greater the arrogation of power by a seemingly all-powerful executive which dominates the House of Commons', he said, 'the greater the incentive and need for judges to protect the rule of law.'[60] The judges, particularly the law lords, have a mixed record, sometimes defending the rule of law against executive encroachment and legislative illegality (in rulings against internment, the use of torture evidence and excessive secrecy in control order cases), but bowing to the executive in most deportation cases. By and large it has been left to groups such as the Campaign against Criminalising Communities (CAMPACC), the Coalition against Secret Evidence (CASE), Cageprisoners, the IRR, Peace & Progress and Helping Households under Great Stress (HHUGS), working with campaigning journalists such as Andy Worthington, human rights organisations and lawyers, to expose and resist injustice in the exclusion and removal of those deemed undesirable.[61]

Abbreviations

ACLEC	Lord Chancellor's Advisory Committee on Legal Education and Conduct
AIT	Asylum and Immigration Tribunal
ALO	airline liaison officer
BID	Bail for Immigration Detainees
CARF	Campaign Against Racism and Fascism
CAS	confirmation of acceptance for study
CG	Country Guidance (applied to Tribunal cases)
CPS	Crown Prosecution Service
CRC	UN Children's Rights Convention
CRE	Commission for Racial Equality
DFT	detained fast track
DNSA	detained non-suspensive appeal
DPP	Director of Public Prosecutions
DSS	Department of Social Security
ECHR	European Convention on Human Rights and Fundamental Freedoms
ECtHR	European Court of Human Rights or 'European Court'
ECJ	European Court of Justice
EEA	European Economic Area
EDM	Parliamentary Early Day Motion
FCO	Foreign and Commonwealth Office
FGM	female genital mutilation
HAC	House of Commons Home Affairs Committee
HMCIP	Her Majesty's Chief Inspector of Prisons
HSMP	Highly skilled migrants programme
IAA	Immigration Appellate Authority
IAS	Immigration Advisory Service
IAT	Immigration Appeal Tribunal
ICIBI	Independent Chief Inspector of Borders and Immigration
ILM	immigration liaison manager
ILPA	Immigration Law Practitioners' Association
IRC	Immigration removal centre
JCWI	Joint Council for the Welfare of Immigrants
LSC	Legal Services Commission
NASS	National Asylum Support Service
NCADC	National Coalition of Anti-Deportation Campaigns
PBS	points-based system
RMJ	Refugee and Migrant Justice
RWLG	Refugee Women's Legal Group
SAL	standard acknowledgement letter
SIAC	Special Immigration Appeals Commission
SSHD	Secretary of State for the Home Department

TUC	Trades Union Congress
UKBA	United Kingdom Border Agency
UKIAS	United Kingdom Immigrants Advisory Service (precursor of IAS)
UNHCR	United Nations High Commissioner for Refugees
UTIAC	Upper Tribunal (Immigration and Asylum Chamber)

CASE REPORTS

AC	Appeal Cases (House of Lords/ Supreme Court)
ECHR	European Court of Human Rights reports
EHRR	European Human Rights Reports
EWCA Civ	Court of Appeal (Civil Division)
EWCA Crim	Court of Appeal (Criminal Division)
EWHC Admin	High Court (Administrative Court)
HLR	Housing Law Reports
Imm AR	Immigration Appeal Reports
INLR	Immigration and Nationality Law Reports
QB	Queen's Bench (high court)
UKAIT	Asylum and Immigration Tribunal (precursor of UT)
UKHL	House of Lords (appellate committee)
UKIAT	Immigration Appeal Tribunal (precursor of AIT)
UKSC	Supreme Court
UKUT (IAC)	Upper Tribunal (Immigration and Asylum Chamber)
WLR	Weekly Law Reports

Notes

The cases cited in the notes are available at www.bailii.org.
All website references were accessed in March 2012.
My own unreported cases are referred to by initial, country if appropriate and year.

INTRODUCTION

1. Refugees, in law, are people who are outside their own country and unable or unwilling to return owing to well-founded fear of persecution on grounds of race, religion, nationality, membership of a particular social group or political opinion. Refugees are recognised, not created, by the grant of refugee status; many refugees remain unrecognised, either because they do not apply for asylum or because they are wrongly refused. Asylum seekers are people who seek recognition and protection as refugees.
2. *R (Q and others)* v. *SSHD* [2003] EWHC 195 (Admin), para 56.
3. See e.g. Zygmunt Bauman, *Globalization: the human consequences*, Cambridge: Polity, 1998.
4. Loitering with intent to commit an arrestable offence, s. 4 Vagrancy Act 1824, which was heavily used to control the movements of young black people in the 1970s until its abolition in 1981.
5. E. P. Thompson, *Writing by candlelight*, London: Merlin, 1980.
6. See A. Sivanandan, 'Imperialism in the silicon age', in *Catching history on the wing: race, culture and globalisation*, London: Pluto, 2008.
7. See Sivanandan, 'Poverty is the new black', in *Catching history*.
8. Zygmunt Bauman, *Modernity and the holocaust*, Cambridge: Polity, 1989, cited in Simon Pemberton, 'A theory of moral indifference: understanding the production of harm by capitalist society', in Paddy Hillyard *et al.* (eds), *Beyond criminology: taking harm seriously*, London: Pluto, 2004.

CHAPTER 1

1. 'Racism 1992', *Race & Class*, Vol. 30, No. 3 (1989).
2. Also known as Sonia, David died tragically in 2010. For an appreciation see IRR News, www.irr.org.uk, 4 November 2010.
3. In the case of *Amuur* v. *France* (1996) 22 EHRR 533, the French government argued that the 'waiting zone' at the international airport was not part of French territory, but the European Court of Human Rights ruled that it was and that asylum seekers held there had to be provided with the guarantees of French law.
4. *SM* (1992).
5. Here and throughout this chapter I refer to 'refugees' in a generic rather than a legal sense, as people in flight from persecution, war or other disaster. Many undocumented migrants fit this description; see e.g. Shahram Khosravi, *'Illegal*

traveller': an auto-ethnography of borders, Basingstoke: Palgrave Macmillan, 2010.

6. See A. Sivanandan, 'Sri Lanka: racism and the politics of underdevelopment', *Race & Class*, Vol. 26, No. 1 (1984); 'Ethnic cleansing in Sri Lanka', IRR News, 9 July 2009.
7. *The Times*, 29 May 1985.
8. *Searchlight*, July 1985.
9. HL Deb. 5 November 1992, cols 1561–72.
10. HC Deb. 18 November 1999, col. 4W.
11. Sixty-four Tamil asylum seekers arrived together and sought asylum. Six were granted exceptional leave to remain (ELR).
12. The men were eventually removed following further legal challenges, although a number of them won an out-of-country appeal and were able to return to the UK as refugees through the efforts of their solicitors, David Burgess and Chris Randall, who went to Sri Lanka to monitor their treatment on return.
13. HC Deb. 17 February 1987, cols 769–70. Quoted by Gerald Kaufman MP at HC Deb. 16 March 1987, col. 715.
14. HC Deb. 16 March 1987, cols 710–12. Ironically, those claiming asylum after arrival were later condemned as bogus and targeted for removal of benefits: see Chapters 2 and 6.
15. HC Deb. 16 March 1987, col. 730.
16. Carrier sanctions were applied across the EU by the Carriers' Liability Directive, 2001/5112.
17. 'Trapped in "le jungle" – but still dreaming of El Dorado', *Guardian*, 4 July 2009. Shahram Khosravi describes a similar journey in *'Illegal' traveller: an auto-ethnography of borders*, Basingstoke: Palgrave Macmillan, 2010.
18. The sanctions were ruled unlawful in the case of *International Transport Roth GmbH v. SSHD* [2002] EWCA Civ 158 because of lack of legal safeguards for hauliers, but they were reinstated with safeguards in the Nationality, Immigration and Asylum Act 2002.
19. 'French police clear the "jungle" migrant camp in Calais', *Guardian*, 22 September 2009.
20. Asylum statistics 1997, Home Office RDS, http://rds.homeoffice.gov.uk/rds/asylum.html.
21. At a European summit: *CARF* 4 (1991). At the Conservative party conference in 1991, home secretary Douglas Hurd said an Asylum Bill was a top priority to curb bogus asylum seekers, and he, Kenneth Baker and John Major spoke of asylum seekers as a 'tidal wave' and 'immigration catastrophe' (*CARF* 5, 1991).
22. Protocol to prevent, suppress and punish the crime of trafficking, UN Doc A/55/383, adopted by resolution A/RES/55/25, 15 November 2000.
23. See John Morrison, 'The dark side of globalisation: the criminalisation of refugees', *Race & Class*, Vol. 43, No. 1 (2001).
24. *R v. Toor* [2003] EWCA Crim 185.
25. 'My God, I had no idea!'
26. *R v. MP* (1995).
27. *MH (Sudan)* (2008).
28. *R v. SSHD ex p Khawaja* [1984] AC 74, the leading case on illegal entry.
29. The appellate committee of the House of Lords, the precursor of the supreme court.

30. *R* v. *Naillie, R* v. *Kanesarajah* [1993] AC 674. The Lords held that migrants did not 'enter' the UK until they passed immigration control.
31. Police figures released in March 1994 showed that racial violence had doubled in five years. There was a spate of firebomb attacks against migrants and refugees. In 1995 politicians including home secretary Michael Howard inveighed against 'bogus asylum seekers' and in January 1996 Howard went to India and Pakistan to tell their populations not to claim asylum in Britain. *CARF* 20, 22, 26, 30 (1994–96).
32. Immigration Act 1971 s. 25A, inserted by Asylum and Immigration Act 1996, substituted by Nationality, Immigration and Asylum Act 2002.
33. See 'Criminalising solidarity', *CARF* 31 (1996).
34. Case files; see also 'Aiding illegal entry laws must go', *CARF* 50 (1999).
35. Council Directive of 20 November 2002 defining the facilitation of unauthorised entry, transit and residence, Council Framework Decision 2002/629/JHA on the strengthening of the penal framework to prevent the facilitation of unauthorised entry, transit and residence, OJ L328, 5 December 2002.
36. Select Committee on European Scrutiny, 25th and 26th report, 3 May 2002, HC 152–xxv and xxvi, paras 11.9ff; Frances Webber, *Border wars and asylum crimes*, London: Statewatch, 2006.
37. See Harmit Athwal, 'Captain criticised for bringing refugees to Felixstowe', IRR News, 16 June 2005. UNHCR commended him. Fishermen and refugee activists in Germany and Italy have been prosecuted for rescuing refugees in distress at sea and landing them.
38. Liz Hales, *Refugees and criminal justice*, Cambridge: Cambridge Institute of Criminology, 1996. Richard Dunstan, analysing arrests of refugees at Heathrow *en route* to Canada or the US in 'Breaches of Article 31 of the 1951 Refugee Convention', *International Journal of Refugee Law*, Vol. 10, Nos. 1/2 (1998), p. 205, cites 53 arrests at Heathrow in the financial year 1993–94, 126 for 1994–95 and 376 for 1995–96, from HC Deb. 30 October 1996, col. 146WA. Although the figures diverge, they confirm the dramatic upward trend.
39. 'The price of asylum', *CARF* 47 (1998); John Morrison, *The cost of survival: the trafficking of refugees to the UK*, London: Refugee Council, 1998.
40. For the distinction between refugees and asylum seekers see Introduction, note 1.
41. *R* v. *Uxbridge Magistrates' Court and others ex p Adimi and others* [1999] EWHC Admin 765, para. 12.
42. *Adimi*, para. 48.
43. *Adimi*, paras 1, 3.
44. *Adimi*, paras 17–18. The demand that refugees claim asylum in the first safe country they reach is not supported by UNHCR or by refugee lawyers who drafted the Convention. But this demand underlies the Dublin Convention 1990 and the Dublin Regulation 2003 ('Dublin II'), informal agreements to return refugees to transit countries and a whole raft of legislation and case law in the UK, built up since the late 1980s. See Chapter 3.
45. *Adimi*, para. 15.
46. It became section 31 of the Immigration and Asylum Act 1999.
47. 'Asylum error to cost millions', *Guardian*, 2 October 2003.
48. *R* v. *Asfaw* [2008] UKHL 31.

49. 'The criminals who aren't: getting the record corrected', IRR News, 19 March 2009.
50. *R* v. *AM* [2010] EWCA Crim 2400.
51. Asylum and Immigration (Treatment of Claimants, etc.) Act 2004, s. 2.
52. Home Affairs Committee, 1st report 2003–4, 16 December 2003, HC 109, paras 11–22.
53. HL Deb. 5 April 2004, col. 1630.
54. Ibid., cols 1627, 1630.
55. *Statewatch*, Vol. 13, No. 6 (2003).
56. *R* v. *Navabi and Embaye* [2005] EWCA Crim 2865.
57. *Soe Thet* v. *DPP* [2006] EWHC 2701 (Admin).
58. *R* v. *Rudolph Alps* [2001] EWCA Crim 218.
59. Under the Sangatte Protocol 1991 and 2000 Additional Protocol (for Eurostar, introduced in June 2001 for France), Le Touquet Treaty (for ferries).
60. Draft Nationality, Immigration and Asylum Act 2002 (Juxtaposed Controls) Order 2003, 8th Standing Committee, 25 June 2003, www.publications. parliament.uk/pa/cm200203/cmstand/deleg8/st030625/30625s01.htm.
61. The map of current ILM locations is at www.ukba.homeoffice.gov.uk/ sitecontent/documents/aboutus/transportindustry/rlon_network_map.pdf.
62. The statutory foundation had been laid by the Immigration and Asylum Act 1999 s. 1 and the Immigration (Leave to Enter and Remain) Order 2000, SI 2000/1161, which allowed immigration officers abroad to grant or refuse leave to enter the UK.
63. An international public interest law organisation which monitors the situation of Roma in Europe and provides legal assistance in upholding Roma rights.
64. *European Roma Rights Centre* v. *Immigration officer Prague Airport and another* [2004] UKHL 55.
65. Immigration and Asylum Act 1999 s. 18; Immigration (Passenger Information) Regulations 2000, SI 2000/912.
66. The legal framework is now the Immigration, Asylum and Nationality Act 2006 ss 32–8 and the Immigration Act 1971 Sch. 2 paras 27, 27B, 27C (as amended and inserted in 1999, 2004 and 2006).
67. 'E-Borders: overview for technology suppliers', UKBA website, www.ukba. homeoffice.gov.uk/.
68. The e-Borders project was meant to be processing 60 per cent of passenger movements to (and from) the UK by December 2009, and 95 per cent by December 2010 (HC Deb. 25 February 2008, col. 1258W), but it has been delayed by technical problems, and the main contractor, Raytheon, was sacked in 2010 and IBM appointed to run another pilot. For more on e-Borders see 'e-Borders plan to tackle "threats"', *Statewatch*, Vol. 15, Nos. 3/4 (2005), 'Pilot prevented arrival of 3,000 passengers May–July 2008', *Statewatch*, Vol. 18, No. 4 (2008).
69. See Liz Fekete, 'From refugee protection to managed migration', *European Race Audit*, No. 43 (2003).
70. UNITED for Intercultural Action, which counts documented deaths at the EU's borders, has calculated that nearly 10,000 people have drowned trying to reach Europe. The true number is likely to be much larger, since many are listed in news reports as 'missing, presumed dead'. See Fortress Europe's interactive map, 'A deadly exodus', available at http://owni.eu/2011/03/04/ app-fortress-europe-a-deadly-exodus. See also Leanne Weber and Sharon

Pickering, *Globalization and borders: death at the global frontier*, Basingstoke: Palgrave Macmillan, 2011.

71. See *CARF* 25 (1994).

72. Liz Fekete, 'The human cost of illegal entry', IRR News, 1 October 2001; 'Spain/Morocco: migrants shot dead at the border fence, Spain deploys army', Statewatch News Online, October 2005.

73. See 'Deaths at Europe's borders, *Race & Class*, Vol. 43, No. 4 (2002); Sharone Backers, 'Risking it all', *Race & Class*, Vol. 43, No. 1 (2001); Liz Fekete, 'Death at the border: who is to blame?', IRR News, 23 July 2003; Webber, *Border wars*.

74. *CARF* 35, 37, 40 (1996–98).

75. 'Remember the Dover 58', *CARF* 57 (2000).

76. The 2002 white paper *Secure borders, safe haven: integration with diversity in modern Britain*, Cm. 5387, proposed processing refugees selected by UNHCR in sites abroad, to prevent unlawful entry. The Gateway scheme was introduced in 2004. Designed to bring only 1,000 particularly vulnerable refugees to the UK annually, it has never met its numerical target.

77. Report of Working Party on a solidarity structure (burden sharing) of the Group of Senior Ministers entrusted with the follow-up to the Conference of Ministers on the movement of persons coming from central and eastern European countries (Vienna Group), Strasbourg, 3 June 1993, cited in Frances Webber, *Crimes of arrival*, London: Statewatch, 1995. See also 'New border regime at Bug river', *Statewatch*, Vol. 13, No. 1 (2003); 'From refugee protection to managed migration: the EU's border control programme', *European Race Audit*, No. 43 (2003); Emre Ertem, 'Virtual walls in the south-east: Turkey on its way to Schengen', *Statewatch*, Vol. 18, No. 4 (2008).

78. See 'The era of global "migration management" begins', *CARF* 54 (1999); 'Exporting Fortress Europe', *Statewatch*, Vol. 15, No. 2 (2005); Jerome Valluy, Migreurop, 'European policies for Morocco', *Statewatch*, Vol. 19, No. 1 (2009); Yasha Maccanico, 'The internal and external fronts: security package and returns to Libya', *Statewatch*, Vol. 19, No. 3 (2009).

79. 'Escape from Tripoli: report on the conditions of migrants in transit in Libya', Fortress Europe (2008). See also 'Dirty dealing with Qaddafi', IRR News, 3 March 2011.

80. Yasha Maccanico, 'EU: controls, detention and expulsions at Europe's borders', *Statewatch*, Vol. 20, Nos. 3/4 (2010).

81. The full title of Frontex is the European Agency for the Management of Operational Cooperation at the External Borders of the Member States of the European Union. Established in October 2004, it became operational in October 2005, using personnel from each member state. Its budget has rocketed from around €6.3m in 2005 to €87m in 2010. For criticism of Frontex' human rights record see *The EU's dirty hands: Frontex involvement in ill-treatment of migrant detainees in Greece*, New York: Human Rights Watch, September 2011.

82. See e.g. Vassilis Tsiamos, 'Notes on the high-tech industry of European border control: migration control and the arms industry in EU security research policy', *Statewatch*, Vol. 19, No. 3 (2009).

83. There are frequent allegations of failure to rescue travellers in difficulty, see '63 refugees left to die at sea after NATO aircraft carrier fails to respond', *Irish Times*, 9 May 2011.

84. *Hirsi Jamaa v. Italy* (27765/09), February 2012. The case was brought by 24 Somali and Eritrean migrants who were among the 200 migrants forced back to Tripoli by Italian military vessels in 2009. By the hearing, lawyers had lost contact with all but six applicants and two had died. Several human rights groups intervened in the case in their support. The case report quotes from many critical human rights reports on interception including *Pushed back, pushed around: Italy's forced return of boat migrants and asylum seekers, Libya's mistreatment of migrants and asylum seekers*, New York: Human Rights Watch, 2009. See also *Frontex Agency: which guarantees for human rights?* Paris: Migreurop, May 2011.

85. An estimated 14,000 refugees, including Libyans and Tunisians but also many Eritrean and Somali, fled to Italy and Malta up to May 2011, with another 1,200 missing, presumed drowned. 'Hundreds risk return to Libya in bid to reach Europe by boat', Geneva: UNHCR, 17 May 2011. The website *Migrants at sea*, http://migrantsatsea.wordpress.com/tag/migreurop/, has links to all these reports.

86. 'Unsafe in Libya, unwanted in Europe', *Independent*, 18 May 2011.

87. These states have not signed the 1967 protocol, which extended the Convention's geographical scope beyond Europe.

CHAPTER 2

1. 'Border staff humiliate and trick asylum seekers – whistleblower', *Guardian*, 2 February 2010.

2. Letter to *The Lancet*, 21 April 1979, quoted in Steve Cohen, *Immigration controls, the family and the welfare state: a handbook*, London: Jessica Kingsley, 2001.

3. See Cohen, *Immigration controls*; Southall Black Sisters website, www.southallblacksisters.org.uk; *Guardian*, 3 February 1979, www.guardian.co.uk/uk/2010/feb/03/airport-virginity-tests-banned.

4. *Immigration control procedures: report of a formal investigation*, London: Commission for Racial Equality, 1985. Home Office notes reproduced as appendices to the report reveal the institutional racism underlying the procedures.

5. *R v. SSHD ex p Honegan* (1995), case files.

6. Quoted in *No easy options: irregular immigration in the UK*, London: Institute for Public Policy Research, 2011.

7. In 1998, one-fifth of the 49,000 Nigerians seeking entry for visit or study were refused (a visa requirement was imposed in 1986). In 2005, nearly 80 per cent of visa applications from young (18–30) Nigerians were refused, and in April 2005 a one-year ban on new applicants in this age group was imposed: 'UK visa delay for young Nigerians', BBC News, 11 April 2005. In 2009, over 50 per cent of applications for entry clearance at Abuja were refused.

8. *R v. SSHD ex p Sunalla* (CO/2362/98).

9. *Landing in Kent: the experiences of unaccompanied children arriving in the UK*, London: Office of the Children's Commissioner, 2011.

10. *Body of evidence: treatment of medico-legal reports for survivors of torture in the UK asylum tribunal*, London: Freedom from Torture, 2011.

11. *Independent*, 16 December 2000.

12. *R v. SSHD ex parte Gurmeet Singh* [1987] Imm AR 489.

13. *R* v. *SSHD ex parte Bugdaycay and Musisi* [1987] AC 514.
14. *Gaima* v. *SSHD* [1989] Imm AR 205; *ex parte Thirukumar* [1989] Imm AR 402.
15. *Vilvarajah* v. *UK* (1991) 14 EHRR 248. In the event the European Court ruled that judicial review before removal was an effective remedy against refusal of asylum.
16. From the 1970s to 2005 appellants appealed to adjudicators and from there to the Immigration Appeal Tribunal (IAT). In 2005, the two-tier system was replaced by the Asylum and Immigration Tribunal (AIT), staffed by immigration judges. In 2010 the two-tier system was restored as the First Tier Tribunal (Immigration and Asylum Chamber) (FTTIAC) and the Upper Tribunal (UTIAC).
17. *R* v. *SSHD ex parte Sivakumaran* [1988] AC 958, HL.
18. Lord Bingham, 'The judge as juror: judicial determination of factual issues', *Current Legal Problems*, Vol. 38, No. 1 (1985), Catriona Jarvis, 'The judge as juror revisited', *Immigration Law Digest* (Winter 2003).
19. Immigration judges' decisions 'should be respected unless it is quite clear that they have misdirected themselves in law': Lady Hale, *AH (Sudan)* v. *Home Secretary* [2008] 1 AC 678, para. 30.
20. M. Akram, *Where do you keep your string beds?* London: Runnymede Trust, 1974.
21. See e.g. Dr Juliet Cohen, 'Errors of recall and credibility: can omissions and discrepancies in successive statements reasonably be said to undermine credibility of testimony?', *Medico-Legal Journal*, Vol. 69, No. 1 (2001), pp. 25–34 (reproduced as a Medical Foundation paper); S.J. Anderson, G. Cohen and S. Taylor, 'Reviewing the past: some factors affecting the variability of personal memories', *Applied Cognitive Psychology*, No. 14 (2000), pp. 435–54.
22. See e.g. J. Herlihy, S. Turner and P. Scragg, 'Discrepancies in autobiographical memories – implications for the assessment of asylum seekers: repeated interviews study', *British Medical Journal*, 9 February 2002, pp. 324–7.
23. *R* v. *Secretary of State for the Home Department ex p Ejon* [1997] EWHC Admin 854.
24. *DS (Angola)* (1999).
25. *BS (Sudan)* (2000).
26. *ST (Libya)* (2006).
27. *YS (Iran)* (2001).
28. *MN (Iran)* (2002).
29. *WM* (1998). The Tribunal and the higher courts have tried to curb immigration judges' reliance on such thinking, as it is so patently daft.
30. *BM and GO (Kenya)* (1998).
31. *MB* (1996); *ST (Libya)* (2006).
32. *TJ (Iran)* (2000); *MY (Sudan)* (2002) (the high court reopened the case on judicial review).
33. *PG (Ivory Coast)* (1999).
34. See text and note 37 below.
35. This is a very frequent reason for rejection of claims.
36. I have seen this frequently in Colombian claims, where paramilitaries send their targets notices of their own funeral before killing them.

37. Asylum and Immigration (Treatment of Claimants) Act 2004 s. 8. This went further than the immigration rules (HC 395 para. 341) which set out similar behaviour which *may* damage credibility.
38. *SM (Iran)* [2005] UKAIT 116; *JT (Cameroon)* v. *SSHD* [2008] EWCA Civ 878.
39. See *No reason at all: Home Office decisions on asylum claims*, London: Asylum Aid, 1995; *Adding insult to injury: experiences of Zairean refugees in the UK*, London: Asylum Aid, 1995; *Still no reason at all*, London: Asylum Aid, 1999; *A betrayal of hope and trust*, London: Medical Foundation, 1995.
40. See e.g. *HK* v. *SSHD* [2006] EWCA Civ 1037.
41. Regular reports are produced on 20 countries (previously 35), with occasional reports on others.
42. *AA (Iran)* (1995); *G (Iran)* (2000).
43. *Beyond belief: the Home Office and Nigeria*, London: Refugee Council, 1995.
44. Natasha Carver (ed.), *Home Office country assessments: an analysis*, London: IAS Research and Information Unit (2003).
45. See *Shirazi* [2003] EWCA Civ 1562. The country guidance system was criticised as inimical to individual justice in *Country guideline cases: benign and practical?* London: IAS, 2005.
46. *Karanakaran* v. *SSHD* [2000] EWCA Civ 11.
47. *S and others* [2002] EWCA Civ 539.
48. *DK (Iraq)* [2006] EWCA Civ 682; *BK (failed asylum seekers, DRC) CG* [2007] UKAIT 98, upheld at [2008] EWCA Civ 1322.
49. *Drrias v SSHD* [1997] Imm AR 346.
50. *LP (LTTE area, Tamils, Colombo risk?) Sri Lanka CG* [2007] UKAIT 76.
51. *MD (Ivory Coast)* v. *SSHD* [2011] EWCA Civ 989.
52. *AM (Cameroon)* [2008] EWCA Civ 100. The facts are set out in detail at [2007] EWCA Civ 131 (when permission to appeal was granted).
53. *R (Saribal)* v. *SSHD* [2002] EWHC 1542 (Admin).
54. The remit of Medical Justice also embraces campaigning around poor health care and brutality in immigration detention.
55. *Adding insult to injury.*
56. Stephanie Harrison case file. The Tribunal upheld the decision, but the high court quashed it.
57. *Mibanga* v. *SSHD* [2005] EWCA Civ 367.
58. *Body of evidence.*
59. In fact, as the Istanbul Protocol indicates, the assessment of consistency between asylum seekers' accounts and their injuries is central to the physician's role.
60. *R (on the application of B)* v. *Special Adjudicator* [2002] EWHC 1469 (Admin).
61. *Mibanga* v. *SSHD* [2005] EWCA Civ 367.
62. *Body of evidence.* Previous surveys include Rhys Jones and Verity Smith, 'Medical evidence in asylum and human rights appeals', *International Journal of Refugee Law*, Vol. 16 No. 3 (2004), pp. 381–410.
63. UKBA, Handling torture claims, non-detained pilot, July–October 2011, Freedom from Torture, www.freedomfromtorture.org.uk/document/referrals/5445.
64. Jack Straw, HC Deb. 11 December 1995, col. 719.
65. *B (Nigeria)* (1995).

66. Now that the Czech Republic, Slovakia, Poland, Hungary and Romania are in the EU, Roma have free movement and do not need to claim asylum. But anti-Roma racism has emerged in deportation drives in several EU states. See e.g. 'EU to raise citizen expulsion policy at September meeting', *EU Observer*, 23 August 2010.

67. The UN Committee for the Elimination of all forms of Racial Discrimination (CERD) report of March 1998 on the Czech Republic, CERD/C/304/Add.47, referred to a six-fold increase in racial attacks, slow investigations, few charges or convictions, harassment and excessive force against Roma. Its 2001 report, CERD/C/304/Add.109, referred to the degrading treatment of minorities by the police. UNHCR's 1999 *Guidelines relating to the eligibility of Czech Roma asylum seekers* said police were sometimes openly sympathetic to skinheads, and the cumulative severe discrimination and violent attacks could amount to persecution.

68. *Horvath v. Secretary of State for the Home Department* [2001] AC 489, a majority judgment. It was strongly criticised by judges in other jurisdictions, e.g. the Australian High Court in *Khawar* [2002] HCA 14, and by UNHCR.

69. *CARF* 57 (2000).

70. *Harakal v. SSHD* [2001] EWCA Civ 884.

71. See e.g. *Police against black people*, London: Institute of Race Relations, 1979; *Policing against black people*, London: Institute of Race Relations, 1987.

72. History repeats itself: in June 2011, a charter flight forcibly returned 26 Tamil refused asylum seekers just days after a Channel 4 documentary, *Sri Lanka's killing fields*, revealed atrocities against Tamils in the aftermath of the civil war.

73. *CARF* 61, 62, 63 (2001).

74. Home Office asylum statistics.

75. Under the Race Relations Amendment Act (now the Equality Act 2010), passed after the Macpherson Inquiry found institutional racism in the police response to the death of Stephen Lawrence.

76. See 'Secret race discrimination', Free Movement, at www.freemovement.org.uk/2011/05/31/secret-race-discrimination/.

77. *RB (Linguistic analysis: Somalia)* [2010] UKUT 329.

78. See John Campbell, 'Language analysis in the United Kingdom's refugee status determination system: seeing through policy claims about "expert knowledge"', *Ethnic and Racial Studies* (2012), dx.doi.org/10.1080/014198 70.2011.634506.

79. *AM (Somalia)* (C5/2009/2370) and others.

80. 'Nationality swapping: isotope analysis and DNA testing – pilot', UKBA Asylum process guidance, www.bia.homeoffice.gov.uk/sitecontent/documents/policyandlaw/asylumprocessguidance/specialcases/guidance/nationality-swapping-DNA-testing?view=Binary.

81. See Genomics Network, Human Provenance Pilot Project resource page, at www.genomicsnetwork.ac.uk/cesagen/events/pastevents/genomicsandidenti-typoliticsworkstream/title,22319,en.html.

82. The asylum policy instructions (API), asylum process guidance, immigration directorate instructions (IDI) are in the 'policy and law' area of the UK Border Agency website, along with country-specific asylum policy and country of origin information.

83. Following the case of *R (Dirshe) v. SSHD* [2005] EWCA Civ 421.

84. *Down and out in London: the road to destitution for rejected asylum seekers*, London: Amnesty International, 2006.

85. This was criticised by John Vine, Independent Chief Inspector of Borders and Immigration, in *Asylum: getting the balance right: a thematic report*, London: ICIBI, 2010. In the Case Resolution Directorate, set up to deal with the backlog of so-called 'legacy' cases, the standard training on asylum, human rights and the immigration rules was just seven days.

86. Under a public service agreement, UKBA contracted to conclude 90 per cent of claims within six months by December 2011. 'Conclusion' meant either the grant of status or removal from the country; *Asylum: getting the balance right*.

87. The IAC, chaired by a former Court of Appeal judge, was set up in association with the Citizens' Organising Foundation following calls from community groups for an authoritative examination of the asylum process. See *Fit for purpose yet?* London: IAC, March 2008.

88. See e.g. *Breaking down the barriers: a report on the conduct of asylum interviews at ports*, London: ILPA, 1999; *Improving the quality of immigration advice and representation*, London: ACLEC, 1998.

89. Jane Apsden, *Evaluation of the Solihull Pilot for the UKBA and the Legal Services Commission*, UKBA, October 2008.

90. See API, 'Early legal advice project guidance', UKBA website, www.ukba. homeoffice.gov.uk/sitecontent/documents/policyandlaw/asylumpolicyinstructions/apis/elap-midland-and-east?view=Binary.

CHAPTER 3

1. *Refusal factory: women's experiences of the detained fast track process at Yarl's Wood Immigration Removal Centre*, London: BID, September 2007.

2. 'The law will continue to be unjust until it is as easy to get an entry certificate in Bombay as it is in Paris', Jo Richardson MP, HC Deb. 19 December 1975.

3. *R v. Secretary of State for the Home Office ex parte Phansopkar* [1976] QB 606.

4. 'Patrials' were UK and Colonies citizens with ancestral connections to the UK and their Commonwealth wives, under the Immigration Act 1971 as originally enacted.

5. *CARF* 24 (1995).

6. *Asylum and Immigration Appeals*, Home Affairs Committee, 2nd report 2003–4.

7. The policy decision to postpone processing of the old claims was ruled unlawful: *R (S) v. SSHD* [2007] EWCA Civ 546.

8. *CARF* 66 (2002).

9. Statement of changes of immigration rules HC 394 as amended, para. 350.

10. *S (Iran)*, March 2007.

11. *Landing in Kent.*

12. *Benkaddouri v. SSHD* [2003] EWCA Civ 1250.

13. *R v. SSHD ex p Deniz Mersin* [2000] EWHC (Admin) 348.

14. *Fast and fair? A report by the Parliamentary Ombudsman on the UK Border Agency*, Parliamentary and Health Service Ombudsman, February 2010.

15. *Shala v. SSHD* [2003] EWCA Civ 233.

16. *EB (Kosovo) v. SSHD* [2009] 1 AC 1159.

17. Under the Dublin Convention 1990 and the Dublin Regulation 2003, which allocated responsibility for deciding asylum claims, generally to the first member state reached by the asylum seeker.

18. Only the presence of minor refugee children or (for children) refugee parents in the UK would stop return to the transit country.

19. Case notes.

20. The Immigration and Asylum Act 1999 s. 11, now the Asylum and Immigration (Treatment of Claimants) Act 2004 Sch. 3.

21. Germany gave refugee status to a tiny percentage of Kosovans fleeing ethnic cleansing in the late 1990s, while all were recognised as refugees in the UK – but Kosovans coming to the UK from Germany were returned there until the Court of Appeal woke up to the huge disparity; see *R v. SSHD ex p Gashi* [1999] Imm A.R. 415. Some EU states refused to accept refugees from non-state persecution, such as Somalis. Disparities like these have lessened since the EU Qualification Directive of 2004, and differences of interpretation of the Refugee Convention can now be litigated in the ECJ at Luxembourg.

22. *MSS v. Belgium and Greece*, (2011) 53 EHRR 2, *NS and others*, C-411/10, ECJ 21 December 2011. For the suspension of removals see HL Deb. 7 June 2011, col. 88WA.

23. Claims from these countries would be certified 'clearly unfounded', and went through an accelerated process, appeals had to be lodged within two days and heard in five, and there was no further appeal to the Tribunal if the certificate was upheld.

24. KPMG Peat Marwick, *Review of Asylum Appeals Procedure: final report*, Home Office/Lord Chancellor's Department, December 1994. See *Statewatch*, Vol. 5, No. 2 (1995).

25. *The Asylum and Immigration Bill 1996: report of the Glidewell Panel*, April 1996. The organisations which set up the panel produced a report, *Providing protection* (1997), many of whose recommendations were subsequently implemented – but not those calling for an end to fast track procedures.

26. See Asylum and Immigration Act 1996 s. 1; Asylum (Designated countries of origin and designated third countries) Order 1996, SI 1996/2671.

27. *R v. SSHD ex p Javed and Ali* [2000] EWHC (Admin) 7, upheld at [2001] EWCA Civ 789.

28. Immigration and Asylum Act 1999 s. 65. An appeal on race discrimination grounds was added in 2000, but has been rarely used because of difficulties of proof and the fact that proving discrimination does not invalidate the immigration decision.

29. Home Office press release 059/00, March 2000.

30. *Statewatch*, Vol. 5, No. 3 (1995).

31. *R (Saadi) v. SSHD* [2002] UKHL 41, upheld by the ECtHR in *Saadi v. United Kingdom* (2008) 47 EHRR 17; see Chapter 8 below.

32. *R (Refugee Legal Centre) v. SSHD* [2004] EWCA Civ 1481.

33. DFT and DNSA intake selection (AIU instruction), www.ukba.homeoffice. gov.uk/sitecontent/documents/policyandlaw/asylumprocessguidance/detention/ guidance/dftandnsaintekeselection?view=Binary. Labour aimed to process a third of claims that way: see *Controlling our borders: making migration work for Britain – five year strategy for asylum and immigration*, Home Office, February 2005.

34. *Fast track asylum determination procedures: how best to represent your clients*, London: ILPA, November 2005.
35. *Fast tracked unfairness: detention and denial of women asylum seekers in the UK*, New York: Human Rights Watch, February 2010.
36. *Fast track to despair*, London: Detention Action, June 2011.
37. See *Working against the clock: inadequacy and injustice in the fast track system*, London: BID, July 2006.
38. *Refusal factory: women's experiences of the detained fast track asylum process at Yarl's Wood Immigration Removal Centre*, London: BID, September 2007.
39. Personal communication, 2006.
40. Nationality, Immigration and Asylum Act 2002 s. 94, with interim provisions in s. 115 covering asylum claims made before the Act was passed.
41. The avowed aim was to reduce asylum claims from these countries, and Lord Brett said that claims from listed countries were reduced by an average of 49 per cent in the first year after listing: HL Deb. 9 February 2010, col. GC147.
42. *R (ZL and VL) v. SSHD* [2003] EWCA Civ 23.
43. A challenge to the legality of including Gambia was dismissed in *R (MD Gambia)* v. *SSHD* [2011] EWCA Civ 121, although the Court of Appeal accepted that Gambia frequently failed to respect human rights.
44. Nigerian men only were listed in the NSA (non-suspensive appeal) process.
45. Nationality, Immigration and Asylum Act 2002 s. 94 (as amended); the original ten states were removed when they joined the EU and their citizens gained free movement rights.
46. Letter from UKBA to Refugee Council, 25 January 2010 on the revised Asylum Procedures Directive.
47. Personal communications, 2000.
48. Case file, 2000.
49. The utter inaccessibility of Home Office caseworkers by phone has been a constant complaint for over two decades, and a BBC survey found that 70 per cent of calls to the Home Office were unanswered or abandoned: see 'Government helplines slow to pick up', BBC News, 13 May 2010.
50. Case file, April 2001.
51. Rules prescribed that notices telling appellants the date of the hearing were 'deemed' received whether they actually arrived or not, and hearings were to go ahead without appellants who failed to appear. Time limits for further appeals were tight and non-extendable: Asylum Appeals (Procedure) Rules 1996 rr. 42, 33, 13 respectively.
52. Appeals were taking over a year to be listed for hearing.
53. The 'deemed service' rule: see *Saleem* v. *SSHD* [2000] EWCA Civ 186. The government injected some flexibility into time limits for second-tier appeals in the Immigration and Asylum Appeals (Procedure) Rules, SI 2000/2333.
54. *R* v. *SSHD ex p Anufrijeva* [2003] UKHL 36.
55. 'Asylum unit "prevents claimants from lodging cases"', *Guardian*, 30 September 2011. See also note 49 above.
56. See UKBA website, 'How to claim asylum', www.ukba.homeoffice.gov.uk/asylum/claimingasylum/howtoclaim/. This makes clear that no help will be given for travel costs.
57. Josie Appleton and Manick Govinda, *UK arts and culture: cancelled, by order of the Home Office: the impact of new restrictions on visiting artists and*

academics, Manifesto Club, 2009; 'Overseas artists boycott Britain in protest at visa clampdown', *Observer*, 10 July 2011.

58. Policy on this has changed since 2004, when applicants could submit forms completed in their own languages provided they had translations prepared if the case went to appeal.

59. UKBA, 'Fees for our services', www.ukba.homeoffice.gov.uk/aboutus/fees/#.

60. See the Independent Chief Inspector's reports on Abu Dhabi, Amman and Istanbul (2010, 2011), available at http://icinspector.independent.gov.uk/.

61. UKBA Business Plan 2011–15.

62. HC Deb. 2 November 1992, col. 43. The Bill became the Asylum and Immigration Appeals Act 1993.

63. HL Deb. 26 January 1993, cols 1169–70.

64. By the Nationality, Immigration and Asylum Act 2002 s. 101 (3), challenged in *R (G)* v. *Immigration Appeal Tribunal* [2004] EWCA Civ 1731.

65. They pointed out the high rate of successful appeals to the second-tier tribunal; see e.g. JUSTICE evidence to Constitutional Affairs Committee, *Asylum and immigration appeals*, 2003–4, HC 211–1 para. 42; *The Asylum and Immigration (Treatment of Claimants) Bill*, Home Affairs Committee 1st report 2003–4, HC 109.

66. Speech at Inner Temple Hall, 3 March 2004, cited in '*A challenge to the rule of law': briefing for peers on the second reading of the Asylum and Immigration (Treatment of Claimants) Bill*, London: ILPA, 2004.

67. *R (Cart, MR Pakistan)* v. *Upper Tribunal and SSHD* [2011] UKSC 28.

68. Nationality, Immigration and Asylum Act 2002 s. 88A, in force April 2008.

69. Cited in *Final report*, Plymouth: Devon Law Centre Asylum Appellate Project, 2010.

70. *Report on an announced inspection of Harmondsworth Immigration Removal Centre 11–15 January 2010*, HM Inspectorate of Prisons, May 2010; 'Harmondsworth expansion adds to risk', IRR News, 29 May 2010.

71. The Office of the Immigration Services Commissioner was set up in 1999. See Part V of the Immigration and Asylum Act 1999.

72. Much of this section is taken from Anne Singh and Frances Webber, 'Excluding migrants from justice: the legal aid cuts', IRR Briefing Paper No. 7 (2010).

73. The LSC would not pay solicitors to travel to see dispersed clients, or travel costs for asylum seekers to visit solicitors.

74. See Chapter 2 for the Solihull pilot, immigration minister Damian Green's announcement at HC Deb. 14 December 2010, col. 662W, and see 'Early Legal Advice Project', on UKBA website, www.ukba.homeoffice.gov.uk/aboutus/your-region/midlands-east/controlling-migration/early-legal-advice-project/.

75. *Justice denied: asylum and immigration legal aid: a system in crisis*, BID and Asylum Aid, April 2005.

76. The Asylum Appellate Project, set up by Devon Law Centre in June 2007 to assist asylum seekers refused representation by solicitors on the basis that their cases were not strong enough, won 79 per cent of funding appeals to the Independent Funding Adjudicator. *Final report*, Asylum Appellate Project.

77. *Report on implementation of Carter proposals for fixed fees in civil legal aid*, Constitutional Affairs Committee, 3rd report 2006–7, HC 223, Vol. I para. 119; Vol. II para. 82.

78. Catherine Baksi, 'Legal aid payment regime blamed for RMJ collapse', *Law Society Gazette*, 24 June 2010.

79. *Landing in Kent.*
80. 'Opening for business: courts to bring world's disputes to UK', *Guardian*, 20 August 2011.

CHAPTER 4

1. The African Union's 1969 Refugee Convention is more generous, providing protection not only to those fearing persecution but also to those who have had to leave their country owing to 'external aggression, occupation, foreign domination or events seriously disturbing public order'.
2. See James Hathaway, *The law of refugee status* (2nd edn), Markham, Ontario: Butterworths, 1996.
3. *SSHD v. Adan* [1999] 1 AC 293.
4. *HM (Iraq)* [2010] UKUT 00331; *GS (Article 15 (c): indiscriminate violence) Afghanistan CG* [2009] UKAIT 00044.
5. *TK (India)* (1995).
6. *CPS (Colombia)* (1994).
7. Heaven Crawley, *Women as asylum seekers*, London: Refugee Women's Legal Group, ILPA and Refugee Action, 1997.
8. Sex is the biological condition while gender is its social reflection.
9. With Nathalia Berkowitz, senior legal and research officer at the IAA. The IAA withdrew the guidelines in 2006, presumably unhappy at being associated with such an enlightened and progressive document.
10. *SSHD v. Savchenkov* [1995] EWCA Civ 47.
11. He became Lord Justice Sedley when he was promoted to the Court of Appeal.
12. *R v. Immigration Appeal Tribunal and SSHD ex parte Shah* [1997] Imm AR 145.
13. *R v. IAT and SSHD ex p Shah; Islam v. SSHD* [1998] 1 WLR 74.
14. *Islam v. SSHD, R v. IAT and another ex p Shah* [1999] 2 AC 629.
15. *Fornah v. Home Secretary* [2007] 1 AC 412.
16. *EM (Lebanon) v. SSHD* [2008] UKHL 64, a case revolving around the prospect of 'flagrant denial' of human rights rather than refugee status.
17. Nearly half won their appeals (compared with 28 per cent of all claims). *Unsustainable: the quality of initial decision-making in women's asylum claims*, London: Asylum Aid, January 2011.
18. Ibid.
19. *Horvath v. SSHD* [2000] UKHL 37. See Chapter 2.
20. *P and M v. SSHD* [2004] EWCA Civ 1640.
21. *RG (Ethiopia) v. SSHD* [2006] EWCA Civ 339.
22. *Januzi v. SSHD* [2006] UKHL 5.
23. See Claire Bennett, *Relocation, relocation: the impact of internal relocation on women asylum seekers*, London: Asylum Aid, 2008, for examples of the inappropriate use of the internal relocation doctrine in women's claims.
24. Case file. See also *PO (Nigeria) v. SSHD* [2011] EWCA Civ 132, where the Tribunal told a victim of sex trafficking by a professional violent criminal that she could safely go to a refuge, in reasoning slated by the appeal court. The decision quashed here was a 'country guidance' case which other Tribunals dealing with Nigerian trafficking victims were bound to follow, so its cavalier approach to the evidence would have affected other trafficked women had its decision stood.

25. *AA (Uganda)* v. *SSHD* [2008] EWCA Civ 579.
26. *B and Hoxha*, [2005] UKHL 19 in which Baroness Hale quoted Rodger Haines QC, 'Gender-related persecution', in UNHCR, *Refugee protection in international law*, Cambridge: Cambridge University Press, 2003, and Heaven Crawley, *Refugees and gender: law and process*, Bristol: Jordans, 2001.
27. *NS (Social Group – Women – Forced marriage) Afghanistan CG* [2004] UKIAT 00328.
28. *MT* (1993).
29. This is not to say that female immigration judges are necessarily more sympathetic or believing of women's accounts than men; they are not. But at least, the impossibility of disclosure to a man is avoided.
30. Peers drew attention to the way the detained fast track is failing refugee women, at HL Deb. 11 October 2011, col. 1525.
31. See e.g. *Iftikhar Ahmed* v. *SSHD* [1999] EWCA Civ 3003 (religious persecution), *R* v. *IAT ex p Jonah* [1985] Imm AR 7, HC (political persecution).
32. *J* v. *SSHD* [2006] EWCA Civ 1238; *HJ (Iran)* v. *SSHD* [2010] UKSC 31.
33. See e.g. *Gomez (Emilia del Socorro Gutierrez)* [2000] INLR 549, IAT.
34. *Savchenkov* v. *SSHD* [1996] Imm AR 28, CA.
35. *Sepet* v. *SSHD* [2003] UKHL 15, upholding the much fuller judgment of the Court of Appeal at [2001] EWCA Civ 681.
36. *BE (Iran)* v. *SSHD* [2008] EWCA Civ 540.
37. *VF (Israel)* (2002).
38. The EU's Qualification Directive, 2004/83, incorporated into the immigration rules HC 395 para. 339 (c) (iv), allows the grant of subsidiary protection to civilians facing a serious and individual threat to life through indiscriminate violence in armed conflict: see *QD (Iraq)* v. *SSHD* [2009] EWCA Civ 620.

CHAPTER 5

1. *Westminster BC* v. *NASS* [2002] UKHL 38, paras 19–20.
2. Economic self-sufficiency was a condition of entry for most non-asylum seeking migrants, though, and recourse to means-tested benefits could result in curtailment of leave or refusal to renew a visa.
3. John Major, Douglas Hurd, Michael Howard and Kenneth Baker all spoke of 'bogus refugees' during the early 1990s, while Norman Tebbitt referred to 'so-called refugees' being involved in large-scale benefit fraud: *CARF* 7 (1992).
4. *Docklands Recorder*, 20 January 1991. The 'luxury block' consisted of asbestos-ridden local authority flats.
5. *Daily Express*, 3 July 1991, quoted in *Immigration controls are out of control: the new Asylum and Immigration Bill*, Manchester: Greater Manchester Immigration Aid Unit, 1993.
6. The National Health Service (Charges to Overseas Visitors) Regulations, SI 1982/863, made under the National Health Service Act 1977. See Steve Cohen, *From ill-treatment to no treatment*, Manchester: South Manchester Law Centre, 1981.
7. *Hackney Gazette*, 13 October 1989.
8. *CARF* 16 (1993).
9. *CARF* 25 (1995).
10. 'Migrants and HIV/AIDS', *CARF* 38 (1997).
11. Case file.

12. *R v. Secretary of State for the Environment ex parte Tower Hamlets Borough Council* [1993] QB 632. The Court quashed Department of Environment guidance to the contrary.
13. Section 4. The Bill fell for lack of time before the 1992 general election but was reintroduced shortly afterwards.
14. Those not claiming asylum at the port but after entry to the country.
15. Conservative Party press release 473/95, 11 October 1995.
16. *Sun*, 12 October 1995.
17. *The Times*, 26 October 1995.
18. *CARF* 30 (1995).
19. *Report on the Social Security (Persons from Abroad) (Miscellaneous) Regulations 1996*, Social Security Advisory Committee, Cm. 3062, 1996.
20. *R v. Secretary of State for Social Security ex parte B, JCWI* [1997] 1 WLR 275.
21. *R v. Royal Borough of Kensington and Chelsea ex p Kihara* (1997) 29 HLR 147.
22. HC Deb. 24 June 1996, col. 37.
23. Asylum and Immigration Act 1996 s. 11.
24. See 'UK: should asylum seekers starve?' *Statewatch*, Vol. 6, No. 5 (1996).
25. Frances Webber, 'Asylum seekers: caught by the Act', *Race & Class*, Vol. 38, No. 3 (1997).
26. *CARF* 36 (1996).
27. National Assistance Act 1948 s. 21.
28. *R v. Hammersmith and Fulham ex p M, The Times*, 10 October 1996. The Court of Appeal upheld the ruling (1998) 30 HLR 10.
29. A grant to local authorities failed to cover costs.
30. Ninety per cent of asylum seekers were in London. Newham housed 20,000, 10 per cent of its population. 'Asylum seekers and local authorities', IRR *London Update*, No. 5, Spring 1998.
31. Immigration and Asylum Act 1999 ss 115, 116. This provision has led to endless legal argument about whether illnesses are 'solely' the result of destitution and so whether councils must help or not.
32. As an interim measure, local authorities continued to provide support, but were paid by central government.
33. *Fairer, faster and firmer: a modern approach to immigration and asylum*, Cm. 4018, July 1998, cited in Liz Fekete, 'The emergence of xeno-racism' in *A suitable enemy: racism, migration and Islamophobia in Europe*, London: Pluto, 2009.
34. Immigration and Asylum Act 1999 s. 97 (2).
35. There were anguished debates about working with the Home Office as charities became enforcers of the draconian rules and began evicting ineligible and refused asylum seekers.
36. At a 1999 conference, I heard a large landlord discussing plans to partition each room in the run-down ex-council tower block she had bought, to maximise profit on the NASS contract.
37. See 'Inquiry into firm's asylum contract', *Guardian*, 3 August 2005.
38. M. Hingorani, 'A right to life: the story of Ramin Khalegi', *Race & Class*, Vol. 43, No. 2 (2001).
39. See 'Defend the Angel Heights Seven', *CARF* 56 (2000).
40. *AA*, case files.

41. 'When they came in the morning', *CARF* 63 (2001).
42. *Token gestures: the effects of the voucher scheme on asylum seekers and organisations in the UK*, London: TGWU, Oxfam, Refugee Council, 2001. See also Arun Kundnani, 'In a foreign land', *Race & Class*, Vol. 43, No. 2 (2001); Fekete, 'The emergence of xeno-racism'.
43. *Another country: implementing dispersal under the IAA 1999*, Audit Commission, June 2000.
44. *Daily Mail*, 6 October, 30 November 1998, see 'Racism and the press in Blair's Britain', *CARF* 48 (1998).
45. 'Wash this human sewage down the drain', *Dover Express*, 1 October 1998.
46. 'Learning the lessons of Dover', *CARF* 52 (1999). The Kent Refugee Action Network brought together local anti-racist, church and migrant support groups and did much to counter the racism asylum seekers faced.
47. See Introduction for this term; see also Liz Fekete, 'The emergence of xeno-racism' in *A suitable enemy*.
48. 'The dispersal of xenophobia', IRR *European Race Bulletin*, Nos. 33/34 (2000).
49. 'Heseltine in attack on asylum cheats', *Daily Telegraph*, 1 January 2001; 'Licence to hate', *CARF* 62 (2001).
50. 'Stop this bogus tabloid nationalism', *CARF* 55 (2000).
51. 'No welcome in Oxford', *CARF* 55 (2000).
52. Liz Fekete, 'The death of Firsat Dag and the failure of Scottish dispersal', IRR News, 1 October 2001. The campaign against these racist attacks led to a heartening joint demonstration against government policies by asylum seekers and local people.
53. 'Refugees pour back to London', 'Nowhere left to run', *Observer*, 31 December 2000; Liz Fekete, 'Asylum seekers, welfare and the politics of deterrence', IRR *European Race Bulletin*, No. 38 (2001).
54. *R (Gezer)* v. *SSHD* [2003] EWHC 860 (Admin), upheld by the Court of Appeal at [2004] EWCA Civ 1730.
55. *Asylum seekers and health*, London: British Medical Association, October 2002; Jenny McLeish, *Mothers in exile: maternity experiences of asylum seekers in England*, London: Maternity Alliance, 2002.
56. Mothers on income support were eligible for an additional amount for formula milk under the Welfare Food Regulations.
57. *T* v. *Secretary of State for Health and SSHD* [2002] EWHC 1887 (Admin).
58. *Migration and HIV Report: improving lives in Britain*, All-Party Parliamentary Group on AIDS, July 2003. See Frances Webber, 'Asylum: from deterrence to destitution', *Race & Class*, Vol. 45, No. 3 (2004).
59. See National Civil Rights Movement website, Civil rights caravan report, www.ncrm.org.uk/caravan/schedule.html.
60. 'Dispersal and the new racism', *CARF* 54 (2000); Liz Fekete, 'Concerns over new national asylum dispersal system', IRR News, 1 March 2000.
61. 'Glasgow welcome', *CARF* 56 (2001).
62. 'We get action over squalid flats from Hell', *Express on Sunday*, 11 June 2000.
63. 'Urge to help asylum seekers', *Liverpool Echo*, 19 July 2001, 'Asylum seekers rehoused after leaving "unfit" blocks', *Inside Housing*, 23 May 2002.
64. 'Asylum seekers' vouchers scrapped', BBC News, 8 April 2002.
65. See *Poverty and asylum*, London: Oxfam and the Refugee Council, June 2002.
66. Cited in *R (Q and others)* v. *SSHD* [2003] EWHC 195 (Admin).

67. 'Dispersal guidelines', NASS *Bulletin* 31; 'Changes in failure to travel policy', NASS *Bulletin* 57; 'Racist incidents', NASS *Bulletin* 81. The EU Reception Directive, 2003/9/EC, which required states to provide support for asylum seekers, made the system slightly less punitive by defining narrowly the situations which could result in removal of support.

68. Nationality, Immigration and Asylum Act 2002 s. 55.

69. Arun Kundnani, 'Nationwide protests against asylum destitution', IRR News, 8 January 2003.

70. HC Deb. 5 November 2002, col. 199.

71. Statement by immigration minister Beverley Hughes, 7 November 2002, cited in *R (Q) v. SSHD* above.

72. Ibid.

73. Radio 4, 'World at One', 20 February 2003.

74. Home Office letter to Inter-Agency Coordination Team, 12 January 2004, cited in Macdonald and Webber, *Immigration law and practice* (6th edn), London: Butterworths, 2005.

75. *R (Q and others) v. SSHD* [2003] EWCA Civ 364.

76. *R (Limbuela) v. SSHD* [2005] UKHL 66.

77. Helen Hintjens, 'Like leaves in the wind: desperately seeking asylum in the UK', *Race & Class*, Vol. 48, No. 1 (2006).

78. *Observer*, 12 June 2005, cited by Hintjens, 'Like leaves in the wind'.

79. See *Shaming destitution: NASS section 4 support for failed asylum seekers who are temporarily unable to leave the UK*, London: NACAB, June 2006.

80. Harmit Athwal and Jenny Bourne, 'Driven to despair: asylum deaths in the UK', *Race & Class*, Vol. 48, No. 4 (2007).

81. *R (Gwveya) v. NASS* [2004] EWHC 2371 (Admin).

82. *The destitution trap: asylum's untold story*, London: Refugee Action, 2006.

83. Initially it was not clear that the provision applied to refused asylum seekers, but this was clarified in 2002.

84. *Salih and Rahmani v. SSHD* [2003] EWHC 2273 (Admin).

85. *Shaming destitution* describes some of the bureaucratic obstacles and poor decisions causing delays.

86. Jon Burnett, 'Condemning the unborn', IRR News, 13 December 2007.

87. *Asylum and Immigration (Treatment of Claimants) Bill, additional clauses*, Joint Committee on Human Rights, 14th report 2003–4, HC 828.

88. Local authorities were obliged to look after children in need, but could not support parents. Nationality, Immigration and Asylum Act 2002 Sch. 3 as amended in 2004.

89. See *Inhumane and ineffective – section 9 in practice*, London: Refugee Council and Refugee Action, January 2006; *The end of the road: the impact on families of section 9*, Oxford: Barnardo's, November 2005.

90. Conference speech, *Guardian*, 2 October 1992.

91. *The treatment of asylum seekers*, Joint Committee on Human Rights, 10th report 2006–7, HC 60-I, paras 120–2.

92. 'G4S, Serco win Border Agency asylum deals', IRR News, 21 March 2012; John Grayson, 'Asylum seeker housing managed by for-profit prison guards? Why not', Open Democracy, www.opendemocracy.net/ourkingdom/john-grayson/asylum-seeker-housing-managed-by-for-profit-prison-guards-why-not, 8 February 2012.

93. *A civilised society: mental health provision for refugees and asylum seekers in England and Wales*, London: MIND, 2009, found that dispersal and enforced destitution increased isolation, diminished self-esteem and confidence and systematised conditions exacerbating psychological distress.

94. *Concluding observations on the UK*, ICESCR, E/C.12/1Add.790, 5 June 2002.

95. In the NHS (Treatment of Overseas Visitors) (Amendment) Regulations 2004.

96. *First do no harm, denying healthcare to people whose asylum claims have failed*, Refugee Council and Oxfam, June 2006.

97. Letter to health secretary Alan Johnson MP, 10 September 2007, on Doctors for Human Rights website, www.phruk.org/index.php?php=true&content=s howitem&table=news&item=86&previouscontent=news&previousphp=true.

98. 'Consultation: refusing entry or stay to NHS debtors. Results of the public consultation on proposed changes to the immigration rules', Home Office, March 2011, www.ukba.homeoffice.gov.uk/sitecontent/documents/ policyandlaw/consultations/nhs-debtors/results-of-consultation-nhs. pdf?view=Binary.

99. *R (YA)* v. *Secretary of State for Health* [2008] EWHC 855 (Admin); [2009] EWCA Civ 225.

100. *R (Tekle)* v. *SSHD* [2008] EWHC 3064 (Admin), which held that the right to normal life, including working, was an aspect of respect for private life (Article 8 of the Human Rights Convention). The judgment on Article 8 was doubted in *R (Negassi)* v. *SSHD* [2011] EWHC 386 (Admin).

101. *ZO (Somalia)* [2010] UKSC 36.

102. Consolidated immigration rules HC 395 as amended, paras 360A, 360C.

CHAPTER 6

1. For the counter-argument (that the power did not exist, except in respect of enemy aliens, but was taken by statute), see Christopher Vincenzi, 'Aliens and the judicial review of immigration law', *Public Law* (1985), p. 93; Prakash Shah, *Refugees, race and the legal concept of asylum in Britain*, London: Cavendish, 2000, both cited in I. Macdonald and R. Toal, *Macdonald's immigration law and practice* (8th edn), London: Butterworths, 2010.

2. See e.g. Peter Fryer, *Staying power: the history of black people in Britain*, London: Pluto, 1984; Ann Dummett and Andrew Nicol, *Subjects, citizens, aliens and others: nationality and immigration law*, London: Weidenfeld, 1990; Dennis Dean, 'The Conservative government and the 1961 Commonwealth Immigration Act: the inside story' in *Race & Class*, Vol. 35, No. 2 (1993); *East African Asians* v. *United Kingdom* (1973) 3 EHRR 76; 'Hong Kong: betrayal by consensus', *Statewatch*, Vol. 5, No. 5 (1995).

3. Of the few concessions to historic ties, exemption from deportation for those already resident was eroded by time, while exemption from the requirement to be able to support family members seeking entry was removed in 1988.

4. See *Secure borders, safe haven: integration with diversity in modern Britain*, Cm. 5387, 2002, p. 40.

5. See 'The economics of managed migration', *CARF* 64 (2001).

6. *Migration: economic and social analysis*, Home Office Research Directorate, January 2001.

7. See Arun Kundnani, 'Managed migration: a permanent crisis', *IRR News*, 8 June 2004.

8. Speech by Harold Wilson to the 1963 Labour Party conference.
9. *Secure borders, safe haven*. While encouraging the 'brain drain' from poor countries, particularly of medical personnel, the government simultaneously disavowed any such intention.
10. The International Convention on the protection of the rights of all migrant workers and members of their families, adopted by the UN General Assembly in 1990. By 1998 only nine states had ratified the Convention, so a Global Campaign was launched by the United Nations Secretariat, intergovernmental agencies and human rights, church, labour, migrant and women's organisations which achieved a further 18 ratifications by 2004.
11. 'Immigrants fight "unfair" law change', BBC News, 16 June 2006.
12. 'Migrant Indians to move court', *Times of India*, 6 February 2007.
13. *Highly skilled migrants: changes to the immigration rules*, Joint Committee on Human Rights, 20th report 2006–7, HC 173, para. 50.
14. *R (HSMP Forum) v. SSHD* [2008] EWHC 664 (Admin).
15. *R (HSMP Forum) v. SSHD* [2009] EWHC 711 (Admin).
16. 'Legitimate expectation' is a legal doctrine which holds individuals and public bodies to promises that others have relied on, in the interests of fairness, unless there is an overriding public interest against being bound. See *R (Coughlan) v. North and East Devon Health Authority* [1999] EWCA Civ 1871.
17. *R (BAPIO Action Ltd) v. SSHD and Secretary of State for Health* [2008] UKHL 27.
18. 'Brown promises new migrant controls to get Britons back to work', *Guardian*, 10 September 2007. The TUC itself had produced a report in June 2007 demonstrating that foreign workers 'make a positive net economic contribution' to the economy, paying more in taxes than they took out in benefits.
19. 'Brown promises Britons first refusal on jobs', *Independent*, 6 June 2007.
20. *Guardian*, 27 February 2007.
21. See 'We want fairness, we want jobs, say workers on the picket lines', *Guardian*, 31 January 2009; Seumas Milne, 'The target of this campaign of strikes is now obvious', *Guardian*, 5 February 2009. David Cameron pointed out that Gordon Brown should never have made the promise – a lesson he was to forget 18 months later.
22. *A points-based system: making migration work for Britain*, Cm. 6741, March 2006.
23. '200,000 jobs barred to non-European migrants', *Guardian*, 12 November 2008.
24. 'Migrant cuts "a threat to UK jobs"', *Guardian*, 31 August 2009.
25. Immigration Act 1971, s. 4, which requires rules regulating entry to the UK to be laid before parliament.
26. 'Immigration cap already in place – for care workers', *Immigration Matters*, 27 November 2010; '150,000 social care workers "paid below legal minimum"', *Guardian*, 3 October 2011.
27. *R (JCWI and ECCA) v. SSHD* [2010] EWHC 3524 (Admin).
28. *SSHD v. Pankina and others* [2010] EWCA Civ 719. The rules said applicants needed to have £800 in the bank; the policy said the money had to be there for the whole of the three months immediately preceding the application.
29. The imposition of unlawful additional requirements continued; the Independent Chief Inspector of the Border Agency, in *Entry clearance in Abu Dhabi and*

Islamabad, November 2010, found that posts at Abu Dhabi and Islamabad were refusing visas to Pakistani PBS applicants for failure to provide documents or evidence which the rules did not demand.

30. Anne Singh, 'The cap that never was', IRR News, 6 January 2011.
31. 'UK carmakers attack cap on immigration', *Guardian*, 28 October 2010.
32. 'High earners exempted from immigration cap', *Guardian*, 16 February 2011.
33. 'Duplicity behind immigration cap', IRR News, 8 July 2010.
34. Tony Blair, 'Why we must attract more students from overseas', *Guardian*, 18 April 2006.
35. *Anwar* v. *SSHD* [2010] EWCA Civ 1275.
36. Although there are many complaints that they go further. Document verification (checking that certificates produced are authentic) has become an area of explicit race discrimination, with students from 'high risk' nationalities routinely having documents subjected to checks, and being refused with no right of appeal when issuing institutions delay in verifying them. See *Briefing for House of Lords debate on HC 1148*, London: ILPA, September 2011.
37. *English UK Ltd* v. *SSHD* [2010] EWHC 1726 (Admin).
38. Statement of changes to the immigration rules, HC 382, July 2010.
39. Until April 2012, sponsors were given 'B', 'A (Trusted)' or 'highly trusted' status, depending on compliance with Home Office requirements (see Chapter 9).
40. See UKBA, 'Highly trusted sponsorship for Tier 4 sponsors – proposed criteria', 18 July 2011; Statement of changes to the immigration rules, HC 908, March 2011.
41. Statement of changes in immigration rules, HC 1148, in force 4 July 2011.
42. 'Visa curbs will cut overseas students by 80,000, says May', *Guardian*, 23 March 2011; 'Student visa changes "will cut immigration"', *Guardian*, 13 June 2011.
43. Earl Attlee, HL Deb. 7 September 2011, col. 356.
44. *Briefing*, ILPA, September 2011.
45. *Guardian*, 2 February 2011.
46. *Guardian*, 16 August 2011.
47. *Observer*, 10 July 2011.
48. Rules have been brought into force with as little as two days' notice.
49. *Guardian*, 21 March 2011.
50. Ibid; Appleton and Govinda, *UK arts and culture: cancelled*, Manifesto Club, June 2009.
51. *Daily Telegraph*, 27 June 2011, www.telegraph.co.uk/comment/letters/8599757/Points-based-visa-system-places-unnecessary-burden-on-artists-making-short-visits-to-Britain.html.
52. *Employment related settlement, Tier 5 and overseas domestic workers: a consultation*, Home Office, June 2011.
53. Theresa May, HC Deb. 29 February 2012, col. 34WS. Those in shortage occupations will be exempt from the earnings threshold, which will apply from April 2016.
54. Migrants admitted for work are currently eligible for settlement in the UK after five years (previously four), subject to character, language and knowledge of life in the UK tests.
55. 'Migration settlement rights to be cut says Home Office', BBC News, 9 June 2011.

56. Kate Roberts, 'UK immigration law and the position of migrant domestic workers', Paper presented at Twenty-first Century Slavery: Issues and Responses on the 23–24 November 2006, organised by the Wilberforce Institute for the study of Slavery and Emancipation (WISE) at the University of Hull. Kalayaan, 2006, www.kalayaan.org.uk/documents/UK%20immigration%20law%20 and%20the%20position%20of%20MDWs.pdf.

57. Wealthy families' servants had their passports stamped 'No employment' when they arrived, but 'Accompanying employer Mr X' would be hand-written over the stamp, tying them to the particular employer.

58. Immigration rules, HC 395 as amended, paras 159A–H.

59. Kalayaan works with North Kensington Law Centre which helps domestic workers to bring tribunal cases, where awards for multiple breaches of employment law have averaged £87,000. M. Lalani, *Ending the abuse: policies that work to protect migrant domestic workers*, London: Kalayaan, May 2011.

60. *The new bonded labour? The impact of proposed changes to the UK immigration system on migrant domestic workers*, Kalayaan and Oxfam, 2008, www.kalayaan.org.uk/documents/Kalayaan%20Oxfam%20report.pdf.

61. Lalani, *Ending the abuse*.

62. See *The impact of proposals to abolish the overseas domestic worker visa*, London: Kalayaan, August 2011; *Response on employment-related settlement, Tier 5 and overseas domestic workers*, London: ILPA, September 2011, p. 26, text and fn. 37.

63. BBC News, 4 September 2011.

64. See note 53 above; Marissa Begonia, 'A step back to Victorian-era slavery for UK domestic workers', Comment is Free, *Guardian*, 11 March 2012.

65. Oliver Pearce, 'Domestic Workers Convention agreed despite UK government', *Independent* blogs, 10 June 2011.

66. 'Coalition "betrays anti-slavery legacy" over domestic workers', *Guardian*, 16 June 2011.

CHAPTER 7

1. *Huang and Kashmiri* [2007] UKHL 11.

2. EEA nationals are citizens of countries making up the European Economic Area, comprising the 27 European Union (EU) countries, Norway, Iceland and Lichtenstein. Swiss nationals are also treated as if they were EEA citizens.

3. As Europe had become more racially mixed, with more and more EEA nationals having family members from Africa, Asia and Latin America, family reunion has become more problematic, especially for extended family members: see e.g. *JO (Nigeria)* [2010] UKUT 478; *KG (Sri Lanka)* [2008] EWCA Civ 13, *Bigia* [2009] EWCA Civ 79, *SM (India)* v. *ECO Mumbai* [2009] EWCA Civ 1426. But EEA family admission is based on free movement rights, enforced by binding judgments of the European Court of Justice in Luxembourg, not on discretionary rules – which makes a big difference.

4. Immigration rules HC 395 as amended, para. 281 (ii). The English language test is not applicable if the applicant is over 65, or has a mental or physical condition preventing them from taking the test, or if there are 'exceptional compassionate circumstances' making it inappropriate.

5. 'Immigrant relatives face five-year wait to claim benefits', *Guardian*, 13 July 2011.

6. See '370,000 migrants on the dole', *Daily Telegraph*, 19 January 2012.

7. *R v. SSHD ex p Arman Ali* [2000] INLR 89, decided eight years after the visa applications.

8. *Mahad v. ECO* [2009] UKSC 16.

9. 'Reforming family migration to promote better integration', UKBA website, 16 September 2011, www.ukba.homeoffice.gov.uk/sitecontent/newsarticles/2011/september/40-migration.

10. Sushma Lal and Amrit Wilson, *'But my cows aren't going to England': a study in how families are divided*, Manchester: Manchester Law Centre, 1986.

11. The unreliability of the tests was described in *Iqbal Haque v. ECO Dacca* [1974] Imm A.R. 51, where an expert said that assumptions about bone growth appropriate for western children were inappropriate for children growing up in Bangladesh. But they continued to be used until public pressure forced an inquiry by Sir Henry Yellowlees, whose 1981 report indicated the dangers to children and the unreliability of the tests. See HL Deb. 25 March 1981, cols 1273–4WA.

12. See Chris Searle, 'Your daily dose: racism and the *Sun*', *Race & Class*, Vol. 29, No. 1 (1987).

13. A policy allowed the admission of over-age children who had been wrongly refused permission to join parents only in 'exceptional compassionate circumstances'.

14. *KP (India)* (2002).

15. *C (Philippines)* (1995).

16. *FA (Algeria)* (2002).

17. See the chapter on family life in Gina Clayton, *Immigration and asylum law* (4th edn), Oxford: Oxford University Press, 2010, or Macdonald and Toal's *Macdonald's immigration law and practice* (8th edn), London: Butterworths, 2010, ch. 11, for a full account of the rules relating to the entry of families.

18. The history of the rules on the admission of foreign husbands is set out in *Abdulaziz, Cabales and Balkandali v. United Kingdom* [1985] ECHR 7.

19. *Trial by separation: women divided from their husbands by the immigration rules*, London: Immigration Widows Campaign, December 1984. Official statistics bore out the claim: see *Abdulaziz, Cabales and Balkandali v. United Kingdom*.

20. *Abdulaziz, Cabales and Balkandali v. United Kingdom*.

21. See e.g. *Bhatia v. IAT* [1985] Imm AR 39 (HC), 50 (CA).

22. Although the questions of primary purpose and the intentions of the parties to cohabit were separate questions, 'evidence bearing on one question will often cast a flood of light on the other': *ex parte Kumar* [1986] Imm AR 446 (CA).

23. Macdonald and Blake, *Immigration law and practice* (4th edn), London: Butterworths, 1995.

24. 'Michael Howard attacks government plans to abolish primary purpose rule', *CARF* 37 (1997).

25. Control of Immigration Statistics, 2nd half and year 1997, 21 May 1998, http://rds.homeoffice.gov.uk/rds/pdfs/hosb1398.pdf.

26. See *Secure borders, safe haven: integration with diversity in modern Britain*, Cm. 5387, 2002, p. 18.

27. *Statewatch*, Vol. 7, No. 3 (1997).

28. Bureaucratic guidance, however, decreed that only specified documentary evidence of violence – an injunction, a court conviction or police caution – was acceptable to prove it, guidance overruled by the Court of Appeal in 2007 as undermining the purpose of the rule: *Ishtiaq* v. *SSHD* [2007] EWCA Civ 386. The rule's utility was further limited by the bar on using public funds, which stopped many migrant women leaving violent partners, since the inability to claim housing benefit prevented access to many women's refuges.
29. *AJ (Pakistan)* (1994).
30. These criteria apply to parents under 65 and other relatives of those settled here. Parents over 65 must satisfy rules relating to dependency.
31. *Singh* v. *ECO New Delhi* [2004] EWCA Civ 1075.
32. See e.g. '102 foreign criminals and illegal immigrants we can't deport', *Daily Telegraph*, 11 June 2011.
33. The policy, known as DP2/93, is set out in the case of *R* v. *SSHD ex p Amankwah* [1994] Imm AR 240, where officials' failure to consider it made their rejection of an overstayer's application to stay unlawful. Amendments in 1996 tightened up the policy.
34. *R* v. *SSHD ex p Amankwah*.
35. DP5/96, modified by 069/99, discussed in *NF (Ghana)* v. *SSHD* [2008] EWCA Civ 906. The policy was withdrawn in 2008.
36. *R (Mahmood)* v. *SSHD* [2001] 1 WLR 840.
37. *Akaeke* v. *SSHD* [2005] EWCA Civ 947.
38. *Chikwamba* v. *SSHD* [2008] UKHL 40.
39. *EB (Kosovo)* v. *SSHD* [2008] UKHL 41.
40. A working group had been set up in 1999, and a joint FCO/Home Office Forced Marriage Unit was set up in 2005.
41. Amrit Wilson, 'The forced marriage debate and the British state', *Race & Class*, Vol. 49, No. 1 (2007).
42. The evidence did not support the argument: see Professor Marianne Hester and others, *Forced marriage: the risk factors and the effect of raising the minimum age for a sponsor, and of leave to enter the UK as a spouse or fiancé(e)*, Draft report 15 February 2007, available on FreeMovement, http://freemovement. wordpress.com/2009/09/05/forced-marriage-unit-warned-home-office-of-risks-in-increasing-spouse-visa-age/; *Domestic violence, forced marriage and 'honour'-based violence*, Home Affairs Committee, 6th report 2007–8, HC 263, paras 110–11.
43. Quoted in Rahila Gupta, 'Mere posturing from the Tories on forced marriage', *Guardian*, 13 October 2011.
44. *Quila and Bibi* v. *SSHD* [2011] UKSC 45.
45. Asylum and Immigration (Treatment of Claimants) Act 2004, ss 19–24, Civil Partnership Act 2004 Sch. 23.
46. *R (Baiai and others)* v. *SSHD* [2008] UKHL 53.
47. The Asylum and Immigration (Treatment of Claimants) Act 2004 (Remedial) Order 2011, SI 2011/1158.
48. Borders, Citizenship and Immigration Act 2009 s. 55, which imposes a stautory duty to consider the welfare of children on anyone exercising immigration functions.
49. Children's rights groups gave evidence to the Joint Committee on Human Rights, which called for the immigration reservation to be lifted in its 10th report of 2002–3, HC 81, and its 10th report of 2006–7, HC 60.

50. The ECtHR had made it clear in cases such as *Uner v. Netherlands* (2007) 45 EHRR 14 that the best interests of children were relevant when deciding whether parents should be deported.

51. *ZH (Tanzania)* v. *SSHD* [2011] UKSC 4.

52. HC Deb. 9 June 2010, col. 11WS; 'Migrants marrying UK citizens must now learn English', 9 June 2010, www.homeoffice.gov.uk/media-centre/press-releases/migrants-learn-english.

53. EDM 870, *Statement of changes in immigration rules (CM 7944)*, 20 October 2010.

54. See Dr Mark Elliott, 'Law, politics and the draft Brighton Declaration', UK Human Rights Blog, 9 March 2012, http://ukhumanrightsblog.com/2012/03/09/law-politics-and-the-draft-brighton-declaration-dr-mark-elliot/.

CHAPTER 8

1. *Q (Algeria)* (2007).

2. *A* v. *SSHD* [2004] UKHL 56. It was not the internment *per se* which the majority held illegal but the fact that the law applied only to foreigners.

3. In *A* v. *SSHD*, Lord Hoffmann proclaimed freedom from arbitrary arrest and detention 'quintessentially British'.

4. Shahram Khosravi, *'Illegal' traveller: an auto-ethnography of borders*, Basingstoke: Palgrave Macmillan, 2010.

5. Case records. See also *Deadly silence: black deaths in custody*, London: IRR, 1991.

6. See *Cell culture: the detention and imprisonment of asylum seekers in the United Kingdom*, London: Amnesty International, 1996.

7. See *United Kingdom: unlawful killing of detained asylum seeker Omasese Lumumba*, London: Amnesty International, November 1993.

8. *CARF* 16 (1993).

9. The first hunger strike in immigration detention was in 1973, the year the 1971 Immigration Act came into force, according to Stephanie d'Orey, *Immigration prisoners: a forgotten minority*, London: Runnymede Trust, 1984.

10. *CARF* 9 (1992).

11. See Mark Ashford, *Detained without trial: a survey of Immigration Act detention*, London: JCWI, 1993.

12. *CARF* 9 (1992).

13. See e.g. Her Majesty's Chief Inspector of Prisons (HMCIP) Tumim's 'grave reservations about the appropriateness' of holding 'distressed, despondent and in some cases desperate' asylum seekers in Pentonville, reported in *Statewatch*, Vol. 4, No. 2 (1994).

14. For details of the close links between politicians and the private security industry see Christine Bacon, *The evolution of immigration detention in the UK: the involvement of private prison companies*, Oxford: Refugee Studies Centre, 2005.

15. *CARF* 43 (1998).

16. 'Campsfield revelations', *CARF* 45 (1998), case files. See also Teresa Hayter, *Open borders: the case against immigration controls*, London, Pluto, 2000, pp. 128ff.

17. *Detention of asylum seekers*, EDM 253, 15 July 1997.

18. Peter van der Vaart, Channel 4 News, cited in 'Refugee detention camp "a shambles"', *Independent*, 6 March 1998.
19. *Saadi and others* v. *SSHD* [2001] EWHC Admin 670 (September 2001), [2001] EWCA Civ 1512 (October 2001), [2002] UKHL 41 (House of Lords). Note the speed with which the Court of Appeal heard the Home Office appeal; appellants generally wait a year or more for a hearing.
20. *Saadi* v. *United Kingdom* [2008] ECHR 80. Six judges strongly dissented from the withholding from asylum seekers of 'fundamental guarantees of individual liberty in a State governed by the rule of law'.
21. The official inquiry into the disturbance and fire commented, 'As they were designed and constructed neither Yarl's Wood nor its sister removal centre, Harmondsworth, were fit for purpose': Stephen Shaw, *Report of the inquiry into the disturbance and fire at Yarl's Wood Removal Centre*, Prisons and Probation Ombudsman, November 2004.
22. Manuel Bravo hanged himself there in 2005 the day before his and his son's deportation to Angola. An inquest jury found he had taken his own life to secure his son's future in the UK. See Harmit Athwal, 'Roll call of deaths of asylum seekers and undocumented migrants', IRR News, 29 October 2010.
23. A *'Bleak House' in our times: an investigation into women's rights violations at Yarl's Wood removal centre*, London: Legal Action for Women, 2006, which found that over 70 per cent of women detained there were survivors of rape or other sexual violence (so should not have been detained), nearly half had been held for over three months, and over half had no legal representation.
24. *CARF* 39 (1997).
25. *Annual Report 1986*, Home Office, Immigration and Nationality Directorate, cited in *Cell culture*.
26. David Blunkett justified accommodation centres for the segregation of asylum seekers on the ground that in the community, they became more difficult to remove: HC Deb. 24 April 2002, col. 353.
27. Khosravi describes irregular migrants and asylum seekers as 'anti-citizens', like dangerous antibodies to be quarantined, in *'Illegal' traveller*.
28. Bacon, *Evolution of immigration detention*.
29. *R (WL Congo)* v. *SSHD* [2011] UKSC 12.
30. *Independent*, 6 March 1998.
31. UN Commission on Human Rights, Report of the Working Group on Arbitrary Detention, Addendum, E/CN.4/1999/63/Add.3.
32. Case notes.
33. *Fairer, faster and firmer – a modern approach to immigration and asylum*, Cm. 4018, July 1998; Operational Enforcement Manual (December 2000), para. 38.
34. Detention Centre Rules 2001, SI 2001/238.
35. *A civilised society: mental health provision for refugees and asylum seekers in England and Wales*, London: MIND, 2009.
36. *R (D and K)* v *SSHD* [2006] EWHC 980 (Admin).
37. *Detention Centre Rule 35 Audit*, UKBA, March 2011. See 'Torture survivors let down', IRR News, 10 March 2011.
38. *R (S)* v. *SSHD and others* [2011] EWHC 2120 (Admin).
39. *R (BA)* v. *SSHD* [2011] EWHC 2748 (Admin).
40. *A betrayal of hope and trust: detention in the UK of survivors of torture*, London: Medical Foundation, October 1994.

41. Enforcement Instructions and Guidance Ch. 55, August 2010.

42. The screening of this documentary led to an investigation by the Prisons and Probation Ombudsman, *Inquiry into allegations of racism and mistreatment of detainees at Oakington immigration reception centre and while under escort*, Prisons and Probation Ombudsman, July 2005.

43. *Outsourcing abuse: the use and misuse of state-sanctioned force during the detention and removal of asylum seekers*, London: Birnberg Peirce, National Coalition of Anti-Deportation Campaigns and Medical Justice, July 2008.

44. Baroness Nuala O'Loan, *Report to the Border Agency on 'Outsourcing abuse'*, March 2010, which, while not finding 'systemic' abuse, found complaints of assault uninvestigated.

45. *Report on the unannounced inspections of three short-term non-residential immigration holding facilities 2–3 August 2005*, HM Inspectorate of Prisons, 2006.

46. Alex Gask, 'Harmondsworth – the full story', *Liberty*, Autumn 2007; 'Riot centre inmates "denied food"', BBC News, 4 March 2008.

47. *Statewatch*, Vol. 17, No. 1 (2007).

48. *A 'Bleak House' in our times*.

49. *Guardian*, 9 February 2010.

50. Report on the UK's record in upholding the provisions of the International Covenant on Civil and Political Rights, UNHRC, July 1995.

51. *Quaquah v. Group 4 Securities Ltd (No 2)* [2001] Prison LR 318.

52. A National Audit Office report in 1995 urged the Home Office to 'consider setting minimum standards for facilities at detention centres', and prisons inspector Judge Tumim's critical report on Campsfield House in 1995 observed that health care needed a 'complete overhaul'.

53. *The treatment of asylum seekers*, Joint Committee on Human Rights, 10th report 2006–7, HC 60.

54. Ibid.

55. Bacon, *Evolution of immigration detention*.

56. Frank Arnold, *Medical implications of immigration detention in the UK*, paper presented to conference at the Refugee Studies Centre, Oxford University, in December 2008. A recent Medical Justice report, *Detained and denied: the clinical care of immigration detainees living with HIV*, London: Medical Justice, March 2011, describes routine failure to provide medication and care to detained HIV patients.

57. Harriet Grant, 'The indefinite detention of foreign prisoners', *Guardian*, podcast 25 February 2011; HL Deb. 29 November 2010, WA 410.

58. *Kambadzi v. SSHD* [2011] UKSC 23.

59. *Abdillaahi Muuse v. SSHD* [2010] EWCA Civ 453.

60. 'The minister versus the judges', IRR News, 5 March 2009.

61. *R v. Governor Durham Prison ex p Singh* [1984] 1 WLR 704.

62. *Detained lives: the real cost of indefinite immigration detention*, London: London Detainee Support Group, 2009. See also *Out of sight, out of mind: experiences of immigration detention in the UK*, London: BID, July 2009.

63. *Muqtaar v. SSHD* [2011] EWHC 2707 (Admin).

64. Simon Hughes MP, in Harriet Grant, 'Indefinite detention'.

65. Immigration and Asylum Act 1999 s. 44.

66. *A nice judge on a good day: immigration bail and the right to liberty*, London: BID, July 2010.

67. BID helped over 2,000 detainees to make their own application in 2009, and has produced a DIY guide, *How to get out of detention*.
68. Sureties should only be demanded if there is evidence indicating that otherwise the person might abscond. Very few do; Richard Dunstan found an absconding rate of 0.59 per cent, in his study *Prisoners without a voice: asylum seekers detained in the UK*, London: Amnesty International, 1994.
69. *Immigration bail hearings: a travesty of justice? Observations from the public gallery*, Oxford: Campaign to Close Campsfield Bail Observation Project, 2011.
70. See Liz Fekete, 'They are children too', in *A suitable enemy: racism, migration and Islamophobia in Europe*, London: Pluto, 2009.
71. Heaven Crawley, *When is a child not a child? Asylum, age disputes and the process of age assessment*, London: ILPA, May 2007.
72. Social services must look after unaccompanied children, but have no such duties towards young adults (apart from care leavers).
73. '£2m paid out over child asylum seekers illegally detained as adults', *Guardian*, 17 February 2012.
74. *R (B) v. London Borough of Merton* [2003] EWHC 1689 (Admin); *A v. London Borough of Croydon*, [2009] UKSC 8.
75. UK Border Agency to Refugee Council, June 2011, in ILPA Bulletin, July 2011.
76. *Guardian*, 6 January 2012.
77. *R (Konan) v. SSHD* [2004] EWHC 22.
78. Crawley and others, *No place for a child: children in UK immigration detention*, London: Save the Children, February 2005.
79. 'No place for a child: a campaign to free children in detention', IRR News, 4 May 2006; *Obstacles to accountability: challenging the immigration detention of families*, London: BID, July 2007.
80. Professor Al Aynsley-Green, *An announced visit to Yarl's Wood immigration removal centre: 31 October 2005*, Children's Commissioner for England, December 2005; Liz Fekete, 'Challenging detention of children', IRR News, 28 March 2006; Children's Commissioner, *The arrest and detention of children subject to immigration control*, 11 Million, April 2009.
81. See also *Significant harm – the effects of administrative detention on the health of children, young people and their families*, Intercollegiate Briefing Paper of The Royal Colleges of Paediatrics and Child Health, of Psychiatry and of General Practitioners, December 2009.
82. Borders, Citizenship and Immigration Act 2009 s. 55.
83. See e.g. *Report on an announced inspection of Yarl's Wood Immigration Removal Centre: 4–8 February 2008*, HM Inspectorate of Prisons; Medical Justice, Ann Lorek and others, 'The mental and physical health difficulties of children held within a British immigration detention centre: a pilot study', *International Journal of Child Abuse and Neglect*, September 2009; *State sponsored cruelty: children in immigration detention*, London: Medical Justice, September 2010; *Detention of children: last resort or first resort?* London: BID and the Children's Society, May 2011. See also, *The detention of children in the immigration system*, November 2009, House of Commons Home Affairs Committee, 1st report 2009–10, HC 73.
84. 'Brown attacked for not scrapping asylum policy that leaves hundreds of children behind bars at Christmas', *Daily Mail*, 14 December 2009.
85. 'Does Barnardo's legitimise child detention?' IRR News, 17 March 2011.

86. 'UKBA accused of breaking pledge to end child detention', *Guardian*, 16 October 2011.
87. See 'Hundreds of children in short-term detention at Heathrow', *Guardian*, 7 July 2011.

CHAPTER 9

1. Immigration and Asylum Act 1999 ss 125, 128–39, Nationality, Immigration and Asylum Act 2002 ss 150–5, Asylum and Immigration (Treatment of Claimants) Act 2004 s. 14.
2. By 2009 it had taken on customs functions, searching for contraband cigarettes and drugs as well as irregular migrants and unauthorised workers. The changes were reflected in the Borders, Citizenship and Immigration Act 2009.
3. Immigration and Asylum Act 1999 ss 20–1.
4. Ibid., s. 126.
5. Ibid., s. 24; Reporting of Suspicious Marriages and Registration of Marriages (Miscellaneous Amendments) Regulations 2000, SI 2000/3164.
6. Nationality, Immigration and Asylum Act 2002 ss 129, 134.
7. Ibid., s. 135.
8. Ibid., ss 136–7.
9. Tony Bunyan, 'Just over the horizon: surveillance and the state in Europe', *Race & Class*, Vol. 51, No. 3 (2010).
10. Proposed by home secretary Michael Howard in 1994.
11. Asylum and Immigration Appeals Act 1993 s. 3; Immigration and Asylum Act 1999 s. 141; Nationality, Immigration and Asylum Act 2002 s. 126; Asylum and Immigration (Treatment of Claimants) Act 2004 s. 15.
12. '"Sleepwalking into a surveillance society?" – Information commissioner', *Statewatch*, www.statewatch.org/news/2004/aug/08uk-info-commissioner. htm. See also 'Now Britain is "surveillance society"', BBC News, 2 November 2006.
13. *Identity Cards Bill*, Joint Committee on Human Rights, 5th report 2004–5, HC 283.
14. *The identity project: an assessment of the UK Identity Cards Bill and its implications*, London: London School of Economics, 2005.
15. HC Deb. 11 November 2003, col. 171; UK Borders Act 2007 ss 5–6, Immigration (Biometric Registration) Regulations 2008, SI 2008/3048 as amended. See 'ID and the final exclusion', IRR News, 4 February 2010.
16. 'Number of biometric residence permits to double', *Guardian government computing*, 27 February 2012, www.guardian.co.uk/government-computing-network/2012/feb/27/biometric-residence-permits-doubled-home-office.
17. Under ss 94ff of the Immigration and Asylum Act 1999; see Chapter 5.
18. Immigration and Asylum Act 1999 s. 127.
19. Home secretary David Blunkett, HC Deb. 24 April 2002, col. 353.
20. SALs had been introduced in 1991 and carried the asylum seeker's photo and identity details.
21. 'UK immigration intros compulsory tags for asylum cases', *The Register*, 27 January 2006; Bianca Bonomi, 'Are homes being turned into detention centres?' IRR News, 14 February 2006.
22. 'New UK terror threat from foreign students', *Daily Telegraph*, 9 July 2007, cited by Scott Poynting and others in 'Universities must not ride the wave of

xenophobia', IRR News, 18 June 2009. For the terrorist policing of students see Liz Fekete, 'The new McCarthyism' in *A suitable enemy: racism, migration and Islamophobia in Europe*, London: Pluto, 2009.

23. Valerie Hartwich, *Students under watch: visa checks and the rise of surveillance in UK universities*, Manifesto Club, September 2011.
24. R *(London Reading College)* v. *SSHD* [2010] EWHC 2561 (Admin).
25. R *(Westech College)* v. *SSHD* [2011] EWHC 1484 (Admin).
26. 'Student visa curbs are damaging our reputation, Universities UK warns', *Guardian*, 2 November 2011.
27. 'Home Office faces legal action over "bogus colleges" claim', *Guardian*, 8 November 2011.
28. R *(Burnley College Ltd)* v. *SSHD* [2011] EWHC 2928 (Admin).
29. Ann Singleton and others, 'Academics refuse to police immigration', *Times Educational Supplement*, 7 May 2009 (reproduced in IRR News, 13 May 2009).
30. Scott Poynting, 'Universities must not ride wave of xenophobia'.
31. Asylum and Immigration Act 1996 s. 8. A statutory defence protected employers who checked and copied a document evidencing the employee's eligibility to work, such as a British passport or one with a permission to work stamp.
32. *CARF* 25 (1995).
33. In provisions of the Nationality, Immigration and Asylum Act 2002, in force from 2004.
34. Immigration, Asylum and Nationality Act 2006 ss 15–19 and 21, the Immigration (Employment of Adults Subject to Immigration Control) (Maximum Penalty) Order 2008, SI 2008/132 and the Immigration (Restrictions on Employment) Order 2007, SI 2007/3290.
35. Immigration minister Phil Woolas, HC Deb. 18 November 2008, col. 315W.
36. *Hard work, hidden lives*, London: TUC Commission on Vulnerable Employment, 2007.
37. See 'Crusade against the undocumented', IRR News, 5 February 2009.
38. 'Castle Douglas hotelier's jail sentence overturned', BBC News, 27 April 2011.
39. The charge was generally working in breach of conditions as a visitor or a student.
40. 'Crusade against the undocumented'.
41. See e.g. *Papers please*, London: Migrants' Rights Network, 2008; *Irregular migration: the urgent need for a new approach*, London: Migrants' Rights Network, 2009; *Hope costs nothing: the lives of undocumented migrants in the UK*, London: Migrant Resource Centre, 2010; Steve Cohen, 'Workers, serfs and slaves: managed migration and employment rights', *Legal Action*, August 2007; Bridget Anderson and Ben Rogaly, *Forced labour and migration to the UK*, London: TUC, 2005; Hsiao-Hung Pai, *Chinese whispers: the true story behind Britain's hidden army of labour*, Harmondsworth: Penguin Books, 2008; *Inquiry into recruitment and employment in the meat and poultry processing sector*, London: Equality and Human Rights Commission, 2009; *Who cares? How best to protect UK care workers employed through agencies and gangmasters from exploitation*, Oxford: Oxfam, December 2009.
42. *Hard work, hidden lives*. The Commission defined 'vulnerable employment' as 'precarious work that places people at risk of continuing poverty and injustice resulting from an imbalance of power in the employer-worker relationship'.

43. Three Chinese nationals were convicted in 2006 of offences including manslaughter, assisting illegal immigration and conspiracy. A film, *Ghosts*, was made by Nick Broomfield about the tragedy and about the use of migrants for low-paid, precarious and temporary work.

44. Gangmasters Licensing Act 2004; see Gangmasters' Licensing Authority website for details of its enforcement regime, http://gla.defra.gov.uk/. Sectors such as care, catering and construction remain unregulated.

45. See Mick Wilkinson, *New Labour, the Gangmasters Licensing Authority and the woefully inadequate protection of migrant workers in the UK*, n.d., www.social-policy.org.uk/lincoln/Wilkinson.pdf. For an analysis of the regulation of gangmasters in the context of neoliberalism see Dr Kendra Strauss, *Challenging hegemonic deregulation? The UK Gangmaster Licensing Authority as a model for the regulation of casual work*, Glasgow: University of Glasgow, n.d.

46. See Amanda Levinson, 'Regularisation programmes in the United Kingdom' in *The regularisation of unauthorised migrants: literature survey and country case studies*, Oxford: COMPAS, 2005; Bridget Anderson, *The devil is in the detail: lessons to be drawn from the UK's recent exercise in regularising undocumented workers*, Working Paper, University of Warwick, 1999.

47. *Recognising rights, recognising political realities: the case for regularising irregular migrants*, London: JCWI, July 2006; Strangers into Citizens website, http://www.strangersintocitizens.org.uk/.

48. *Strangers into Citizens campaign*, EDM 1371, 27 April 2007.

49. 'Illegal migrants' right to work wins support of public in poll', *Independent*, 27 April 2007.

50. *No easy options: irregular immigration in the UK*, London: IPPR, see Frances Webber and Jon Burnett, 'IPPR: fuelling popular racism?' IRR News, 28 April 2011.

51. See 'Joy vanished into Britain's child-sex trade – why aren't we looking for her?' *Observer*, 16 October 2011; 'Children lost from care in trafficking cases', *Guardian*, 19 October 2011.

52. See 'Number of biometric residence permits to double'.

53. Presentation by Nadine Ballantyne at PICUM/Praxis workshop, 'Building strategies to protect children in an irregular migration situation in the United Kingdom', London, 6 October 2011.

54. Fizza Qureshi, Doctors without Borders Project London presentation at PICUM/Praxis workshop.

55. 'Immigrants must pass test on British history, says Cameron', *Daily Telegraph*, 11 October 2011.

56. See *Right to come and stay for all, not amnesty for some*, Manchester, No One is Illegal, n.d, available on www.noii.org.uk.

CHAPTER 10

1. *Border controls*, Home Affairs Committee, 1st report 2000–1, HC 163, para. 63.

2. 'Passport control officers to get uniforms in Reid reforms', *Guardian*, 24 July 2006.

3. These figures exclude those removed after refusal of leave to enter. Control of immigration statistics 2007, 2008, 2009; immigration statistics 3rd quarter 2011; www.homeoffice.gov.uk/publications/science-research-statistics/

research-statistics/immigration-asylum-research/immigration-brief-q3-2011/
removals.

4. See A. Sivanandan, 'New circuits of imperialism', in *Communities of resistance:
black struggles for socialism*, London: Verso, 1990.

5. See Liz Fekete, *A suitable enemy: racism, migration and Islamophobia in
Europe*, London: Pluto, 2009.

6. Refugee Action has this Home Office contract, previously held by the
International Organization for Migration (IOM), requiring it to secure the
voluntary return of a specified annual number of people who would otherwise
be removed. See Frances Webber, 'How voluntary are voluntary returns?' *Race
& Class*, Vol. 52, No. 4 (2011).

7. Statement of immigration rules for control after entry, October 1972.

8. Overstayers were subject to deportation until 1999, when they became subject
to administrative removal.

9. *R v. Nazari* (1980) 1 WLR 1366.

10. *R v. Immigration Appeal Tribunal ex p Bakhtaur Singh* [1986] 1 WLR 910.

11. Immigration Act 1988, s. 5. Illegal entrants had no pre-removal appeal rights
until 2000, when the human rights appeal was introduced.

12. The adjudicator on his appeal read 41 letters from MPs, three from peers,
eleven from clerics, three from social work organisations, 14 from community
and educational organisations, 52 from branches of his union NALGO, and
eleven from other trade unions and trade councils. There were also many letters
from individuals testifying to Mr Idrish's qualities as a social worker, 'as well
as a number which would seem primarily critical of successive governments'
restrictive immigration policies', and petitions with thousands of signatures.
The appeal was allowed.

13. Mendis's was one of three public sanctuaries in churches and temples in 1987,
and less publicly, a Hindu temple in Wimbledon gave shelter to a group of
around 60 Tamils, providing them with mattresses and food, until stopped
by the local authority on planning grounds. See Paul Weller, *Sanctuary: the
beginning of a movement*, London: Runnymede Trust, 1987.

14. The policies were withdrawn in 2008. See Chapter 5.

15. 'Private life' has been interpreted as including all the ties a person has with
the host country: see e.g. *Beldjoudi v. France* (1992) 14 EHRR 801, ECtHR.

16. 'Family life' includes the relationship between spouses and partners, and
between minor children and their natural or adoptive parents, but not
relationships between adult siblings, or between adult children and their
parents, unless there is particular dependency. See Macdonald and Toal,
Macdonald's immigration law and practice (8th edn), London: Butterworths,
2010, 8.81ff.

17. *Border controls*, HAC, para. 69.

18. Alasdair Palmer, 'Blunkett should know that his plan can't work', *Daily
Telegraph*, 2 June 2002. Palmer thought that Blunkett had the right idea, but
that the judges would thwart him. He was wrong.

19. 'Blunkett uses TV to pillory asylum seekers', *The Times*, 24 May 2002; on
lottery funding to the NCADC see *Daily Mail*, 10 August 2002, *Guardian*,
13 August 2002; on Ahmadi family see *Guardian*, 12 September 2002.

20. See 'UN condemns British policy on deportees', *Observer*, 12 June 2005, cited
in Hintjens, 'Like leaves in the wind: desperately seeking asylum in the UK',
Race & Class, Vol. 48, No. 1 (2006).

21. *Financial Times*, 27 October 2004, cited in Liz Fekete, *The deportation machine: Europe, asylum and human rights*, IRR, 2005.

22. *KH (Article 15 (c) Qualification Directive) Iraq CG* [2008] UKAIT 23; *QD (Iraq)* v. *SSHD* [2009] EWCA Civ 620.

23. 'New government seeks to bully judges', IRR News, 10 June 2010.

24. 'European court demands halt to forcible return of Iraqi asylum seekers', *Guardian*, 5 November 2010.

25. See 'Deportation flights to Iraq resume despite UN warning', *Guardian*, 9 March 2011.

26. See *AA and LK* v. *SSHD* [2006] EWCA Civ 501, reversing *AA* v. *SSHD* [2005] IAT 144; *HS (Returning asylum seekers) Zimbabwe CG* [2007] UKAIT 94; *RN (Returnees) Zimbabwe CG* [2008] UKAIT 83; *EM (Zimbabwe)* [2011] UKUT 98.

27. See 'Enforced returns to Zimbabwe will resume', 14 October 2010, www.homeoffice.gov.uk/media-centre/news/enforced-returns.

28. *SSHD* v. *AH (Sudan)* [2007] UKHL 49.

29. See 'Asylum-seekers are sent back to Darfur', *Independent*, 7 July 2008; 'Sent back by Britain. Executed in Darfur', *Independent*, 17 March 2009.

30. *Observer*, 24 October 2004, cited in Fekete, *The deportation machine*.

31. *AG* v. *SSHD* [2006] EWCA Civ 1342.

32. *Sufi and Elmi* v. *United Kingdom* [2011] ECHR 1045.

33. *NA* v. *United Kingdom* [2007] ECHR 602. See *Preventing harm to refugees and migrants in extradition and expulsion cases: Rule 39 indications by the European Court of Human Rights*, Council of Europe Parliamentary Assembly Committee on Migration, Refugees and Population, Doc. 12435, November 2010.

34. *Report of Secretary-General's panel of experts on accountability in Sri Lanka*, United Nations, March 2011.

35. See 'Deported Tamils "face torture" on return to Sri Lanka', *Guardian*, 15 December 2011.

36. HC Deb. 16 June 2011, col. 975.

37. See e.g. Catherine Ramos, *Unsafe return: refoulement of Congolese asylum seekers*, Stockton-on-Tees: Justice First, November 2011.

38. *BK (failed asylum seekers) DRC* [2007] UKUT 98 (IAC).

39. See Fekete, 'They are children too', in *A suitable enemy*.

40. FCO Migration Directorate, ILPA mailing, June 2010, p. 19.

41. ILPA mailing, November 2010, p. 36; see also 'Simone Troller: orphans of war deserve our support', *Independent*, 14 June 2010.

42. See Chapter 3.

43. The Secretary of State interprets the provision, Article 6, as allowing children to be returned to the first state where they claimed asylum: see *R (BT and others)* v. *SSHD* [2011] EWCA Civ 1446.

44. The words of Justice Collins, in *R (T)* v. *SSHD, R (M)* v. *SSHD* [2010] EWHC 435 (Admin).

45. Ibid.

46. *Landing in Dover*, Children's Commissioner, January 2012. The UKBA's chief executive ordered an end to the practice in November 2011.

47. See 'How the deportation story emerged', BBC News, 9 October 2006.

48. UK Borders Act 2007, ss 32–8.

49. 'Fit for purpose?' *Socialist Lawyer*, 44 (2006).

50. See Liz Fekete and Frances Webber, 'Foreign nationals, enemy penology and the criminal justice system', *Race & Class*, Vol. 51, No. 4 (2010).

51. Control of immigration statistics.

52. *AK (Rwanda)* (2008).

53. Refugee Convention, Article 33 (2).

54. Nationality, Immigration and Asylum Act 2002, s. 72. The presumption of danger to the community could be rebutted. The regulations were the Nationality, Immigration and Asylum Act 2002 (Specification of Particularly Serious Crimes) Order 2004. Refugees cannot be deported, however, if there is a risk of torture or inhuman or degrading treatment.

55. *The Nationality, Immigration and Asylum Act 2002 (Specification of Particularly Serious Crimes) Order 2004*, Joint Committee on Human Rights, 22nd report 2003–4, HC 1212.

56. *EN (Serbia)* v. *SSHD* [2009] EWCA Civ 630. The court also ruled that the presumption that a crime was 'particularly serious' could be rebutted.

57. See 'Segregation policy for foreign national prisoners condemned', IRR News, 26 February 2010.

58. *Foreign national prisoners: a thematic review*, HM Inspectorate of Prisons, July 2006.

59. *R (Equalities and Human Rights Commission)* v. *Ministry of Justice and others* [2010] EWHC 147 (Admin).

60. See 'We must regain the right to kick out foreign criminals', *Daily Express*, 30 June 2011, '"Undesirable and dangerous" criminals cannot be deported from Britain, say Euro judges', *Daily Mail*, 28 June 2011; Adam Wagner, 'More poor human rights reporting on Somali foreign criminals case', UK Human Rights blog, 30 June 2011, http://ukhumanrightsblog.com/2011/06/30/more-poor-human-rights-reporting-on-somali-foreign-criminals-case/.

61. 'British judges are "overzealous" in their use of the Human Rights Act', *Daily Express*, 31 October 2011.

62. See George Eaton, 'Theresa May's cat story unravels', *New Statesman* blog, 4 October 2011; 'Foreign criminals, the press and the judges', IRR News, 29 June 2011.

63. HC Deb. 19 December 2011, cols 1065–6.

64. 'Judges too politicised, says supreme court appointee', *Guardian*, 9 November 2011. For a rebuttal of the argument see Stephen Sedley, 'Judicial politics', *London Review of Books*, Vol. 34, No. 4 (23 February 2012).

65. Izmir Declaration, High level conference on the future of the European Court of Human Rights, 26–27 April 2011, www.coe.int/t/dc/press/news/20110427_declaration_en.asp; 'Human rights: the assault continues', IRR News, 8 September 2011. The draft Brighton declaration for agreement in April 2012 contains radical suggestions for diluting the Court's jurisdiction; see 'Xenophobia drives assault on European Court', IRR News, 23 March 2012.

66. 'Top European judge slams UK "xenophobia"', *Guardian*, 24 November 2011; 'Human rights chief issues warning to UK', *Observer*, 11 December 2011.

67. *D* v. *United Kingdom* (1997) 24 EHRR 423.

68. *Bensaid* v. *United Kingdom* (2001) 33 EHRR 10.

69. See 'AIDS, drug prices and generic drugs', on www.avert.org/generic.htm.

70. *Towards universal access: scaling up priority HIV/AIDS interventions in the health sector*, Geneva: WHO, UNAIDS and UNICEF, 2009.

71. *N* v. *SSHD* [2005] UKHL 31.

72. N v. *United Kingdom* (2008) 47 EHRR 39.
73. *FM (Zimbabwe)* v. *SSHD* [2011] EWCA Civ 168.
74. *RS* v. *SSHD* [2010] UKUT 363 (IAC). Return to death caused by discriminatory denial of medication is akin to a refugee case, while death caused by poverty and inability to access drugs is seen as in the 'natural order of things' regardless of deeper causes.
75. *CA* [2004] EWCA Civ 1165.
76. *LN (Ghana)*, 2005. Since then, the supreme court has confirmed the need to consider the effect of parents' removal on children, see *ZH (Tanzania)* v. *SSHD* [2011] UKSC 4.
77. *Guardian*, 20 March 2008.
78. Harmit Athwal, *Driven to desperate measures 2006–2010*, London: IRR, 2011.
79. *R (Soumahoro)* v. *SSHD* [2002] EWHC 2651 (Admin), case note.
80. *R (Soumahoro)* v. *SSHD* [2003] EWCA Civ 840.
81. See *J* v. *SSHD* [2005] EWCA Civ 629.
82. *M* v. *Home Office* [1994] 1 AC 377. The ruling made legal history, establishing that ministers of the crown could be subjected to legal sanctions.
83. See e.g. *R (Collaku)* v. *SSHD* [2005] EWHC 2855 (Admin), in which judge Collins deplored the practice.
84. *R (Karas)* [2006] EWHC 747 (Admin).
85. *Karas*, para. 84.
86. *R (Anufrijeva)* v. *SSHD* [2003] UKHL 36, see Chapter 3.
87. *Karas*, para. 87.
88. Ibid., para. 82.
89. Examples taken from NoBorders network website, www.noborders.org.uk, and see Fekete, *A suitable enemy*.
90. *R (Medical Justice)* v. *SSHD* [2010] EWHC 1925 (Admin), 26 July 2010, upheld by the Court of Appeal at [2011] EWCA Civ 1710.
91. David Blunkett, 'Judges have no answers to immigration challenges', 26 July 2010, http://davidblunkett.typepad.com/media_centre/2010/07/blunkett-judges-have-no-answers-to-immigration-challenges.html.
92. *Guardian*, 14 October 2010.
93. 'Abused, humiliated and abandoned: what really happens when the UK deports failed asylum seekers', *Independent*, 5 July 2010, cited in Liz Fekete, 'Accelerated removals: the human cost of EU deportation policies', *Race & Class*, Vol. 52, No. 4 (2011).
94. 'Staff on deportation flights played "Russian roulette" with lives', *Guardian*, 8 February 2011.
95. See 'G4S in spotlight again as new abuse claims emerge', *Guardian*, 22 October 2010.
96. *Death in police custody of Joy Gardner*, London: Amnesty International, August 1995.
97. *Harm on removal: excessive force against failed asylum seekers*, London: Medical Foundation, 2004.
98. *Detention undercover: the real story*, BBC1, 2 March 2005.
99. *Outsourcing abuse: the use and abuse of state-sanctioned force during detention and removal of asylum seekers*, London: Birnberg Peirce, Medical Justice and NCADC, July 2008; see Chapter 8.

100. *Report on an unannounced short follow-up inspection of Tinsley House Immigration Removal Centre*, HM Inspectorate of Prisons, October 2009.

101. *Detainees under escort: inspection of escort and removals to Jamaica*, HM Inspectorate of Prisons, March 2011, *Detainees under escort: Inspection of escort and removals to Nigeria*, HM Inspectorate of Prisons, April 2011.

102. *Out of control: the case for a complete overhaul of enforced removals by private contractors*, London: Amnesty International, July 2011.

103. 'Police investigate alleged assault on Nigerian mother on deportation flight', *Guardian*, 3 October 2011.

104. Jessica Hurd, in *Harm on removal*.

105. See 'Men "thrown off flight" for raising concerns about deportation', *Guardian*, 1 November 2010.

106. '"Air rage" lets asylum seekers stay in UK', *Scotland on Sunday*, 13 May 2007.

107. *Announced full inspection of Tinsley House IRC*, HM Inspectorate of Prisons, July 2011.

CHAPTER 11

1. *R v. SSHD ex p Hosenball* [1977] 1 WLR 766.

2. Ibid.

3. The one exception to the exclusively male SIAC appellants was Ekaterina Zatuliveter, the alleged Russian spy.

4. Committee on Immigration Appeals, chaired by Sir Roy Wilson QC (Cmnd. 3387, 1967). The government responded by the Immigration Appeals Act 1969, which allowed Commonwealth citizens (but not aliens) to appeal against exclusion, removal and other immigration decisions. See Macdonald and Toal, *Macdonald's immigration law and practice* (8th edn), London: Butterworths, 2010, p. 1462.

5. Paul Gordon, *Deportations and removals*, London: Runnymede Trust, 1984.

6. *R v. SSHD ex p Cheblak* [1991] 1 WLR 890.

7. 'Prisoners of "War", 'Detentions as a result of the Gulf war', *Statewatch*, Vol. 1, Nos. 1 and 2 (1991).

8. *Detroit Free Press v. Ashcroft* 303F 3d 681 (6th cir. 2002) at 683, quoted by Lord Bingham, 'The rule of law', 6th David Williams lecture, 10 November 2006.

9. *Chahal v. United Kingdom* [1996] 23 EHRR 413; 'Howard's way blocked', *Statewatch*, Vol. 6, No.6 (1996).

10. See Special Immigration Appeals Commission Act 1997; Special Immigration Appeals Commission (Procedure Rules) 2003, SI 2003/1034.

11. *SSHD v. AF* [2009] UKHL 28. For control orders see CAMPACC website, www.campacc.org.uk; Coalition Against Secret Evidence (CASE) website, http://coalitionagainstsecretevidence.com; the Joint Committee on Human Rights' annual reports on renewal of control order legislation; Lord Macdonald of River Glaven, *Review of counter-terrorism and security powers*, Cm. 8003, January 2011; Victoria Brittain, 'Besieged in Britain', *Race & Class*, Vol. 50, No. 3 (2009), Victoria Brittain, *The meaning of waiting*, London: Oberon, 2010 (performed at the Purcell Room, March 2010). Control orders were replaced by the very similar terrorism prevention and investigation measures (TPIMs) in December 2011.

12. In practice, the Secretary of State rarely gives further disclosure, electing not to rely on the undisclosed material, which generally leads to revocation of the order. See note 27.

13. *RB (Algeria)* v. *SSHD* [2009] UKHL 10, following an ECtHR case, *Maaouia* v. *France* (2000) 33 EHRR 1037, where the judges held that decisions about immigration status or deportation were not about 'civil rights or obligations' and did not attract the fair trial guarantees of Article 6 of the Convention.

14. See Lord Phillips in *RB (Algeria)*, paras 80ff.

15. *W (Algeria)* v. *SSHD* [2012] UKSC 8, overruling SIAC and the Court of Appeal.

16. *R (Cart)* v. *Upper Tribunal* [2009] EWHC 3052 (Admin).

17. *Home Secretary* v. *Rehman* [2003] AC 153, per Lord Hoffmann at para. 53.

18. See Brian Barder, 'On SIAC', *London Review of Books*, Vol. 26, No. 6 (18 March 2004).

19. See the exposition by Magnus Hornqvist, 'The birth of public order policy', *Race & Class*, Vol. 46, No. 1 (2005), of the growth of 'a concept of security that has broken away from the logic of the law. The focus is shifted to what a person might do instead of what the person has done ... The judicial determination of guilt is replaced by the administrative assessment of risk.' This describes the SIAC process perfectly.

20. Barder, 'On SIAC'.

21. See 'Lawyer attacks anti-terror laws', BBC News, 20 December 2004.

22. *M*, SC/17/2002, 8 March 2004; *Sihali*, SC/38/2005, 14 May 2007 and the 'Russian spy' case, *Zatuliveter*, SC/103/2010, November 2011. In *T*, SC/31/2005, 22 March 2010, SIAC revoked a deportation order on the ground that its subject had outgrown his previous terrorist interests. The judgments are all available on the SIAC website, www.justice.gov.uk/tribunals/special-immigration-appeals-commission.

23. The designation allowed the men to be interned under provisions of the Anti-Terrorism, Crime and Security Act 2001 later declared unlawful by the House of Lords.

24. *Ajouaou and others*, SC/1/2002, 29 October 2003.

25. *Ajouaou*, paras 160, 173.

26. *J1*, SIAC, 15 April 2011.

27. *SSHD* v. *AN* [2008] EWHC 372 (Admin). He was alleged to have acted as a link with overseas extremists, been involved in attack planning, travelled repeatedly to the Middle East, openly advocated support for extremists, and facilitated extremists to travel abroad for terrorist purposes. Three 'extremist' associates were named after a legal battle, but he never got any further disclosure of the detail or the evidence behind these allegations, which he strongly denied, and the control order was revoked after the Secretary of State refused to provide more detail.

28. *MI*, SIAC, 10 May 2011, para. 9.

29. Cageprisoners held an exhibition of national security detainees' artistic work in June 2008: see Victoria Brittain, 'The art of internment', *Guardian*, 12 June 2008. See also 'Fighting ghosts: an interview with Husein Al Samamara', IRR News, 1 July 2010.

30. See *VV* v. *SSHD*, SC/59/2006, 2 November 2007.

31. See Lawrence Archer, *Ricin! The inside story of the plot that never was*, London: Pluto, 2010; Gareth Peirce, 'Was it like this for the Irish?' in *Dispatches from the dark side: on torture and the death of justice*, London: Verso, 2010.

32. See Peirce, *Dispatches*, 'MI5 tip-off to CIA led to men's rendition', *Guardian*, 28 March 2006, 4 September 2011; see also Andy Worthington, 'As the UK government announces compensation for ex-Guantanamo detainees, is the return of Shaker Aamer part of the deal?' 16 November 2010, on www.andyworthington.co.uk.

33. *A, B, C, D* v. *SSHD*, 2 October 2003, upheld by the Court of Appeal at [2004] EWCA Civ 1123.

34. *A* v. *SSHD (no 2)* [2005] UKHL 71, where Lords Bingham, Nicholls and Hoffmann dissented from the majority view that the use of torture had to be proved (rather than accepted as a real risk) before excluding evidence.

35. *OO (Jordan)* v. *SSHD* [2009] UKHL 10.

36. *Othman* v. *UK* [2012] ECHR 56; 'Human rights court risks corroding support for civil liberties, warns PM', *Guardian*, 25 January 2012.

37. *Chahal* v. *UK*, note 9 above.

38. *Saadi* v. *Italy* (2009) 49 EHRR 30 (Grand Chamber), where the British government intervened.

39. For strong criticism of such assurances see UN High Commissioner for human rights, Statement to the Council of Europe Group of Specialists on Human Rights and the Fight against Terrorism, 29–31 March 2006; 'Diplomatic assurances not an adequate safeguard for deportees, UN special rapporteur warns', UN press release, 23 August 2005; Thomas Hammarberg, 'Torture can never, ever be accepted', 27 June 2006; 'Diplomatic assurances – no protection against torture or ill-treatment', London: Amnesty International, December 2004, 'UK human rights: a broken promise', London: Amnesty International, February 2006; 'Empty promises: diplomatic assurances no safeguard against torture', New York: Human Rights Watch, April 2004, 'Still at risk', New York: Human Rights Watch, April 2005, 'Not worth the paper they're written on', New York: Human Rights Watch, August 2005, 'Dangerous ambivalence: UK policy on torture since 9/11', New York: Human Rights Watch, November 2006.

40. *A and others* v. *SSHD*, SC/33–39, 20 October 2005.

41. *AS and DD* v. *SSHD*, SC/42 & 50/2005, upheld by the Court of Appeal as *AS (Libya)* v. *SSHD* [2008] EWCA Civ 289.

42. *Othman* v. *UK*, where deportation was refused because of the risk of trial by torture evidence, but the judges expressly approved the diplomatic assurances which they said protected Othman from a real risk of torture. See 'Abu Qatada decision causes alarm – to rights activists', IRR News, 26 January 2012.

43. *Roberts* v. *Parole Board* [2005] UKHL 45, where the House of Lords (with human rights judges Bingham and Steyn dissenting) approved a closed procedure to protect informants.

44. Hard-fought provisions of the Coroners and Justice Act 2009 (not in force at the time of writing) allow inquests to be replaced by secret inquiries in sensitive cases: see 'Labour forces secret inquests Bill through the Commons', *Independent*, 10 November 2009. Home secretary Theresa May sought unsuccessfully to withhold evidence of MI5 activities from the 7/7 inquests: *Guardian*, 22 November 2010.

45. *R (Mohamed)* v. *Secretary of State for Foreign Affairs* [2010] EWCA Civ 65, 'Seven paragraphs which tell a sorry tale', IRR News, 11 February 2010.

46. *Al Rawi and others* v. *Security Services and others* [2010] EWCA Civ 482, upheld by the supreme court at [2011] UKSC 34.

47. 'Campaigners to shun UK inquiry into detainee "torture"', BBC News, 4 August 2011.
48. *Justice and security: green paper*, Cm. 8194.
49. Adam Wagner, 'More secret trials? No thanks', UK human rights blog, 31 January 2012.
50. Much of the material in this section is taken from Amanda Weston, 'Deprivation of citizenship by stealth', IRR News, 9 June 2011, based on a seminar given at the IRR.
51. Passed in response to pressure for the deportation of Abu Hamza, a former preacher at Finsbury Park mosque and naturalised British citizen who was convicted in February 2006 of incitement to murder and racial hatred.
52. British Nationality Act 1981 s. 40, amended by Nationality, Immigration and Asylum Act 2002. The new law did not help the home secretary in Abu Hamza's case, since he had already been stripped of his Egyptian citizenship, and could not be rendered stateless. See *Abu Hamza v. SSHD*, SC/23/2003, on SIAC website, www.justice.gov.uk/tribunals/special-immigration-appeals-commission.
53. British Nationality Act 1948, s. 25; British Nationality Act 1981 s. 40 (unamended).
54. All recipients of these notices so far have been male.
55. *Guardian*, 28 January 2011.
56. See Peter Spiro, 'David Hicks' British citizenship: now you see it, now you don't', Opinio Juris blog, 5 September 2006.
57. See *MH and others v. SSHD* [2009] EWCA Civ 287.
58. 'British "al-Qaida member" killed in US drone attack in Somalia', *Guardian*, 23 January 2012.
59. 'Democracy, the rule of law and the role of judges', *European Human Rights Law Review*, No. 3 (2006), pp. 243–53.
60. Ibid.
61. See these organisations' websites: CAMPACC is at www.campacc.org.uk; CASE is at http://coalitionagainstsecretevidence.com; Cageprisoners is at www.cageprisoners.com; the IRR is at www.irr.org.uk; Peace & Progress is at www.peaceandprogress.org; HHUGS is at www.hhugs.org.uk; Andy Worthington's website is at www.andyworthington.co.uk; see also Peirce, *Dispatches*.

Index